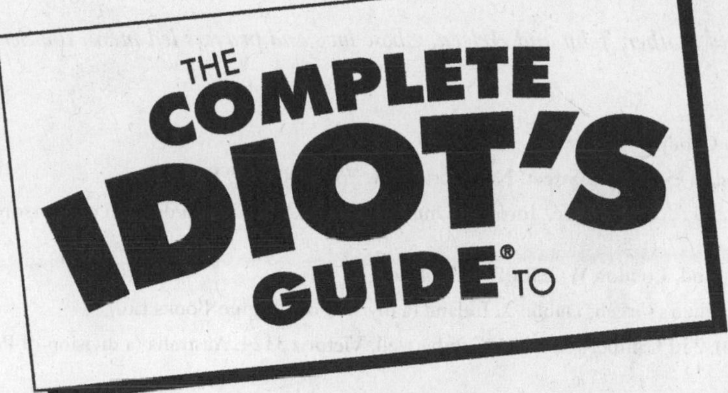

The Last Days

by Richard H. Perry

A member of Penguin Group (USA) Inc.

To my father and mother, John and Arleen, whose love and prayers led me to the Scriptures.

ALPHA BOOKS

Published by the Penguin Group

Penguin Group (USA) Inc., 375 Hudson Street, New York, New York 10014, U.S.A.

Penguin Group (Canada), 10 Alcorn Avenue, Toronto, Ontario, Canada M4V 3B2 (a division of Pearson Penguin Canada Inc.)

Penguin Books Ltd, 80 Strand, London WC2R 0RL, England

Penguin Ireland, 25 St Stephen's Green, Dublin 2, Ireland (a division of Penguin Books Ltd)

Penguin Group (Australia), 250 Camberwell Road, Camberwell, Victoria 3124, Australia (a division of Pearson Australia Group Pty Ltd)

Penguin Books India Pvt Ltd, 11 Community Centre, Panchsheel Park, New Delhi—110 017, India

Penguin Group (NZ), cnr Airborne and Rosedale Roads, Albany, Auckland 1310, New Zealand (a division of Pearson New Zealand Ltd)

Penguin Books (South Africa) (Pty) Ltd, 24 Sturdee Avenue, Rosebank, Johannesburg 2196, South Africa

Penguin Books Ltd, Registered Offices: 80 Strand, London WC2R 0RL, England

International Standard Book Number: 978-1-59257-561-9
Library of Congress Catalog Card Number: 2006927535

14 13 8 7 6

Interpretation of the printing code: The rightmost number of the first series of numbers is the year of the book's printing; the rightmost number of the second series of numbers is the number of the book's printing. For example, a printing code of 06-1 shows that the first printing occurred in 2006.

Printed in the United States of America

Publisher: *Marie Butler-Knight*
Editorial Director: *Mike Sanders*
Managing Editor: *Billy Fields*
Executive Editor: *Randy Ladenheim-Gil*
Senior Development Editor: *Phil Kitchel*
Senior Production Editor: *Janette Lynn*
Production Editor: *Kayla Dugger*
Copy Editor: *Krista Hansing*
Cartoonist: *Shannon Wheeler*
Cover Designer: *Bill Thomas*
Book Designers: *Trina Wurst/Kurt Owens*
Indexer: *Julie Bess*
Layout: *Ayanna Lacey*
Proofreader: *Aaron Black*

Contents at a Glance

Contents

Appendixes

Introduction

For many people, the idea of the Last Days brings to mind concerns and fears about the end of the world, the Antichrist, the Mark of the Beast, world war, and the Battle of Armageddon. For centuries, humanity has been preoccupied with the idea that someday the world will come to an end. These thoughts and concerns have often been fueled by the Bible, earthquakes, famines, wars, or writers like Nostradamus, Jeane Dixon, and Tim LaHaye.

When we hear about the Last Days, generally we have more questions than answers. Is the world really going to end? Should I be concerned about the future? Are any of the things I've heard true? Where are we in relation to the Last Days?

The concept of the Last Days originates with the Bible. Therefore, I use the Bible as the primary resource for explaining what lies ahead according to Last Days prophecy. This book outlines the major prophetic events of the Last Days so that you will be able to determine when they are predicted to occur. This book was written based on the belief that the Bible is the collected wisdom of God as told to his prophets and disciples through the ages and recorded for all of mankind. You will find no argument herein about the accuracy of the Bible as a record of God's word.

Throughout the book you will find timelines, graphic presentations of the timing of key Last Days events. These timelines point out for you the timing of some things that are believed to have happened in the past, as well as when things are indicated, according to biblical prophecy, to occur in the future.

How to Use This Book

This book is divided into five parts:

Part 1, "Bible Basics," describes what some well-known religions believe about the Last Days and the end of the world. From there we go on to examine the biblical foundations that shape Christian beliefs about the Last Days and the end of the age. Then you will see how Bible prophecy was fulfilled by Jesus Christ at the beginning of the first century.

Part 2, "Signs of the Times," talks about the many signs and events that the Bible says will indicate that the end of the age is approaching.

Part 3, "Sound the Trumpets," introduces key End Times players, those who the Bible says will lead the world through its darkest hour. You will also find out about many signs and miracles that are predicted to occur to deceive people about what's going on.

Part 4, "The Great and Dreadful Day Is Dawning," covers the Day of the Lord, perhaps the most significant time prophesied throughout the Bible, and what the Bible says will be happening as that day unfolds. Some of the events you will read about include the Second Coming of Christ, the resurrection and rapture, and the Final Battle, popularly called Armageddon.

Part 5, "The Last Day," explains what the Bible says about the Kingdom of God on earth. In closing, we explore how different groups interpret the timing of End Times events.

Extras

To help your understanding of the Bible's Last Days, the following sidebars pop up regularly throughout the book.

The Prophet Says

These are direct quotes of Last Days prophecies from the Old and New Testaments as they relate to the topics being discussed in the chapter.

Prophetic Pitfalls

These highlight incorrect assumptions that have been or could be made regarding biblical prophecies, and provide information to make sure you understand the correct approach.

def•i•ni•tion

Throughout the book, I use popular and biblical terms to identify and describe people, places, and things pertinent to a discussion of the Last Days. I identify and define these terms for you. There is also a listing of the terms in Appendix B.

Acknowledgments

Thanks to the editorial staff at Alpha and Penguin for their perseverance and dedication to this challenge. Thanks to Randy Ladenheim-Gil, executive editor, for her vision and patience; to Phil Kitchel, senior development editor, for his remarkable skill and perceptive questioning; and to Janette Lynn, senior production editor, for her organizational skill and determination to deliver on time.

I also want to thank my literary agent Jacky Sach, of BookEnds, who introduced me to Alpha and their best-selling approach to informative books.

Thanks also to the artists and designers who have contributed their graphic skill to the presentation of this work on the Last Days.

Part 1

Bible Basics

If you're reading this book to learn what is ahead for the world, you have come to the right place. The Last Days are also popularly called the End Times.

As I begin to guide you through the Last Days, I will tell you and show you, from the Bible, what is being prophesied about the future. Not only will you understand a biblical day, but you will see what else the Bible tells us about God's timetable.

In this first part of the guide to the Last Days, you will learn about biblical days, the appointed times of God, early prophecies about the kingdom that is to come, and some important teaching about the King Himself.

Chapter 1

Last Days

In This Chapter

- The end of the world as we know it
- What different religions think about End Times
- Not all Christians agree
- The skeptics chime in

We've all heard people talking about it: End Times, Last Days, Judgment Day … it sounds so ominous. What does it really mean? Is the world really coming to an end? And if it is true, why don't we do something about it? We watch the news, and it looks so frightening: war, nuclear weapons, greed, famine, earthquakes, global warming, and out-of-control weather.

We look around the world and see huge disparities in wealth, health care, and basic necessities. Is this what the Bible foretold? Are the Last Days truly upon us? This book takes a look at what the Bible says about the Last Days, also referred to as the End Times. If we believe that the Bible is the Word of God, we can look at this source of information regarding the future and decide for ourselves what may or may not be looming ahead.

Is the Sky Falling?

The Bible tells of a series of signs that indicate the world is nearing the end of the age and the *Second Coming* of Christ. The "end of the age" refers to the time when this present age changes and becomes the age of righteousness promised in the Bible. The Bible can be interpreted as a road map of things to come in the Last Days. As we look around us in confusion and fear, unsure why the world seems to be falling apart, we can turn to this road map for an idea of what, perhaps, might be in store for us.

def•i•ni•tion

The **Second Coming** is a popular expression for the return of Jesus Christ to earth. According to the Bible, the First Coming of Jesus Christ, also known as the Messiah, occurred in A.D. 32, when He rode into Jerusalem as King. The Bible says that Christ will return at the end of the age to establish the Kingdom of God on earth.

def•i•ni•tion

The **Last Days** and **End Times** are synonymous expressions for the period of time leading up to the Second Coming of Jesus Christ and the end of the age.

What Do People in the News Say?

It does sometimes seem like the world is collapsing around us today. With a growing population and a dwindling supply of resources to meet the world's increasing needs, we find references to the *Last Days* in publications like *The New York Times*, *The Chicago Tribune*, *Newsweek*, and *TIME* from journalists, religious leaders, and even politicians.

James Watt, President Reagan's first Secretary of the Interior, told the U.S. Congress in 1981 that protecting natural resources was unimportant in light of the imminent return of Jesus Christ. In public testimony, he said, "After the last tree is felled, Christ will come back."

Jerry Falwell, in 1999, stated that Jesus Christ could return within 10 years. He went on to say that before that can happen, the Antichrist must appear. Falwell said, "Is he alive and here today? Probably."

Bill Moyers addressed the potential for the *End Times* during his acceptance of the Harvard Medical School's Global Environment Citizen Award in 2004. Here is some of what he had to say:

> *So what does this mean for public policy and the environment? Go to Grist to read a remarkable work of reporting by the journalist, Glenn Scherer—"The Road to Environmental Apocalypse." Read it and you will see how millions of Christian fundamentalists may believe that environmental destruction is not only to be disregarded but actually welcomed—even hastened—as a sign of the coming apocalypse.*

> *As Grist makes clear, we're not talking about a handful of fringe lawmakers who hold or are beholden to these beliefs. Nearly half the U.S. Congress before the recent election—231 legislators in total—more since the election—are backed by the religious right. Forty-five senators and 186 members of the 108th congress earned 80 to 100 percent approval ratings from the three most influential Christian right advocacy groups. They include Senate Majority Leader Bill Frist, Assistant Majority Leader Mitch McConnell, Conference Chair Rick Santorum of Pennsylvania, Policy Chair Jon Kyl of Arizona, House Speaker Dennis Hastert, and Majority Whip Roy Blunt. The only Democrat to score 100 percent with the Christian coalition was Senator Zell Miller of Georgia, who recently quoted from the biblical book of Amos on the Senate floor: "'The days will come,' sayeth the Lord God, 'that I will send a famine in the land.'" He seemed to be relishing the thought.*

Pat Robertson, former GOP presidential candidate and host of *The 700 Club*, feels that we must be getting close to the End Times. In 2005, Robertson spoke on CNN's *Late Edition* following a catastrophic earthquake, devastating hurricanes in the U.S., and the killer tsunami in Asia. He said, "These things are starting to hit with amazing regularity."

In 2005, Mahmoud Ahmadinejad, president of Iran, said that his mission is to prepare Iran for the End Times by paving the way for the arrival of the Islamic End Times prophet, Imam Mahdi.

These people are not the only ones talking about this.

What Do We Say?

As morality deteriorates and violence increases, talk of the end of the world increases. We hear it at work, at home, and on the Internet, TV, and radio. We are surrounded by …

- Terrorist threats from the Middle East
- The threat of frightening and devastating war between Eastern and Western civilizations
- Excessive interest in violence and eroticism, as seen on television; in books, films, and magazines; and online
- Worldwide natural disasters, such as flooding, tsunamis, earthquakes, hurricanes, and famines

- A breakdown of moral, social, and ethical values
- Power shortages, rising gasoline prices, water shortages, rising medical costs, and medical shortages
- Fears of apocalyptic diseases, such as HIV/AIDS, bird flu, and other health emergencies
- Internal division and violence within countries

Are these indications of the Last Days?

Many people are frightened and concerned that we cannot continue like this and that we are seeing some of the signs of the *end of the age*. It often seems that we are on the brink of the apocalypse.

def•i•ni•tion

The **end of the age** is a biblical expression for the moment of time when Jesus Christ returns and the world changes from this present age to an age of peace and righteousness.

In a poll conducted by *TIME* and CNN in 2002, 59 percent of Americans said that they believed that the prophecies of the Bible's Book of Revelations are going to come true. Almost 25 percent also reported that they believe that the 9/11 terrorist attacks were predicted in the Bible.

What are the biblical signs that the end is coming? We examine those in this book. For now, I'll list several biblical signs that the end is near.

What Does the Bible Say?

The Bible tells us that the following signs will be indications that we are approaching the end of the age and the return of Jesus Christ. These are not necessarily in chronological order.

- Israel will be reborn as a Jewish nation.
- Earthquakes, famines, pestilences, and fearful events will increase.
- The Jewish Temple will be rebuilt in Jerusalem.
- A Middle Eastern kingdom will rise to world power.
- World war will occur.
- Peace in Jerusalem will be brought about as a result of a treaty with the leader of the Middle Eastern world power.

- A Middle Eastern leader will enter the Jewish Temple and declare that he is God.
- God's people will experience a time of unprecedented persecution.
- Signs will take place in the heavens and miracles will occur on earth.
- The nations' armies will gather for a great and final battle at Jerusalem.
- Jesus Christ, the Messiah, will return.

Now, before we go on to learn more about the Bible's teachings, let's briefly discuss what some other religions have to say about the End Times.

The Last Days in Various Religions

Teaching on the Last Days and the end of the age is not limited to Christianity. Almost all religions address the topic of the end of the world as we know it. They have their own terminology and beliefs, which are often similar to biblical prophecies. Within every religion, people have significant differences of belief, including what is believed about the Last Days. I provide some of the general beliefs of various religious groups for comparison, but keep in mind that in each group there are different beliefs than those presented.

American Indian Perspective

Perhaps you will not be surprised to learn that there are similar End Times beliefs among several of the native tribes and nations of the Americas. For example, according to a revered Sioux medicine man, Ogalala, the world will grow out of balance and natural disasters such as floods, fires, and earthquakes will increase. Then a "White Buffalo Calf Woman" will be born and return balance, harmony, and spiritual awakening to the world. Some tribal leaders feel that this may have begun when a white buffalo was born in 1994.

The Hopi believe that the world was created by God (Taiowa). When most of mankind did not obey God, Taiowa killed them with a great flood. Subsequently, two more worlds were created and destroyed. We are currently living in the Fourth World.

Several Hopi tribal leaders have prophesied that the coming of the white man to the Americas signaled the arrival of the End Times. Several aspects of their End Times prophecies seem to coincide with the coming of the white man to what is now known as American soil. For example, their teachings include these prophecies:

- Strange beasts like "white buffalo with great horns" will fill the land. This has been interpreted as cattle.
- Iron snakes and stone rivers will cross the earth. This has been interpreted as railroads and roads.
- The land will be criss-crossed with a giant spider web. This has been interpreted as highways.
- The sea will be turned black. This has been interpreted as oil spills.

The Hopi prophecies also tell of a "great dwelling place" crashing to earth. During this time, the earth will be shaken and the white men will battle people in other lands. Smoke will rise in the deserts, and there will be great destruction and other signs that the end is near. Many will die, but those who understand will live in the places of the Hopi people and will be safe. Then the "True White Brother" will return and plant the seeds of wisdom in people's hearts. This will be the coming of the Fifth World.

The ancient and modern Maya believe that the universe has been renewed four times. The fourth renewal produced the "true humans." The first two universes were destroyed by great floods and the third universe by fire. The Mayan calendar will complete its first great cycle in A.D. 2012. The proximity of this date has caused some to speculate that this will signify the Mayan "coming of a great change." Others speculate that there will be another "end of the universe."

— Last Days Timeline —

Day 1	*Day 2*	*Day 3*	*Day 4*	*Day 5*	*Day 6*	*Day 7*
1,000 years	2,000 years	3,000 years	4,000 years	5,000 years	6,000 years	7,000 years
Adam	Noah	Abraham	David	Christ		

Mayan Calendar Ends A.D. 2012 (↑ Day 6)

Now let's move from the Americas to an East Indian perspective.

Buddhist Perspective

Buddhists, like Hindus, believe in a pattern of spiritual rebirths cycling from creation to destruction, leading to the final rebirth. According to Buddha's recorded sayings in the *Sutta Pitaka*, mankind will go through a moral deterioration. During this time, Buddha's teachings and 10 moral behaviors disappear gradually over 500 years and are replaced by 10 amoral behaviors. This breakdown results in poverty and lawlessness.

In the Middle Ages, when 500 years had passed from the time prophesied, commentators revised the time to 5,000 years. One commentator, Buddhaghosa, predicted that Buddha's teachings would disappear step by step in stages. Near the end of the final stage, a Fifth Buddha, Maitreya, who is said to currently reside in heaven, would arise to renew the teachings of Buddhism and rediscover the path to Nirvana.

Prophetic Pitfalls

L. Ron Hubbard, founder of Scientology, claimed that he was the fulfillment of the Buddhist's Maitreya prophecy in a poem called "Hymn of Asia," written between 1955 and 1956. So far, it doesn't appear that he has fulfilled the prophecy.

Hindu Perspective

The Hindus believe that a manifestation of divinity (Lord Vishnu) is called an "Avatar." The doctrine of the Avatars appears in the sacred writings of the Bhagavad Gita (500–200 B.C.). Hindus believe that Lord Vishnu has been incarnated in nine Avatars over four ages. One of the Avatars is known as Krishna. They believe that we are currently in the fourth age and that the tenth incarnation, Kalki Avatar, will appear during this age. The present age (Kali) is considered an age of brokenness, darkness, and doom. The next incarnation, Kalki Avatar, is to end evil and restore truth and righteousness. They believe that the next Avatar will appear riding on a white horse and wielding a sword.

Baha'i Perspective

The Baha'i believe that the Second Coming of Jesus, the coming of the Fifth Buddha, and other religious prophecies of a second coming were fulfilled in the person of Baha'u'llah. Baha'u'llah was born in Iran in 1817 and died in the Holy Land of Israel in 1892. The Baha'i believe that Baha'u'llah was the manifestation of God for the current age, just as Moses, Abraham, Christ, Muhammad, Krishna, and Buddha were in the past. Each manifestation of God was to establish one of the world's great religions.

The Baha'i predict an imminent catastrophic global calamity that will lead to world peace. First there will be a secular "lesser peace" (sulh al-Akbar), then a greater spiritual peace or "most great peace" (sulh al-a zam). The Baha'i blend many of the teachings of other major religions, including those of the Bible's End Times.

Judaic Perspective

The sacred books of Judaism include the *Tanakh*, all the books of the Old Testament; the *Torah*, the first five books of the Old Testament; and the *Talmud*, a collection of rabbinic discussions of Jewish law, customs, legends, and stories. The End Times are called *acharit hayamim* (end of days).

The Talmud states that the world as we know it will last only 6,000 years. Although some Jews interpret the time specified in Scripture as symbolic, Orthodox Jews take it literally. By their calendar, the year 2006 is the year 5766. In Judaism, there is a great deal of mystery and uncertainty about these dates in relation to the end of days.

The Prophet Says

About the end of days, a time of war and suffering, the Old Testament says, "'On the mountains of Israel you will fall, you and all your troops and the nations with you. I will give you as food to all kinds of carrion birds and to the wild animals. You will fall in the open field, for I have spoken,' declares the Sovereign Lord. 'I will send fire on Magog and on those who live in safety in the coastlands, and they will know that I am the Lord.'" (Ezekiel 39:4–6)

Many Jews believe that at the end, there will be a great battle between *Magog and Israel* in which many will die on both sides. God will intervene and save the Jewish people in this final battle. After God has defeated the enemy, He will establish a kingdom of righteousness over the whole earth. This future era of peace and spiritual awakening is called the Olam Haba (Future World).

They also believe that the Mashiach, or Messiah, has not arrived yet but can come at any time. Some traditions say that Elijah the prophet will announce the imminent arrival of the Messiah. The Messiah is to come from the lineage of King David, will rebuild the Jewish Temple, and will gather the Jewish exiles to Israel. During the End Times, the Sanhedrin (a Jewish court of law comprised of 71 Jewish sages) will be reestablished, and the nation will focus on the Torah and the law. Exactly when the Messiah will come in relation to the End Times events is a topic of debate among the Jewish people.

Islamic Perspective

The Koran and other Islamic commentaries provide some very interesting details regarding the Islamic beliefs about the End Times. Much of the Islamic End Times material presents a picture similar to that of the Judaic and Christian writings. Mohammed (A.D. 570–632) wrote down the Koran, which Sunni Muslims consider to be the Word of God. Shiite or Shia Muslims also consider other inspired commentaries as part of the sacred text, much the way certain Jews respect the Talmud.

— Last Days Timeline —

Day 1	*Day 2*	*Day 3*	*Day 4*	*Day 5*	*Day 6*	*Day 7*
1,000 years	2,000 years	3,000 years	4,000 years	5,000 years	6,000 years	7,000 years
Adam	Noah	Abraham	David			

Mohammed A.D. 570-632

Muslims also expect there to be signs indicating that the end is near. The signs include moral and social deterioration, and natural and cosmic disasters. Certain contemporary Islamic interpreters believe political events, such as the "Christian West" invading the Muslim lands, will also be a sign.

Islamic prophecy regarding the End Times involves three major players. It is believed that they will appear in a certain order during the End Times.

The *Dajjal* (Antichrist or, more accurately, Antimohammed) is expected to appear first. It is believed that he will most likely be Jewish. He will perform miraculous signs, even raising someone from the dead. He will also claim to be Allah. The Dajjal will be successful until the return of the prophet *Isa* (Jesus).

During the time of the Dajjal, *Mahdi*, a great prophet of Allah (God) and Muslim leader, will appear. According to some Shiites, Imam Mahdi disappeared in A.D. 941, and when he returns, he will reign on earth. The writings go so far as to tell us that Mahdi will appear at the age of 40 and come to power following the death of a ruler. There will be a dispute among the Muslim people, but he will unite the Muslims and spread Islam throughout the world. He will make treaties with the Romans (the West), and the last of the treaties will last for seven years. Mahdi will be in power for seven years before his death.

Prophetic Pitfalls

In the news, **Muqtada al-Sadr**'s Mahdi Army of more than 10,000 **militia** has recently pledged military support to Iran if the United States or Israel were to attack Iran.

During the time of Dajjal and Mahdi, *Isa* (Jesus) will descend from heaven. Mohammed wrote that Jesus, the prophet to the Jews, was not killed on the cross but was taken into heaven by Allah. Isa (Jesus) is said to return from heaven descending with angels at the time of a great battle. Mahdi will lead the Muslims into battle against the Dijjal and the Jews, but Mahdi will not be able to defeat or kill the Dijjal.

At the appearing of Isa, the Dijjal will retreat, but Isa will kill the Dijjal with his sword. The Jews will be killed, and all the surviving people will revert to Islam and return to their own countries.

The reign of Isa will last 40 years from the time he appears. During his reign, Islam will be the worldwide religion, and peace, harmony, and tranquility will pervade the world. Also during the 40 years, no one will die, animals will not harm anyone, and the land will be extremely fruitful. Furthermore, during the 40 years, Isa will marry and live for 19 years before he dies and is buried next to Mohammed.

After a time, there will be another great battle when *Yajuj and Majuj* (Gog and Magog) invade the world and destroy it. Then Allah will bring the world to an end.

Muslim End Times apocalyptic literature has become highly popular in certain Islamic circles in the last 20 years. One source of the current interest is the 1987 book *The Anti-Christ*, by Said Ayyub. Said Ayyub is to many Muslims what Hal Lindsey is to many evangelical Christians. In his book, he interpreted events of the modern world in terms of the Muslim traditions and the Bible, and identified the United States as the "Great Satan."

The current president of Iran, Mahmoud Ahmadinejad, seems very serious about the idea of the End Times. On November 16, 2005, in a speech to senior clerics in Tehran, Ahmadinejad said his main mission was to "pave the path for the glorious reappearance of Imam Mahdi (May God Hasten His Reappearance)." Ahmadinejad wants Iranians to prepare for the coming Mahdi by turning the country into an advanced Islamic society and by avoiding the excesses of the West.

Mormon Perspective

Mormonism, whose major denomination is the Church of Jesus Christ of Latter-Day Saints, was founded by Joseph Smith Jr. He presented the Book of Mormon in 1830. Their very name, Latter-Day Saints, indicates that they believe that we are in the Last Days.

The Mormons believe that many signs will occur before the Second Coming of Jesus Christ. Several of the signs happened in the 1800s during the early days of the Mormon Church. Some of the remaining signs include the rebuilding of a temple in Israel; the building of a Mormon Temple in Jackson County, Missouri; wars among the nations; and the preaching of the restored Gospel in all nations.

Then Jesus Christ will return and usher in a 1,000-year era of peace. During this period, called the Millennium, Satan will be bound. At the end of the Millennium, Satan will be loosed and there will be war on earth again. The world will then be destroyed by fire, but all Mormons will be saved from the destruction. Then every person who has lived since the beginning of time will be resurrected, judged, and placed either in outer darkness or into one of three heavenly kingdoms.

Jehovah's Witness Perspective

The Jehovah's Witnesses, also known as the Watchtower Society, have a detailed theology about the End Times. They believe that the Greek word in the New Testament often translated as "coming" should be translated as "presence." By their calculations, Jesus returned to earth in an invisible coming or "presence" in 1914 and now rules over the earth.

Jehovah's Witnesses do not believe in an end of the world or planet, but rather in a conclusion of present things. The following is a list of events to occur:

- Christ will return and Satan will be thrown down to earth with his angels.
- Peace and security will come before destruction.
- The beast of Revelation (Antichrist), using the world political system of the United Nations, will destroy Babylon the Great (all false religion).
- Satan will attack true Christians.
- God will war against the nations at Armageddon.
- Christ will reign for 1,000 years.
- Satan will be let loose, will gather followers, and will be destroyed with his followers.
- Christ will turn the Kingdom over to the Father.

As you can see, there are similarities and differences among the different religions, as well as differences among believers within each religion. Next we talk a little about how the different religions view Jesus, and then we talk about some different End Times views among Christians.

Various Christian Views

As you know from our brief review of different End Times beliefs, a number of religions recognize Jesus. Some say He was a prophet, a teacher, or even a Christ. However, for purposes of distinction, Christians recognize and accept that Jesus Christ, the Messiah, is and was Almighty God.

Following is a list of some religions with an indication of who each believes Jesus of Nazareth to be.

- Christianity: Almighty God
- Jehovah's Witnesses: Michael, the archangel
- Mormons: A god
- Islam: A prophet
- Judaism: A false messiah
- Baha'i: A christ

Even though Christian religions believe that Jesus is who He claimed to be, they still do not all believe the same thing about the Last Days or His return. These differences in belief are also present within denominations and even local church bodies. Christian beliefs on the End Times are so divergent that most churches today avoid the topic, for fear of upsetting some of their members.

Let's start our brief discussion about Christian End Times views with the early church.

Early Church (A.D. 100–1800)

The early church leaders seemed to take a literal view of End Times events. They basically believed that the Antichrist would rise to power and then there would be a terrible time of persecution and suffering for the followers of Christ. Then Christ would return to defeat the Antichrist and deliver His people into the Kingdom of God. The Roman Catholic Church played an integral part in early church development.

Roman Catholic

Today the Roman Catholic Church is a very hierarchical organization led by a pope. The Roman Catholic Church reserves the right to interpret Scripture for its members. Regarding the End Times, it officially takes few doctrinal stands on the many prophetic events and issues. However, the Roman Catholic Church does believe that the church has been in the Last Days for almost 2,000 years.

The Roman Catholic Church believes that, under the New Testament covenant, God is building His kingdom in the members of His church. Then at the "end of time," the world as we know it will reach completion.

The Prophet Says

John wrote, "They came to life and reigned with Christ a thousand years. (The rest of the dead did not come to life until the thousand years were ended.) This is the first resurrection. Blessed and holy are those who have part in the first resurrection. The second death has no power over them, but they will be priests of God and of Christ and will reign with him for a thousand years. When the thousand years are over, Satan will be released from his prison." (Revelation 20:5–7)

The Roman Catholic Church has taken two doctrinal positions regarding the Last Days. First, there will be no literal 1,000-year reign of Christ on earth. Around A.D. 400, St. Augustine interpreted the 1,000 years as a metaphor for the time of the Last Days church. In Chapter 5, we discuss briefly how and why this belief developed. It remains part of church doctrine.

The Roman Catholic Church is also against the relatively new theology known as dispensationalism (which we discuss in a minute). The church rejects the following dispensational beliefs:

- Two plans are in place for God's people: one for Israel and another for the church.
- There will be a 1,000-year Kingdom of God on earth.
- A secret rapture of the church will take place.

However, Catholics do believe that the Antichrist will rise to power near the end of the age and then there will be a time of trial for the church. The Second Coming of Jesus Christ will occur when the Kingdom of God has reached completion.

Protestant and Evangelic

The most popular End Times view of the Protestant Evangelic church in the United States is based on a relatively new theology referred to as *dispensationalism.* This view has become increasingly popular in the United States since it was originally developed by John Nelson Darby in the 1830s. One of its most famous supporters was Cyrus Ingerson Scofield (1843–1921), who footnoted the dispensational view into his now famous Scofield Reference Bible.

The dispensation view was further popularized by Hal Lindsey in his 1970 best-selling book *The Late Great Planet Earth.* Then in 1995, Tim LaHaye and Jerry Jenkins wrote *Left Behind,* which became part of a Last Days series of books that have sold more than 60 million copies. With the increasing popularity of this view, many more authors and teachers have jumped on this bandwagon, making it the most popular End Times view in the United States. Even non-Christians are familiar with it. However, very few people who are familiar with this view know about the theology of dispensationalism. What they do know about is the *rapture.*

def•i•ni•tion

The **rapture,** according to the dispensationalists, is a "secret" removal of Christ's followers from the earth before the great persecution of the others begins. The time of tribulation following the removal of the Christians is when the Antichrist persecutes God's followers. The **dispensationalists** say that those persecuted will be Jews and "Tribulation Saints" (new followers of Christ).

def•i•ni•tion

The **Great Tribulation** is the last three and a half years of this present age, which will conclude with the Second Coming of Jesus Christ. The Bible identifies the Great Tribulation as a period of unprecedented persecution and death for God's people.

Dispensationalism, as you might guess by its name, is a relatively complex and involved theological system. What has made this End Times view so popular is one key component: the rapture, or, more specifically, the pre-Tribulation rapture. The dispensational view says that the followers of Jesus Christ will be removed from the earth before the period known as the *Great Tribulation.* Essentially, Christ's followers are out of here before the trouble starts. This form of "tribulation avoidance" is why the rapture is so popular. After all, who would want to face a future that includes the Great Tribulation?

About America's infatuation with the rapture, Bill Moyers, in 2005, said, "In this past election, several million good and decent citizens went to the polls believing in the Rapture index. That's right—the Rapture index. Google it and you will find that the best-selling books in America today are the 12 volumes of the *Left Behind* series written by the Christian fundamentalist and religious right warrior, Timothy LaHaye. These true believers subscribe to a fantastical theology concocted in the 19th century by a couple of immigrant preachers who took disparate passages from the Bible and wove them into a narrative that has captivated the imagination of millions of Americans."

But there are still others.

Dissenting Opinion

Some believe that everything will continue on indefinitely. They don't believe in a Second Coming (the physical and visible return of Jesus Christ to earth) or in a future earthly Kingdom of God. They say that these times are no different than any other time on earth.

The Bible prophesied that people would feel this way in the Last Days. The Apostle Peter, in his second New Testament letter, told Christ's followers that in the Last Days, scoffers will not believe that Christ will actually return to earth and set up the promised kingdom. Peter said that scoffers would ask, "Where is this Second Coming He promised?" They will continue to pursue their own desires, believing that nothing has changed and that everything will go on the way it always has from the beginning.

The Prophet Says

The Apostle Peter wrote, "First of all, you must understand that in the last days, scoffers will come, scoffing and following their own evil desires. They will say, 'Where is this "coming" he promised? Ever since our fathers died, everything goes on as it has since the beginning of creation.'" (2 Peter 3:3–4)

Who are these scoffers that Peter mentioned, and what do they believe about the Second Coming?

Worldly Skeptics

Some people believe that the world will continue on, with no end in sight.

Albert Schweitzer, in 1899, wrote *The Mystery of the Kingdom of God*. Using the Gospel of Matthew, Schweitzer argued that Jesus believed that the world was about to reach a catastrophic end and that it would happen before His disciples completed their mission. Several years later, Schweitzer developed his idea in a second book titled *Quest of the Historical Jesus.* Basically, Schweitzer believed that Jesus was wrong. He concluded that each of the Second Coming Gospel accounts in Matthew 24, Mark 13, and Luke 21 refer to a Second Coming that never happened and never will.

If Schweitzer and others who share his opinion are correct, this would mean that not only was Jesus not who He said He was, but also that He was not even a true prophet because prophets of God do not make false predictions.

In 1919, existentialist Karl Barth wrote *Epistle to the Romans.* In Barth's view, regardless of what the New Testament writers might have believed, the Second Coming is an ever-present spiritual reality but will not be a physical reality. There will be no literal Second Coming. The theme of the Second Coming is to be a reminder of the eternal reign of Christ in our lives.

Many other scholarly books written in the last 70 years have expressed variations of Barth's and Schweitzer's theories. Some variations of these two views have even crept into modern church doctrine.

But scholarly unbelievers are not the only skeptics.

Christian Skeptics

When Peter mentioned Last Days scoffers, he was warning Christ's followers about scoffers in the organized church. The Christian skeptics referred to by Peter would be familiar with the idea of the Second Coming and God's promise to establish a kingdom of righteousness on earth. So what was Peter warning them about? There was no reason Christ's followers would need to be warned about skeptics outside the church because they would not know Christian beliefs.

Before we discuss the answer to that question, let's list, in chronological order, some Bible basics regarding the Second Coming, the 1,000-year Kingdom of God on earth and Final Judgment.

- Jesus of Nazareth, the Messiah, also called Christ, will physically and visibly return from heaven to earth.
- When Christ returns, He will judge His followers at what Scripture calls the Judgment Seat of Christ.
- When Christ returns, He will establish His kingdom in Jerusalem.

- He will reign over the world for 1,000 years.
- After the 1,000 years, everyone else will be judged at Christ's Great White Throne.

Now let's discuss some forms of skepticism that exist in the organized Christian church today.

— Last Days Timeline —

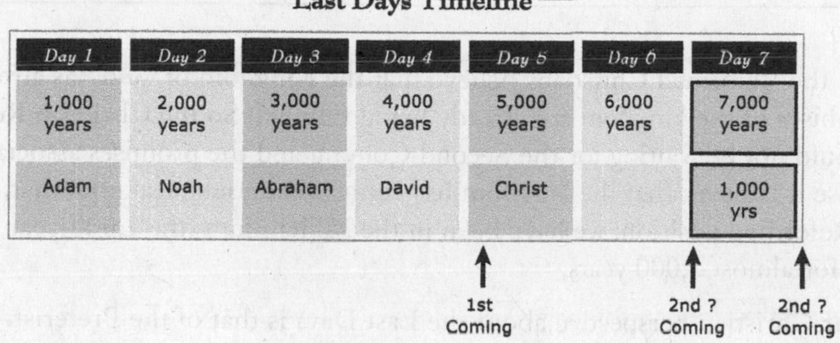

Day 1
Day 2
Day 3
Day 4
Day 5
Day 6
Day 7
1,000 years
2,000 years
3,000 years
4,000 years
5,000 years
6,000 years
7,000 years
Adam
Noah
Abraham
David
Christ
1,000 yrs
1st Coming
2nd ? Coming
2nd ? Coming

Reformed Skeptics

Christian Reformed eschatology has some of its roots in Judaism and some in Roman Catholicism.

The Jews expected that when the Messiah came, he would immediately set up the Kingdom of God in Jerusalem. The Christian Reformed view borrows from the Jewish expectation and says that the Kingdom of God began in A.D. 32 with the First Coming of Jesus the Messiah. Therefore, the Christian Reformed view has Jesus currently reigning over the earth from heaven.

We have already seen that the Roman Catholic Church also believes that the church is currently in the 1,000-year reign of Christ on earth. Both the Christian Reformed view and that of the Roman Catholic Church believe that the kingdom is progressing and maturing toward completion.

However, the Reformed belief and the Catholic belief differ from the Jewish belief. The Judaic belief is that, when the Messiah comes, the kingdom will immediately be physically set up with the Messiah ruling from David's throne in Jerusalem.

The Prophet Says

"For to us a child is born, to us a son is given, and the government will be on his shoulders. And he will be called Wonderful Counselor, Mighty God, Everlasting Father, Prince of Peace. Of the increase of his government and peace there will be no end. He will reign on David's throne and over his kingdom, establishing and upholding it with justice and righteousness from that time on and forever. The zeal of the Lord Almighty will accomplish this." (Isaiah 9:6–7)

Because the Reformed Christians believe that the Kingdom of God has already begun, the promises of the kingdom are already being fulfilled. So the Christian Reformed view would not be waiting for the Second Coming and the promises associated with it because it believes that the kingdom has come. We should also note that, according to the Reformed position, we have been in the Millennium (the 1,000-year reign of Christ) for almost 2,000 years.

A similar Christian perspective about the Last Days is that of the Preterist. *Preterist* means "past." The Preterist view is that everything that was prophesied in the Bible about the Second Coming and the end of the age was fulfilled by the year A.D. 70. Therefore, they also believe that we are in the 1,000-year reign of Jesus Christ.

As we can see, there are several variations of the view that the world is currently under Christ's rule. Within this view, the only thing remaining is final judgment. Some within this view believe that Jesus will visibly return for the judgment, and some do not.

Now that we have briefly discussed some major religions' views on the Last Days, we begin a careful and comprehensive look at what the Bible has to say. The Bible (Old and New Testaments) represents the earliest comprehensive documentation regarding the Last Days and the end of this world as we know it. We discuss some of the basic foundational teachings of Scripture before we examine the future prophecies to the Last Days. The discussion in this book of the Last Days considers all the major biblical prophecies, so you will be able to see for yourself what the Bible has to say on the topic.

The Least You Need to Know

- Many people are talking about the Last Days and the End Times.
- Although the religions of the world have different points of view on the End Times, many things that they believe are very similar to one another and to biblical prophecy.
- Christians may be united in who they believe Jesus is, but they have many different points of view regarding His return and His Millennial reign.
- The skeptics also have different points of view about the Last Days.

Chapter 2

First Days First

In This Chapter

- From God's patterns to God's plans
- A lesson from the Garden of Eden
- Understanding the biblical Last Days
- What last day is it now?

This book covers the Last Days as they are foretold in the Bible. The first thing you'll need to know is what a "day" is in God's plan. This is one of the essential building blocks on your way toward understanding the Last Days. In this chapter, you will read about God's perspective on the Last Days and begin to understand where we are in the Last Days.

First Things First

Before we talk about the signs and events that will occur during the Last Days, it will help you to understand a few biblical basics. We take the approach that everything in *the Bible* was inspired by God to reveal something to mankind, and that God wants us to know who He is, who we are, what He has done, and what He is going to do. The God of the Bible tells us that if we want to know the truth, we can read what is written and understand it. "For we do not write you anything you cannot read or understand." (2 Corinthians 1:13)

In The Beginning

The Bible tells us that God has a definite character and awesome capabilities. God declares in Scripture that He is all-powerful. "Sovereign Lord, you have made the heavens and the earth by your great power and outstretched arm. Nothing is too hard for you." (Jeremiah 32:17)

def•i•ni•tion

The *Bible, Scripture,* and the *Word of God* are synonymous. The **Bible** is made up of two parts. The Old Testament, containing 39 books, was written before the First Coming of Jesus Christ. The New Testament, containing 27 books, was written after the First Coming of Jesus Christ.

Claiming to be "all-powerful" is very different from claiming to be simply "powerful." Consider the creation account. We are told that God created everything in heaven and on earth in six days and rested on the seventh day. Now, if the God of the Bible was just *very* powerful, He may have needed six days to create the heavens, the earth, and all that is in them. And if God was just *very* powerful, He may also have needed a day to rest.

However, the God of the Bible is not just *very* powerful—He is *all-powerful.* He could have created everything in a flash, in the twinkling of an eye!

When God created the heavens and the earth, He used seven days and nights to show His plan for creation. He wants us to know what He is going to do. "I make known the end from the beginning, from ancient times, what is still to come." (Isaiah 46:10) While God was creating the universe, He was also establishing a pattern of making His purposes known and revealing part of His plan for the world.

Biblical Days

Next, let's look at how Scripture explains what a "day" is. Basically, the Bible presents two different "days." One is the 24-hour period we're familiar with. But when I say "Last Days," I am referring to the other type of day, a much longer period of time. Let's start by exploring the answers to the following questions:

- How long is a biblical day?
- How many days will there be?

- How many days have been completed?
- How many days are left?

Once we answer these questions, we will be ready to understand the Last Days.

Day One, Day Two ...

The Bible says the events of creation took place in six days, with the seventh day designated by God as a day of rest. God's pattern and plan started like this:

- **Day 1:** The light was created. Light was separated from the dark, marking off day and night.
- **Day 2:** The sky was created to separate the water from the earth and sky.
- **Day 3:** The land and seas were separated on the earth, and vegetation was created.
- **Day 4:** The sun, moon, and stars were created, to mark off the times and the seasons.
- **Day 5:** The birds of the air and the creatures of the sea were created.
- **Day 6:** The creatures of the land were created. Man was created, male and female, and given dominion over the earth.
- **Day 7:** The day of rest was established.

By the end of the sixth day, God had finished creating everything. On the seventh day, a day of rest, God blessed His creation and made it holy. These are the basic aspects of the creation week, the seven-day pattern God set for His creation, and God's plan for the world.

Seven Day Creation Timeline

Day 1	*Day 2*	*Day 3*	*Day 4*	*Day 5*	*Day 6*	*Day 7*
Light and Dark	Earth and Sky	Land and Sea	Moon and Stars	Fish and Foul	Animals and Man	Rest

God's seven 24-hour days of creation is an Old Testament metaphor for His greater plan. The New Testament tells us that the Last Day is the seventh day, also known as

God's Sabbath-rest. We are also told in the New Testament that the last biblical day is an extended period of time which we will discuss shortly. Therefore, God's greater plan for the world takes place over seven *biblical* days. God will work out His purposes for man in "six days" and then, on the "seventh day," the Sabbath rest, He will complete His work: restoring all of creation to a right relationship with Himself. This book focuses on Days 6 and 7, and the transition from Day 6 to Day 7.

Trouble in Paradise

Before we leave the creation story, we can learn an important lesson about carefully and accurately understanding what God has said as opposed to what we *think* He said. The lesson in this story about correctly handling the Word of God is repeated throughout Scripture and will help us as we study the prophecies about the Last Days.

In Genesis, we are told that things went wrong soon after God placed the first humans, Adam and Eve, in the Garden of Eden. This story demonstrates the importance of reading God's Word carefully. A careless reader (or listener) will not understand God's plan and may be deceived into acting contrary to his own best interest. This theme is repeated throughout the Bible, and many warnings about deception are associated with the Last Days Scripture. Therefore, it's appropriate for us to consider the story of Adam and Eve in more detail.

Initially, Adam was close to God. They spent time together, and God instructed Adam regarding his responsibilities. God also issued Adam a command: "You are free to eat from any tree in the garden; but you must not eat from the tree of the knowledge of good and evil, for when you eat of it you will surely die." (Genesis 2:16–17) The command and the warning were clear, so what could go wrong—and what can we learn from it?

The Devil Made Me Do It

In the garden, Eve saw that the fruit of the tree was good for food, pleasing to the eye, and useful for gaining wisdom. She wanted to eat the fruit but knew it was forbidden.

Faced with the temptation, Eve tried to recall what God had said. Most likely, *Satan*, through the serpent, planted a seed of doubt in Eve's mind about

def•i•ni•tion

Satan is the devil, the great dragon, the ancient serpent. He is a powerful angel who rebelled against God and strives to rise to the throne of God by destroying the people and plans of God.

God's command. The serpent told Eve that she would not die. Instead, the serpent explained, God did not want her to eat of this tree because she would be like God and would know good from evil.

Notice what Eve did in her conversation with the serpent to set her up for the fall. Eve said to the serpent, "We may eat fruit from the trees in the garden, but God did say, 'You must not eat fruit from the tree that is in the middle of the garden, and you must not touch it, or you will die.'" (Genesis 3:2–3)

Although it appears that Eve's misinterpretation of what God said is subtle, it may have contributed to her disobedience. It also should serve as another lesson to us regarding the careful interpretation of what God has said.

Eve did eat from the forbidden tree, and she gave some of the fruit to Adam, who ate it as well. This disobedience had consequences. God told Adam that because he had listened to Eve and eaten what was forbidden, He would put a curse on the earth, and man would have to work hard all his days to produce food to eat. God explained that this would be man's life until man returned to the dust of the earth. This curse, a punishment for disobedience, will be lifted on the Last Day of God's plan for man.

Now, if we compare what God said to what *Eve* said He said, we find that the two statements are different. Eve added to the words God had spoken, and she also left out some words. Eve's misinterpretation or poor recollection may or may not have contributed to her disobedience. However, the lesson to readers of the Bible is clear: adding to or taking away from God's Word changes the meaning. If we change the meaning, we will not know what the Bible says about the Last Days. Therefore, this book attempts to carefully and correctly interpret what God has said in Scripture about the Last Days.

It's interesting that this first lesson in the Bible is essentially the same as the Bible's final warning. In the last few verses of the last chapter in the last book of the Bible, God warns us not to add to or take away from His Word. "I warn everyone who hears the words of the prophecy of this book: If anyone adds anything to them, God will add to him the plagues described in this book. And if anyone takes words away from this book of prophecy, God will take away from him his share in the tree of life and in the holy city, which are described in this book." (Revelation 22:18–19)

The Prophet Says

"Hear now, O Israel, the decrees and laws I am about to teach you. Follow them so that you may live and may go in and take possession of the land that the Lord, the God of your fathers, is giving you. Do not add to what I command you and do not subtract from it, but keep the commands of the Lord your God that I give you." (Deuteronomy 4:1–2)

It's as though the God of the Bible is saying, "Trust Me, I said what I meant and I meant what I said." (If you would like some guidance on how to correctly interpret Scripture, see Appendix A.)

A Day with the Lord

Equipped with the seven-day creation pattern and our lesson from Eve, let's return to our list of questions about a biblical day. To understand what is meant by the biblical Last Days, we need to know what a day is. Our first question is, how long is a biblical day?

Both the Old Testament and the New Testament answer this clearly. In Psalm 90:4, we are told that a thousand years in God's view are like a day in our view. And to ensure that we understand that nothing changes with God and His purposes, in 2 Peter 3:8–9, we are reminded that, with God, a day is like a thousand years and a thousand years are like a day. Therefore, we should not get impatient. He will fulfill His plan in time. From what He says, it seems that God thinks His followers have a tendency to be impatient and forgetful!

God, who is timeless and dwells in eternity, is communicating His schedule to us who dwell in time. With these passages we are able to determine the scope of God's greater plan. When God says a day is a thousand years and a thousand years is a day, He is repeating the same message for emphasis.

Our next question is, how many days will there be? To this we will apply the creation pattern of seven days. So, there are a total of seven days, or 7,000 years, in God's greater plan for creation and mankind. As I mentioned earlier, we are told in the New Testament that the Last Day is the seventh day and that the Last Day will be 1,000 years in duration. Therefore, we can determine from what Scripture states that there will be seven biblical days of 1,000 years in God's greater plan.

When a Day Is Not a Day

Our next question is, how many days have been completed so far? The biblical record lists the age in which fathers begat sons, from Adam all the way to Abraham, Isaac, and Joseph. From these genealogies we are able to calculate that there were 1,656 years from Adam to Noah and the Great Flood. From these we also know that there were 2,200 years from Adam to the time of the Hebrew patriarch, Abraham.

Therefore, from Adam to Abraham, there were just over 2,000 years. If a thousand years is a day, this means two days passed before Abraham came on the scene in Day 3.

— Last Days Timeline —

Day 1	*Day 2*	*Day 3*	*Day 4*	*Day 5*	*Day 6*	*Day 7*
1,000 years	2,000 years	3,000 years	4,000 years	5,000 years	6,000 years	7,000 years
Adam	Noah	Abraham				

↑ Here

From the time of Abraham onward, Scripture does not provide a year-by-year account. However, the historical record provides information we can use to determine the passing of time. Combining the scriptural account and the historical record, we are able to approximate the time that has passed.

I outline God's seven-day plan incorporating the explanation that one day equals a thousand years so you can see the biblical week and the amount of time it represents.

- Day 1: From 1 to 1,000 years
- Day 2: From 1,000 to 2,000 years
- Day 3: From 2,000 to 3,000 years
- Day 4: From 3,000 to 4,000 years
- Day 5: From 4,000 to 5,000 years
- Day 6: From 5,000 to 6,000 years
- Day 7: From 6,000 to 7,000 years

Approximately another thousand years passed from the time of Abraham to King David. David began his reign about 1,000 years before Christ. The Hebrew people had entered into slavery in Egypt; then, after many years, Moses led them out of slavery through the desert to the land God had promised. Joshua picked up where Moses left off and the Hebrews entered into the Promised Land. There they were governed by judges until God gave His people their first king, Saul. The time from Abraham to Saul lasted several hundred years and completed Day 3. King David succeeded Saul, which brings the time of David to the beginning of Day 4.

— Last Days Timeline —

Day 1	Day 2	Day 3	Day 4	Day 5	Day 6	Day 7
1,000 years	2,000 years	3,000 years	4,000 years	5,000 years	6,000 years	7,000 years
Adam	Noah	Abraham	David			

↑ Here (Day 4)

What a Difference a Day Makes

From the reign of King David in the Promised Land through a turbulent history, another 1,000 years, Day 4, passed. During this period, Israel had a succession of kings and violent wars with her neighbors. In about 600 B.C., Israel was conquered by Nebuchadnezzar, king of Babylon. Exiled in Babylon, the prophet Daniel received several visions regarding the Last Days. Daniel also received a prophecy indicating the precise timing of when the *Messiah* would come to His people. Jesus Christ arrived on the scene at the beginning of Day 5. From the time of Jesus' First Coming, in A.D. 32, the world has been in the Last Days.

> **def•i•ni•tion**
>
> **Messiah** is a Hebrew word that means "the anointed one of God." In the New Testament, the term for the anointed one is *Christ*. Christ is a title; Jesus is His name. That is why He is called, Jesus Christ. According to the New Testament, Jesus is the Messiah.

The first days of God's biblical week included Days 1, 2, and 3. Day 4 is the middle of the week. Days 5, 6, and 7 are the Last Days. The New Testament writers indicated that they considered themselves to be in the Last Days when they wrote, "In the past God spoke to our forefathers through the prophets at many times and in various ways, but in these last days he has spoken to us by his Son, whom he appointed heir of all things, and through whom he made the universe." (Hebrews 1:1–2) Therefore, Jesus Christ's First Coming was at the beginning of Day 5, and Day 5 was the first of the Last Days.

> **The Prophet Says**
>
> David saw the coming of the Messiah. "This is the day the Lord has made; let us rejoice and be glad in it. O Lord, save us; O Lord, grant us success. Blessed is he who comes in the name of the Lord." (Psalm 118:24–25)

From the time of Christ's First Coming to today, almost 2,000 years have passed. That means almost two more days. Our calendar today is dated from the approximate time of Christ's birth. Don't forget that the birth of Jesus Christ and His First Coming are two different dates. It has been calculated today that Jesus was actually born around 4 B.C. However, His First Coming is dated at A.D. 32, when Jesus rode into Jerusalem as king, just as prophesied in Psalm 118:24 and Zechariah 9:9 and described in the Gospel of John 12:15.

The Day That the Lord Has Made

There are differences of opinion as to when the First Coming of Jesus Christ took place. As you know, it's important to our study of the Last Days because we want to know when Day 5 starts. Some think His coming was at His birth, while others think it was when John the Baptist baptized Him in the Jordan River. For our purposes, we want to rely on the scriptural record to determine the timing.

The Prophet Daniel gave the prophecy from which we can calculate the precise time of the First Coming. Daniel wrote, "Know and understand this: From the issuing of the decree to restore and rebuild Jerusalem until the Anointed One [Messiah], the ruler [king], comes, there will be seven 'sevens' [7 years], and sixty-two 'sevens' [7 years]." (Daniel 9:25) Daniel's prophecy states that from the decree to rebuild Jerusalem, which was issued by King Artaxerxes in 445 B.C., there would be a total of 69 sevens of years until the Messiah the king comes. Sixty-nine sevens of years equals 483 years.

This is what Scripture declares as the First Coming of Jesus Christ, the Messiah, which took place in A.D. 32—that's 483 years from the issuing of the decree. You should also realize that the reason 445 B.C. and A.D. 32 do not add up to 483 years is that the world's calendar has undergone numerous changes. From 445 B.C. to A.D. 32 is 483 years using the biblical 360-day year calendar.

In other words, 2,000 years, or two days, have already passed since the birth of the Christ child. However, because the First Coming of Christ occurred in A.D. 32, we still have a few years left until a full two biblical days have elapsed from the First Coming of Christ.

You should also realize that because the biblical record does not account for every year since Adam, we cannot know exactly how many years have passed since creation. We can, however, estimate how much time has passed. Based on the estimates, we are getting very close to the end of Day 6 and the beginning of Day 7.

So, the answer to our question concerning how many days are left is that there is one full day left in the Last Days, Day 7, and at least several years before we reach the end of Day 6 and the beginning of Day 7.

— Last Days Timeline —

Day 1	Day 2	Day 3	Day 4	Day 5	Day 6	Day 7
1,000 years	2,000 years	3,000 years	4,000 years	5,000 years	6,000 years	7,000 years
Adam	Noah	Abraham	David	Christ		

We are Here.

Remember that God set aside Day 7 as a Sabbath rest. This is what Scripture reveals about Day 7 in Hebrews 4:9–10. There still remains a Sabbath rest for the people of God. Anyone who enters God's Sabbath rest will also rest from his or her own work, as God rested from His work. This Sabbath rest is also referred to in Scripture as the Last Day. I explain more about the Last Day as we go.

Today Is the Day

Now that you have the basic picture of the biblical week, let me show you how Scripture refers to the Last Days. The term *Last Days* is recorded eight times in Scripture. The first mention of the Last Days was by the prophet Isaiah. In Isaiah 2:2–4, he referred to the Last Days when describing the final state of affairs on earth, or Day 7. He wrote that in the Last Days, the kingdom of the Lord and his temple will be above all the other kingdoms. All the nations of the world will come to His kingdom to learn the ways of God so they can live by them. The law of the land will come from Jerusalem, and the Lord God will judge between the nations and settle their disputes. The nations will beat their swords into plowshares and pruning hooks, and no longer will they train for war.

Although Isaiah's picture of Last Days is specifically referring to Day 7, it is not the only prophecy about the Last Days. Most prophecies regarding the Last Days are not so heartening. Most of the time when we read about the Last Days, we read about Day 6. Because the world has already gone through all of Day 5 and most of Day 6, we should realize that the world does not seem to be moving naturally in the direction of the Kingdom of God. The Kingdom of God will be one of righteousness and peace. History and the current state of the world would indicate, as does the Bible, that the world is going from bad to worse. So that we have the full picture, let's review some other biblical prophecies about the Last Days.

When the Apostle Paul wrote in 2 Timothy 3:11, he said there will be terrible times in the Last Days. Paul is not describing Day 7. The Last Days he is describing will be more like what the world has seen in Days 5 and 6. More than likely, Paul is referring to the last part of Day 6, the time we live in.

James also records a sobering warning regarding the Last Days in James Chapter 5. He warns, listen, you rich people, weep and wail because of what is coming. Your wealth has deteriorated and your goods are gone. Your things testify against you and consume your flesh like fire. Because you have hoarded wealth in the Last Days, you're in for some really bad times. James is prophesying about events that haven't yet happened but that occur very near the end of Day 6. It's a prophecy about what happens just before we reach Day 7, the Sabbath rest. We can see from these prophecies that there will be a big difference between Day 6 and Day 7.

After Two Days

We have answered all our questions about a day, in the context of God's seven-day plan. We know how long a day is and where we are in God's seven-day week. Now I would like to show you how Jesus expressed His mission using God's 1,000-year day. If Jesus Christ's First Coming took place in A.D. 32, by A.D. 2033, Christ will have been gone for 2,000 years, or two days.

In Luke 13:32, Jesus said, "Tell him I will drive out demons and heal people today and tomorrow, and on the third day I will reach my goal." According to the Bible, Jesus' goal is the Kingdom of God on earth, Day 7, the Sabbath rest. The Bible states that Christ will reign for 1,000 years in the Kingdom of God on earth. Therefore, Jesus Christ must return at the beginning of Day 7. We will cover the return of Christ and the coming Kingdom of God in more detail in subsequent chapters.

Prophetic Pitfalls

The Bible declares that Jesus Christ will return to earth and reign in Jerusalem in the Kingdom of God. Scripture indicates that His Second Coming will be just as real, both physically and visibly, as His First Coming.

The Last Day

Jesus Christ returned to heaven in A.D. 32, about 40 days from His resurrection. So, He has been gone for almost two days, Day 5 and 6. Christ's prophecy seems to be saying that He will return from heaven after two days, and on the third day, He will achieve His goal.

The prophet Hosea said something very similar. He indicated that after two days, God will restore Israel and He will live with them. Hosea also indicated that as sure as the sun will rise, the Lord will appear and deliver his people after two days.

When we can picture God's seven 1,000-year days in our mind, many things that we read in Scripture take on a prophetic significance.

Now that we have this picture of Day 7, the Last Day, let's read a brief discourse by Christ. Here in the Gospel of John Chapter 6, Jesus describes what He will do for His followers on the last day: "I will lose no one that the Father has given me, but I will raise them up at the last day. Because everyone who believes in Me will live forever, I will raise them up at the last day."

Later in the Gospel of John Chapter 11, we read a conversation between Jesus and Martha. Their conversation explains that being raised at the Last Day is describing what happens at *the first resurrection.* Jesus told Martha that her brother would rise again. Martha, who had often listened to Jesus teach, said, "I know my brother will rise again in the resurrection at the last day."

def•i•ni•tion

The First Resurrection is the harvest gathering and the change that will take place in all the followers of Christ, both dead and living, at the return of Christ, as in Revelation 20:5. Scripture explains this as the raising of the dead and the changing of those left alive at that time.

The Least You Need to Know

- God's followers are not to add to or take away from the Word of God.
- God's day is a thousand years long, and there are seven days in His plan for mankind.
- We are in the last years of Day 6, and there remains a Sabbath rest, Day 7.
- Jesus has been gone almost two days; He said after two days, He would reach His goal.

Chapter 3

God's Appointed Times

In This Chapter

- The times as written in the Law
- The times as revealed in the feasts
- The times as spoken of by the prophets
- The present age and the coming age

Within God's greater plan, He has set times and seasons when key events are to take place. Each of these appointed times reveals something about what He is planning to do and when.

In the Bible, God employs several ways to reference His appointed times. By understanding each of these, we will be better able to identify the signs related to them and determine where in the Last Days we are.

In this chapter, we review God's seven-day plan, study His seasonal plan, touch on the times of God, and examine the ages of God as they relate to this age and the coming age.

Israel and the Law

In Chapter 1, we discussed how God revealed part of His plan with the seven-day creation week. Now we are going to see how God again shows a seven-day pattern with the Ten Commandments.

— Last Days Timeline —

Day 1	Day 2	Day 3	Day 4	Day 5	Day 6	Day 7
1,000 years	2,000 years	3,000 years	4,000 years	5,000 years	6,000 years	7,000 years
Adam	Noah	Abraham	David	Christ	Church	Kingdom
		↑ Here				

Before we get to the Commandments, let's talk about how the Bible refers to the "people of God." Abraham, the patriarch of the Jewish people, was a Hebrew. He had a son, Isaac, who had a son, Jacob. God changed Jacob's name to Israel. Israel was the father of 12 sons and their descendants. Twelve tribes were formed, and each tribe carried the name of one of Israel's sons. These tribes are known as the tribes of Israel. The peoples who make up the 12 tribes of Israel are all referred to as Israelites and are also called God's "chosen people." About 3,650 years ago, the Israelites lived in Egypt and eventually spent years in slavery to the Egyptians.

Pre-Law Days

Not long after the Israelites left Egypt, under Moses' leadership, they began to complain because they were running out of food. Moses asked God what he should do, and God told him that He would provide for the people. God told Moses that He would send birds for meat in the evening and bread in the morning. God said that He would provide the food the people needed each day, but He had specific instructions about how they were to gather the bread. God told them they could gather the bread each morning for their needs that day; however, they could not gather bread on the seventh day. The seventh day was set aside as holy unto the Lord, and no one was to work on the Sabbath rest. Therefore, God said He would provide a double portion of food on the sixth day so no one would need to work on the Sabbath. God gave them these instructions before He wrote the Ten Commandments. Step by step, God was incorporating His seven-day plan into their daily lives and emphasizing the significance of the seventh day, the Sabbath rest.

A Day in the Law of God

Three months after they left Egypt, the Israelites came to Mount Sinai and set up camp there. On Mount Sinai, God told Moses that if the people of Israel obeyed Him fully and kept His commandments, they would be His people and He would make them a kingdom of priests and a holy nation. The people agreed that they would do everything God said, and God made a covenant with them.

On Mount Sinai, God wrote the Ten Commandments on stone tablets as instructions for the Israelites. In the Ten Commandments, God revealed the respect that He was due, reminded them of the Sabbath rest, and told them how to behave toward one another. These are God's Ten Commandments, as recorded in Deuteronomy 5:6–21:

1. I am the Lord your God. Have no other gods before me.
2. Do not make for yourself an idol in the form of anything in heaven above or on the earth beneath or in the waters below. Do not bow down to them or worship them; for I am a jealous God.
3. Do not misuse My name.
4. Observe the Sabbath day by keeping it holy. Six days you will do all your work, but the seventh day is a Sabbath rest to the Lord your God. Do not work on the Sabbath.
5. Honor your parents, as the Lord your God has commanded you, so that you may live long and that it may go well with you.
6. Do not murder.
7. Do not commit adultery.
8. Do not steal.
9. Do not give false testimony against your neighbor.
10. Do not covet your neighbor's wife. Do not set your desire on your neighbor's house or land, or anything that belongs to your neighbor.

The Prophet Says

"And the Lord said to Moses, 'Go to the people and consecrate them today and tomorrow. Have them wash their clothes and be ready by the third day, because on that day the Lord will come down on Mount Sinai in the sight of all the people.'" (Exodus 19:10–11)

It is obvious that the Sabbath rest is a very important part of God's plan for man. God wrote more in the commandments to explain His Sabbath rest than He did in any of the other commandments. He also placed the commandment about the Sabbath rest after those about mankind's responsibilities to God but before those addressing mankind's responsibilities to one another.

Not only was the observance of the seventh day written in stone, but the Sabbath rest was being woven into the fabric of the Israelites' day-to-day existence, establishing the seven-day cycle we refer to as a week. God also stated that the law of the Sabbath rest was an eternal covenant, a sign between God and His people forever. God wanted His people to understand its importance and realize what it meant in God's plan for them. The people of God were to rest 24 hours out of each seven-day week as a foreshadowing of the coming 1,000-year Sabbath rest of Day 7.

God's Seasonal Feasts

Within His covenant of the law, God revealed much more about His purposes and plans for mankind. After God inscribed His commandments in stone, He instructed the Israelites to celebrate seven holy feasts each year, at appointed times. God gave the seven feasts to Israel as reminders of what God had already done and as indicators of what God was planning to do. Just as the seasonal cycles in nature include spring and fall harvests, God showed His people that there would be spring and fall harvests in His plan for them as well.

God also instructed the Israelites to make a sanctuary for Him as His dwelling place among them. This sanctuary is called the tabernacle, and it is an elaborate tent, made exactly as God instructed. The tabernacle is to be God's dwelling and the center of worship for the Israelites. God also instructed them to make a finely crafted chest of acacia wood, completely overlaid with pure gold. This golden chest was the Ark of the Covenant; in it they placed the stone tablets of the covenant.

Each of the seven Feasts of God represents an appointed time of Christ's work. The four spring and summer feasts signify what Christ would do (and now has done) at the time of His First Coming. The three fall harvest feasts represent what Christ will do at the time of His Second Coming during the Last Days.

The Prophet Says

"Remember that you were slaves in Egypt, and follow carefully these decrees. Celebrate the Feast of Tabernacles for seven days after you have gathered the produce of your threshing floor and your winepress. Be joyful at your Feast …." (Deuteronomy 16:12–14)

The seven feasts outline God's timetable and plan for His creation, culminating with the Sabbath rest, Day 7.

God spelled out the feasts in detail. The feasts involved the sacrifice of animals for the forgiveness of sins. The animal was to be sacrificed on the altar and burned over a fire. These were to be joyous occasions of celebration. Today these feast celebrations would look like an elaborate religious barbeque.

Next we cover each of the seven Feasts of God, including how the Israelites were to remember that feast and how Christ fulfills it.

Signs of Spring

The four spring and summer feasts of Passover, Unleavened Bread, Firstfruits, and Pentecost reveal God's bigger plan, just as the seven days of creation do. These feasts signify one advent of Christ and point to things He would accomplish. These feasts were fulfilled by Christ in about A.D. 32.

The First Feast, Passover, commemorates when the Israelites were in Egypt in bondage to Pharaoh, and God prepared to bring them out of their slavery. He instructed them to sacrifice a lamb and place its blood on the door frame of their house as a sign to protect their firstborn from death when the destroying angel passed over. (The destroying angel, a.k.a. the Destroyer, is first identified in the story of the Exodus, but we will find him referred to again in the Book of Revelation.) This miraculously protected them and also provided them the means of escaping from their Egyptian slavery. God told the Hebrews to remember these events by celebrating a Passover feast each year. When their children asked about the meaning of the Passover sacrifice, they were to explain how the Lord spared His people when He struck down the Egyptians.

Scripture explains that Jesus Christ fulfilled this feast when He sacrificed Himself, making a new covenant in His blood that protects His followers from eternal death and provides a means of escape from sin. "For Christ, our Passover lamb, has been sacrificed." (1 Corinthians 5:7)

The Second Feast, of Unleavened Bread, commemorates when God brought the Hebrews out of Egypt and into the desert. During their flight from Egypt, they ate unleavened bread (bread without yeast) for the first seven days. In Scripture, leaven always represents sin. Not using leaven symbolized their cleansing from the bondage of sin. God told the Israelites to remind their sons each year that they use no yeast and eat only unleavened bread for seven days because of what the Lord God did for His people when He brought them out of Egypt. This is covered in Exodus 13:7–8.

Jesus Christ, the one without sin, later sacrificed Himself and died a sinner's death to cleanse His followers from their sin.

The Third Feast, Firstfruits, comes at the end of the seven days of the second feast and signifies that God delivered the firstborn of Israel from death. The Feast of Firstfruits is to be celebrated each year using the first of the early harvest. The term *firstfruits* also means a promise of things yet to come.

The resurrection of Christ from the dead accomplished God's plan for the firstfruits of the harvest, guaranteeing His followers the promise of the resurrection and the eternal life to come in the Kingdom of God. Scripture reveals that Christ's new covenant provides the way for anyone who puts their faith in Christ to be grafted into the line of Abraham and receive the promises and the Kingdom of God.

The Heat of Summer

The Fourth Feast, or Pentecost, celebrates the day when God gave the Hebrew people His law on Mount Sinai, establishing His covenant with them. It is celebrated each year in late spring. Pentecost signifies the early or spring harvest also called the Feast of Weeks or Feast of Harvest.

Following His resurrection and ascension into heaven, the Bible says that Christ gave the Holy Spirit to His followers, establishing His new covenant with them. This new covenant, under the Spirit of God, began when the Holy Spirit fell like fire on Christ's followers during a Pentecost celebration not long after His ascension into heaven. The people were filled with the Holy Spirit and began to speak in other tongues as the Spirit enabled them. This is recorded in Acts 2:1–4.

The Fall Harvest

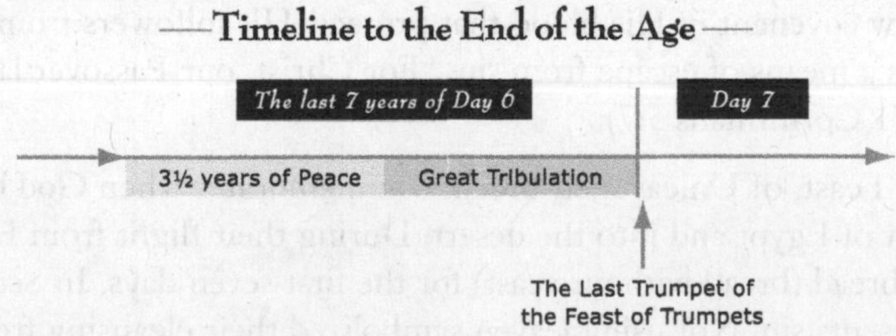

The Bible says that the three remaining fall harvest feasts of Trumpets, Atonement, and Tabernacles will be fulfilled by Christ at His Second Coming, as the world transitions from Day 6 to Day 7.

The sounding of trumpets alerted the Israelites to the impending Fifth Feast, the annual fall harvest gathering. The final trumpet blast signaled the time to assemble and begin the fall harvest feasts. This is recorded in Leviticus 23:23–25.

During the Last Days, the first six trumpets of God, as recorded in the Book of Revelation Chapters 8 and 9 (which we study in more detail later), will warn of the impending fall harvest, a harvest of the people of God. The seventh and last trumpet, in Revelation Chapter 11, will signal the return of Christ, the resurrection of Christ's followers, and the establishment of the Kingdom of God on earth.

The Prophet Says

"But in the days when the seventh angel is about to sound his trumpet, the mystery of God will be accomplished, just as he announced to his servants the prophets." (Revelation 10:7)

The Sixth Feast, the Day of Atonement, is the day when God judges the people and atones for the sins of His people. It's also called the Day of Judgment or the Day of Redemption, because it signifies God's judgment and redemption of His people. The annual feast day was to be a day when the people of God would do no work and would refrain from worldly things. This is described in Leviticus 23:26–31. This foreshadows the time when Jesus Christ will return and will judge the world, condemning the disobedient and rewarding His followers.

The Seventh Feast is known as the Feast of Tabernacles, the most joyous of God's harvest feasts. It serves as a reminder to the Israelites of the time they spent in temporary dwellings during the Exodus from Egypt to the Promised Land. This is recorded in Leviticus 23:33–36.

The Bible tells us that Christ will fulfill this final harvest feast when He establishes His kingdom and reigns on earth with His followers for 1,000 years. We are told that Christ will resurrect His followers and change them from their temporary dwellings (bodies of flesh) into their permanent dwellings (resurrected bodies). Therefore, Christ's followers will have permanent bodies at Day 7 when they enter the promised Kingdom of God on earth. This change is written of in 1 Corinthians 15:50–52. Another aspect of the Feast of Tabernacles is that Christ will live, or tabernacle, with His people. This is referenced in Leviticus 26:11.

God's Timing

God's predetermined times for carrying out His plans are specified by His holy feasts. It's interesting that the Hebrew word for *feast* means "appointed time."

The Bible speaks of "time" in much the same way you and I speak of time. However, God also uses "time" in the context of His overall plan, including the time of His Last Days. I also use the term "the End Times" interchangeably with the term "the Last Days." In Scripture, the concept of the Last Days is synonymous with the biblical terms *later times, last times*, and *time of the end.*

The Prophet Says

Daniel was told this about his prophecies: "'Go your way, Daniel, because the words are closed up and sealed until the time of the end.'" (Daniel 12:9)

The prophet Daniel's writings are key to understanding God's End Time plan. The expression "time of the end" appears several times in Daniel's prophecies. God tells His followers, in Daniel 12:9, that Daniel's prophecy will be sealed until the Last Days. When the prophecies of Daniel are unsealed, the people of God will understand them.

Changing Times

The New Testament writers refer to God's End Times in speaking of changes that will become more prevalent in the world. In 1 Timothy 4:1–2, Paul wrote that in the last times, people will abandon the true faith and follow deceiving spirits and things taught by demons. He said these deceptive teachings will be taught by hypocritical liars, people with their own motivations.

Jude wrote that in the last times, individuals will make fun of the truth and follow their own instincts and ideas. He warns the followers of Christ to remain in the Spirit of God and build themselves up in the faith as they wait for Christ to return and bring them into eternal life.

End Times

In the Old Testament, several writers recorded prophecies referring to the various times in the context of God's plan. One particular reference that several prophets repeat is to the "time of Israel's distress" or "Israel's time of trouble." In Jeremiah 30:7, the prophet says that the time of Israel's trouble will be so terrible that there will be none like it. This future time of Israel's trouble is also known as the *Great Tribulation.* We discuss the Great Tribulation in greater detail in Chapters 10 through 14.

def•i•ni•tion

The **Great Tribulation** is the 3.5-year period of unparalleled persecution and suffering of God's people brought on by Satan through the Antichrist and the False Prophet. This is the period of time recorded in Scripture, being referred to as 42 months, 1,260 days, and a time, times and half a time. (A "time" is a 360-day prophetic year. Therefore, a time, times and half a time equals 3½ years.) This period begins with the abomination that causes desolation and ends with the return of Christ at the end of the age, as written in Matthew 24:21.

From Age to Age

Yet another interval of time referred to in the Bible, called an "age," provides an important perspective to our understanding of the Last Days. The Bible indicates that there have been ages in the past and there will be ages in the future. Of the various intervals of time mentioned in the Bible, the "age" appears to be one of the longest. The Bible does not state when the present age began. It may have begun in the Garden of Eden or it may have begun after the Great Flood. However, the important thing for us to understand is that we are in the present age and that the next age is "the age to come." Jesus often referred to this present age and the age to come when He was discussing the coming Kingdom of God. The age to come is the Kingdom age in which God will fulfill all His prophetic promises. We will be discussing this in greater detail as we go through the book.

Before we go any further, I would like to clarify something about the Last Days. Some have gotten the impression, from certain biblical translations or things they've heard, that the Bible says that there will be an end to the world when Christ returns. This is because some Bibles translate the Greek word *aion* as "world," while others translate it as "age." Technically, both are true. The Bible indicates that mankind is destined for a great change as we move from this age to the next age. So great is the change that the prophet Isaiah describes it as God making a new heaven and a new earth. In Revelation Chapter 21, it's recorded that John has a vision of a new heaven and a new earth, and that the first heaven and the first earth pass away.

The Old Testament prophets also used the idea of "age" when they describe how God will fulfill His promises eternally. Isaiah says that the people of God will be saved by the Lord eternally and that their deliverance will be everlasting, to ages eternal.

According to Scripture, God will transition mankind from this present evil age into the age to come. This change will be cataclysmic; it will not be like the past transitions from one biblical 1,000-year day to the next. It is described as being like God's creation of the first heaven and the first earth. It's also compared to the days of Noah, when God destroyed the living things of the earth with a flood and started over.

So there will be an end to the first earth, but God will make a new one. Scripture refers to the new earth as being restored because it is the time when God restores everything. As we study this coming transition and the Last Days, I talk about this age and the age to come.

This Present Evil Age

Jesus spoke often of the present age in contrast to the age to come. He indicated that it is important that His followers understand the implications of the two ages. The Bible says that the way people live in the present age determines their future in the coming age. In Matthew 12:32, Jesus says that anyone who speaks against Him can be forgiven, but anyone who speaks against the Holy Spirit, won't be forgiven, either in this age or in the age to come. According to Scripture, an unforgiven person is not allowed in God's kingdom.

—Timeline to the End of the Age—

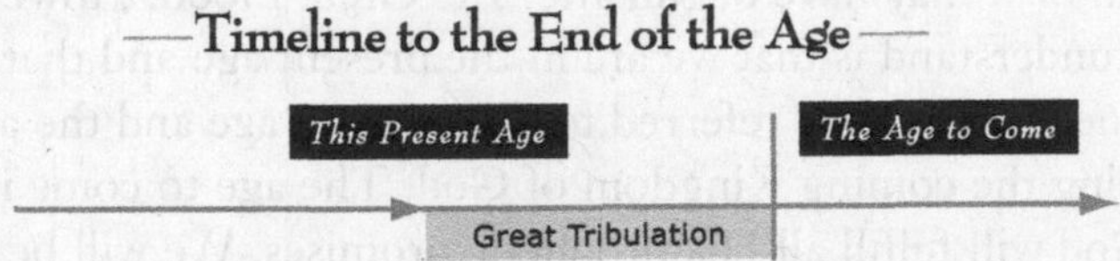

Jesus also seems to indicate that, just as the transition would be great from this age to the next, so would be the reward. In Luke 18:29–30, Jesus encourages His followers by assuring them that they will be greatly rewarded in the coming age, including the promise of eternal life. Jesus tells them that they may have to give up home and family in their pursuit of God, but it will be worth it in the end.

The Apostle Paul, in his two letters to the Corinthians, spoke about this present evil age, warning of its deceptive leaders and their ways that he said would come to nothing. Paul explained that the deception of this age has its origin in Satan, who he said is the ruler of the present evil age.

The Age to Come

Not only is the tremendous contrast between the two ages spoken of many times, but the Bible also tells of a great transition that the world must undergo to enter the age to come. Consistent with the harvest theme of God's fall feasts, in Matthew 13:37–41, Jesus explains His parable about the end of this age. He says that He is the one who planted the good seeds in the world and that the good seeds are His followers and belong to the Kingdom of God. The bad seeds are sons of Satan, the Devil, and the Devil planted them. At the end of the age, the sons of the Devil and all who do evil will be burned in the fire. Jesus concludes by saying that His angels are the harvesters who will gather His followers into the Kingdom of God.

Another of Jesus' teachings about the transition from this age to the age to come provides some clues to the dramatic transition that will be experienced by those entering the age to come. In Luke 20:34–36, Jesus is recorded as saying that people in this age marry and carry on their lives. However, He says that the people who are worthy to enter the age to come will not marry. He also says that they will be changed in the resurrection, that they will be immortal, with spiritual bodies like those of the angels. They will live forever.

During the final days of Jesus' first time on earth, Jesus was sitting on the Mount of Olives when His disciples came to him and asked what sign He would give to indicate that His return and the end of the age were near. In Matthew Chapter 24, Mark Chapter 13, and Luke Chapter 21, the disciples record the many signs and events that Jesus explained will take place before the end of the age and His return.

On one of His last occasions with His disciples, Jesus told them that He would be with them in spirit as they carried on making disciples, to the very end of the age.

As we can see, God provides many pieces of information about the timing of His plan for the Last Days. We have now discussed God's days of the week, seasons of the year, times, and ages. Understanding these measures of time will help us as we go through this guide to the Last Days.

The Least You Need to Know

- Understand that the Sabbath rest is 1,000 years and begins at the return of Jesus Christ.
- God's spring and summer feasts have been fulfilled by Christ, and the fall feasts will be fulfilled at Christ's Second Coming.

- One of God's final periods of time is called the "time of Israel's trouble," which is also called the Great Tribulation.
- The present age is nearly over, and the age to come will be ushered in with a new heaven and a new earth.

Chapter 4

Thy Kingdom Come

In This Chapter

- God reveals His management style
- God picks a king after His own heart
- The Son of David will be King of Israel
- Prophecies about the coming King

The God of the Bible lets his people know what He is going to do in the future in many different ways. In this chapter, we see how King David and his son, King Solomon, reveal characteristics of the future King of Israel who will rule during Day 7. Each demonstrates an aspect of what God has planned for His people on the Last Day, when He sets up His eternal kingdom on earth.

The Old Testament prophets provide us with many details about the future King, the Kingdom of God, and how and when the kingdom will come into being. Some of their prophecies foretell the life and person of Jesus of Nazareth, but the vast majority of their prophecies describe a Second Coming, an event of cataclysmic and spectacular magnitude that will establish the future Kingdom of God on earth. In this chapter, we primarily discuss prophecies of the First Coming and reserve those about the Second Coming for subsequent chapters.

God Governs

In the previous two chapters, we discussed how God uses the days of the week and seasonal harvests to show what He is planning to do and when He will do it. Now we see how He uses Israel's leaders and kings to reveal how He will govern in His future kingdom.

> **The Prophet Says**
>
> The Israelites were told, "When you enter the land the Lord your God is giving you and have taken possession of it and settled in it, and you say, 'Let us set a king over us like all the nations around us,' be sure to appoint over you the king the Lord your God chooses." (Deuteronomy 17:14–15)

Shortly after God made His covenant with the Israelites, God advised Moses through his father-in-law to appoint capable men from all the tribes of Israel as judges to govern the Israelites. Moses took this advice and instructed these judges in God's Law so that they would be able to judge the simple cases themselves and refer the difficult cases to Moses. In this way, Moses was able to manage well over one million Israelites. This system of governance lasted throughout their journey across the desert and continued when they reached the land that God had promised them.

With the Ark We Can

The Israelites entered the Promised Land under the leadership of Joshua, who had been anointed by God before Moses died to replace him. With the Ark of the Covenant going before the Israelites, Joshua miraculously led them through the Jordan River, even though it was at flood stage. Once across the Jordan River, he had them set up the Tabernacle of God and the Ark of the Covenant on the plains of Gilgal, on the eastern border of Jericho. From their base camp at Gilgal, Joshua led the Israelites in many battles against the Canaanites in the Promised Land, beginning with the miraculous victory when Jericho's mighty walls collapsed and they defeated the city.

Up Close and Personal

The Bible tells us that God wanted to be the Israelites' king and led them through the judges and the prophets. It's described as though God doesn't want to be too far removed from His people. You may recall that in the creation story, God wanted to walk with Adam in the garden. Similarly, He doesn't want to give the Israelites a king because He is to be their king. As we go through the scriptural account of the history of Israel's kings and kingdoms, we find that God always wants to remain close to His people.

Kings of Israel

During the first 300 years in the Promised Land, God's judges continued to rule over the Israelites. Then God chose a prophet and judge named Samuel. Though God seems to have wanted a more direct relationship with the people, the Bible indicates that the Israelites wanted a king like the other nations. Eventually, God gave in to their request and had Samuel anoint Saul as the first king over Israel. Saul reigned as king for about 50 years until God had Samuel anoint another to succeed as king and replace the line of Saul. God chose to replace Saul because he failed to obey the word of God. (Never mind how.)

God instructed Samuel to anoint a young shepherd named David to be king over Israel. God chose David and his lineage because David was a man after God's heart. Even though David had been anointed by God to be king, he respected Saul as God's first anointed and did not resist him or attempt to succeed Saul. When Saul was killed in battle with the Philistines, David was made king over Israel.

The Heart of David

Scripture tells us that David was courageous as a youth and a man, and that he and his men accomplished valiant feats of daring and bravery. It's written that he was revered by all of Israel and highly favored by God. David was a warrior king, and under King David, Israel prospered and was victorious over her enemies. David wanted to please God in all he did and wanted to build a permanent house for the Lord. However, God told David that he was not the one to build His temple. Although King David did not build a temple for God, he did bring the Tabernacle of God and the Ark of the Covenant from the site in Gilgal to the city of David, in Jerusalem.

During David's reign, God revealed to David that his son would be the one to build God's temple. There were two components to this prophecy. First, the prophecy said that David's son Solomon would be the one to build the first Temple of God in Jerusalem. Though some of David's other sons attempted to succeed to his throne, Solomon was anointed as the next king of Israel before David died. When David died, Solomon was made king, and he built the first Temple of God in Jerusalem.

def•i•ni•tion

Son of David is a prophetic name for the anointed one of God, the coming Messiah, the Christ, the future King of Israel who will reign from David's throne forever.

The second aspect of the prophecy has not been fulfilled yet. In addition to telling him that his son would build the temple, God told David that the Messiah would come through David's lineage and would reign on David's throne. The Bible says that Jesus Christ, who is also known as the *Son of David*, will build God's eternal temple. The Apostle Paul describes the eternal temple as being built of the followers of Christ, with Jesus Christ as its chief cornerstone. This is recorded in Ephesians 2:19–21.

The Wisdom of Solomon

When Solomon became king, God asked him what he wanted. Solomon asked for a wise and discerning heart so that he would be able to lead the great people of Israel. Because Solomon did not ask for something for himself, God granted him not only the wisdom he asked for, but also such riches and honor that no king would be his equal during his lifetime. Solomon used his great wealth and wisdom to build the first Temple of God, as had been prophesied.

The Prophet Says

"'The days are coming,' declares the Lord, 'when I will fulfill the gracious promise I made to the house of Israel and to the house of Judah. In those days and at that time I will make a righteous Branch sprout from David's line; he will do what is just and right in the land. In those days Judah will be saved and Jerusalem will live in safety. This is the name by which it will be called: The Lord Our Righteousness.' For this is what the Lord says: 'David will never fail to have a man to sit on the throne of the house of Israel ….'" (Jeremiah 33:14–17)

In choosing Solomon to build the first Temple of God in Jerusalem, God was accomplishing a specific task and also revealing wisdom and honor that would belong to the future Son of David when He rules from Jerusalem.

Solomon's Temple

The Bible tells us that Solomon's temple was magnificent, made by Israel's finest craftsmen from the best materials available. We are told that Solomon spared none of his great wisdom and wealth in constructing the Temple of God. All the articles of the temple were made of pure gold, and the wooden interior was covered in pure gold. When the temple was completed, King Solomon had all of David's gold and silver articles dedicated to the temple and brought into its treasuries. All the leaders of the tribes and the priests assembled in Jerusalem for the dedication. Solomon's temple was dedicated during the fall harvest feasts of the seventh month, and the Ark of the Covenant was brought from the tabernacle of David into Solomon's temple and put in the Most Holy Place. The Most Holy Place is the inner sanctuary of the temple, which contained the Ark of the Covenant, signifying the presence of God.

The Prophet Says

Jesus said to the angel of the church, "I am coming soon. Hold on to what you have so that no one will take your crown. Him who overcomes I will make a pillar in the temple of my God." (Revelation 3:11–12)

King Solomon's dedication celebration in Jerusalem was so lavish that the number of sheep and cattle sacrificed could not be counted. Hundreds of priests participated in the joyous festival. They sang and played instruments accompanied by 120 priests sounding trumpets. The whole of Jerusalem was in joyous celebration marveling at the magnificent Temple of God. When the priests withdrew from putting the Ark of the Covenant in the Most Holy Place, the glory of the Lord filled the temple.

Just as God reveals His plans through the kings He chooses, He also reveals the importance of His temples. Solomon's temple is a foreshadowing of God's final, Last Day temple, which we discuss in the final chapters.

Good Kings, Bad Kings

After Solomon, many kings ruled over Israel in the Promised Land over a nearly 500-year period. A few of the kings followed the commandments and decrees of the God of the Israelites, but many were disobedient and went their own way, following other gods and doing things detestable to God. In His law, God had instructed His people that He would bless them when they were obedient and punish them when they were not. This principle of God does not change.

The Prophets of Doom

During the last 250 years of the reign of the kings of Israel, God sent His people prophets. The prophets during this time were Joel, Amos, Hosea, Micah, Isaiah,

> **The Prophet Says**
>
> Jeremiah warned the Israelites, "This is what the Lord Almighty, the God of Israel, says: Reform your ways and your actions, and I will let you live in this place. Do not trust in deceptive words, and say, 'This is the temple of the Lord, the temple of the Lord, the temple of the Lord!'" (Jeremiah 7:3–4)

Nahum, Jeremiah, Habakkuk, Zephaniah, and Obadiah. The prophets warned the people and the kings to turn back to God and away from their wicked ways. We are told that the prophets' messages almost always fell on deaf ears and hard hearts. During the same period, there were many false prophets, and God's prophets were always ostracized, often beaten, and even killed because of their message. The false prophets were popular with the kings and the people because they told them what they wanted to hear. The tribes of Israel did not stay united and ended up dividing into separate kingdoms.

Who Lost the Ark?

At the end of the time of the kings, there were just two kingdoms remaining, Judah and Israel. The prophet Jeremiah was one of the last prophets during this time, and he foresaw the coming defeat of Jerusalem by Babylon and the exile of the Israelites. Ultimately, both remaining kingdoms fell. When Judah was defeated, Jerusalem and Solomon's temple were destroyed. In about 575 B.C., the Israelites were taken in exile to Babylon. However, when the Babylonian army looted and destroyed the temple, they did not find the sacred articles of the temple or the Ark of the Covenant. Scripture does not indicate what happened to the sacred items, and they remain lost to this very day. I discuss prophecies relating to the missing articles and their importance to the Last Days in Chapter 9.

Since the defeat and exile of the last king and kingdom of the Israelites, the nation of Israel has been without her king. It has been almost 2,500 years, and Israel still does not have a king ruling from David's throne, as prophesied.

Prophecies of the Coming King

As we discussed, several of the prophets spoke and wrote about a future king of Israel who would rule righteously from David's throne. They also described a glorious future Kingdom of God that would encompass the whole world.

The prophet Jeremiah said that God would raise a righteous king from David's offspring who will gather the Israelites from all nations and rule over them in wisdom. The prophet Micah wrote of the kingdom of the Lord coming in the Last Days. He envisioned a future with the Lord ruling over many nations and peoples from His temple in Jerusalem. He described the people of the world as streaming to the Lord's kingdom to learn the ways and wisdom of God. This prophecy is recorded in Micah 4:1–3.

The prophet Micah predicted the birthplace of Israel's future ruler. He wrote that, although Bethlehem was small, out of her would come the one who would rule over Israel. This is recorded in Micah 5:2. The prophet Zechariah wrote very specific details about what the coming would look like. He wrote that Jerusalem would be loudly rejoicing when her king would come riding on the colt of a donkey. These details are recorded in Zechariah 9:9–10.

Isaiah Tells All

No prophet of God wrote more about the future King of Israel than Isaiah. Isaiah prophesied that the house of David would see a son born of a virgin and He would be called "God with us." Isaiah wrote that the kingdom would be on this child's shoulders, that this king would reign from David's throne, and that His kingdom would never end. These accounts are recorded in Isaiah 7:14 and 9:6–7.

In another prophecy, Isaiah wrote that one from the house of David who seeks justice and righteousness would establish His throne in love and faithfulness. In another he wrote of Christ as proclaiming good news to the poor, freedom to the captives, and the year of the Lord's favor. In addition to these descriptions of the future King, Isaiah described in detail the suffering and death of the Christ. The depictions of Christ's suffering are recorded in Isaiah Chapters 52 and 53. From Isaiah's many prophecies, readers of Scripture can see the coming Son of David from His birth to His sacrificial death and His triumphal return. Isaiah prophesied so extensively about the First Coming of the Messiah that some people call Isaiah's writings the Old Testament's Gospel of Jesus Christ.

Isaiah provides his readers with extensive, vivid accounts of the Second Coming. We discuss Isaiah's Second Coming prophecies in more detail; for now, just keep in mind that Isaiah described the coming Day 7 kingdom similarly to the other prophets.

Daniel Tells Time

The prophet Daniel had many visions and prophecies about the Last Days, including details about the events leading up to the coming Kingdom of God on earth at Christ's Second Coming. The Book of Daniel also provides information that can be used to calculate the date of Christ's First Coming.

— Last Days Timeline —

Day 1	*Day 2*	*Day 3*	*Day 4*	*Day 5*	*Day 6*	*Day 7*
1,000 years	2,000 years	3,000 years	4,000 years	5,000 years	6,000 years	7,000 years
Adam	Noah	Moses	David	Christ	Church	Kingdom

↑ Time of the Kings and the Prophet Daniel

It will help your understanding of the Bible's account of the Last Days if you understand more about Daniel's prophecies of the First Coming of Christ. Daniel received his prophecies in around 550 B.C. Daniel's prophecy stated that the Messiah would come 483 years after the decree to restore and rebuild the city of Jerusalem. The only decree that called for the rebuilding of Jerusalem is in Nehemiah Chapter 2. It states that in the month of March (the Jewish month of Nisan) in the twentieth year of King Artaxerxes (445 B.C.), the king decreed that Nehemiah would go to Jerusalem and rebuild the city.

Using the biblical calendar of twelve 30-day months per year, and taking into consideration calendar changes, we can calculate from Daniel's prophecy that the Messiah would come in April A.D. 32.

Before I move on to the other prophets' descriptions of the coming Messiah, I should point out that this same prophecy is in Daniel Chapter 9, also describing some other key events that will take place in the Last Days, just before Christ's Second Coming.

Prophets Tell More

As you have now read, many of the prophets provided details about the coming Messiah and King of the Jews. Let's quickly summarize the major prophecies and put the events they foretell in chronological order:

1. **Micah:** He will come from Bethlehem.
2. **Isaiah:** He will be born of a virgin.
3. **Isaiah:** A son will be born, and He will rule on David's throne, upholding righteousness forever.
4. **Isaiah:** He will preach good news to the poor.

5. **Zechariah:** The King will come humbly, riding on the colt of a donkey.
6. **Daniel:** The anointed one, the King, will come in A.D. 32.
7. **Isaiah:** He will suffer, die, and then see the light of life. God will assign Him a portion among the great.

The Last Old Prophet

After the last Old Testament prophet, Malachi, in about 425 B.C., Scripture remained silent as to what God was doing until the time of the New Testament. The long silence was finally broken when the angel Gabriel announced to Zechariah that his wife, Elizabeth, would give birth to a son whose name would be John.

Their son would become known as John the Baptist, who we are told came in the spirit of Elijah to prepare the way for the Lord and turn the hearts of God's people to righteousness. Six months after Gabriel's announcement to Zechariah, Gabriel also announced to a young virgin named Mary that she was to give birth to a son, whose name was to be Jesus. It is recorded that the angel Gabriel declared that Jesus would be called the Son of God and the Son of David, and that God would give Jesus the throne of His father David to reign over forever.

First Coming, Second Coming, Which Coming?

Woven into the many writings of the Old Testament prophets are numerous accounts and descriptions of the future Messiah and His arrival on earth. Some of these accounts, such as those I mentioned earlier, address the First Coming. Other prophecies are so different from those regarding the First Coming that they describe either another Messiah or two different arrivals of one Messiah. However, Scripture is clear that there is only one Messiah.

Because the vast majority of the prophecies about the Messiah relate to the Second Coming, we discuss them in subsequent chapters. However, so you see what I am talking about, let me give you a couple examples of the prophet's Second Coming descriptions.

The King's Kingdom

In addition to the prophecies we discussed earlier, Isaiah wrote about the coming of one who would rule the world from David's throne in an account that does not mention the birth of the Christ child or His suffering and sacrificial death. Instead, this account describes the scene of the Second Coming as one in which the whole earth is broken and thoroughly shaken. Isaiah identifies the time as the Day of the Lord, when the Lord will punish those in the heavens and on the earth for their guilt and rebellion. This day (the Last Day) will come many days after the moon and the sun go dark. After this we are told that the Lord Almighty will reign with His people gloriously from Mount Zion in Jerusalem. This account is recorded in Isaiah 24:17–23.

Ezekiel's version of the Second Coming of the Messiah goes something like this: the Lord will gather the Israelites out of all the nations and bring them back to their land; His people will be united under one shepherd, and David will rule over them forever. God will dwell with His people and will be their God. Ezekiel writes that the whole world will know that God makes His people holy because He will put His Temple with them forever.

These prophetic accounts are examples of prophecies that have not yet been fulfilled. They describe the Second Coming of the King, and, as you have already read, they will take place at the end of the age as we go into the Last Day, Day 7.

Name That Messiah

Before we leave the prophets and their prophecies about the future king, let's take a look at some of the names they used for the Messiah. Then you will know who they are referring to as you read their prophecies.

Isaiah 2:9–19	The Lord Almighty
Isaiah 8:6	Wonderful Counselor, Prince of Peace
Isaiah 10:17	The Light of Israel
Isaiah 10:20	Holy One of Israel
Isaiah 11:10	Root of Jessie
Isaiah 15:5	One from the house of David
Isaiah 40:10	Sovereign Lord
Isaiah 62:11	Savior
Isaiah 66:15	The Lord
Daniel 7:13	One like the Son of Man
Daniel 9:25	Anointed One, the ruler

Jeremiah 30:9	David their King
Ezekiel 37:25	David my servant
Hosea 3:5	David their King
Joel 2:11	The Lord
Zechariah 6:12	The Branch
Zechariah 9:9	Your King
Zechariah 9:14	The Lord

We have now seen how God governs His people and who He selected for His royal lineage. We have also sampled a few of the many prophecies about a future Son of David. In the next chapter, we will see how some of these prophecies have been fulfilled.

The Least You Need to Know

- In God's government, God wants to be the king and likes to be close to His people.
- God has a plan for a future king, who will come from the line of David.
- The Old Testament prophets wrote many details describing the Messiah.
- The Old Testament prophets also described two different arrivals of the Messiah.

Chapter 5

The King Is Just Visiting

In This Chapter

- The first signs of the King
- What the King had to say for Himself
- What the King said about His kingdom
- What the King said about His return

Four hundred years after the Old Testament prophets completed their prophecies about the coming of the Messiah, He showed up right on cue. We looked at the prophecies in the previous chapter; in this chapter, we see how they were fulfilled. Not only did Jesus Christ fulfill many of the prophecies, but He also explained a great deal about how He would fulfill the remaining prophecies.

While Jesus was with the people, He taught them about the current Kingdom of God and His future Day 7 kingdom. He explained that when He left earth, He would be gone for a long time and then would return to settle accounts and set up the new order.

Born to Be King of the Jews

In Chapter 3, we discussed several of the Old Testament prophecies that pointed to the time of the First Coming of the Son of David, the Messiah, King of the *Jews.* These prophecies describe His birth, life, and death. I also mentioned a couple prophecies that describe the Second Coming of the Messiah. These Second Coming prophecies describe the Messiah's return in terms of a glorious heavenly appearance, followed by His eternal reign from David's throne in Jerusalem.

> **def•i•ni•tion**
>
> The terms ***Jews,*** *Jewish people, Israelites,* and *Hebrews* are used interchangeably to refer to the people of God. For our purposes, this terminology is not just referring to people who live in a certain country.

Now we examine what Scripture says about the fulfillment of the First Coming prophecies. Seeing how prophecies have already been fulfilled is an indicator of how those yet to be fulfilled will be.

We are about to discuss how the people knew, from Scripture, about the Messiah and His imminent arrival. This should reassure us that the God of the Bible wants His people to know and understand what He is going to do ahead of time.

Jesus of Nazareth

When the New Testament period begins, more than 400 years have passed since the last Old Testament prophecies about the coming Messiah and the eventual establishment of His Kingdom on earth. As the curtain rises on the New Testament period, several prophecies of Isaiah and the other prophets were beginning to be fulfilled in the person of Jesus of Nazareth. We are told of Jesus' miraculous birth, that He was born of the Spirit of God through a virgin in the town of Bethlehem, Israel. He was born into the family of Joseph, who was a descendant in the line of King David.

> **The Prophet Says**
>
> "But you, Bethlehem Ephrathah, though you are small among the clans of Judah, out of you will come for me one who will be ruler over Israel, whose origins are from of old, from ancient times." (Micah 5:2)

Shortly after Jesus' birth, the Romans imposed King Herod, who believed the child was the one prophesied to become King of the Jews. He attempted to have the Christ child killed. Scripture records that an angel of God warned Joseph of the danger and told him to flee to Egypt. Years later, after Herod had died, an angel told Joseph that it was safe to return to Israel. Joseph took Jesus and his mother, Mary, back to Israel, and they settled in Nazareth. In the Old Testament, each of these events in Jesus' life was foretold as a sign of the Messiah. The Bible indicates that these events fulfill some of the prophecies about the Messiah you read about in Chapter 3.

In the New Testament, we are told that Jesus grew up in Nazareth with Joseph, Mary, and His brothers and sisters. At the age of 30, in what is now dated as approximately A.D. 29, He began His public ministry when He came from Galilee to the Jordan River to be baptized by John the Baptist. Soon afterward, Jesus began to teach in the Jewish synagogues and preach in the Israeli countryside. He taught with such knowledge and authority about the Kingdom of God that the people were amazed.

In his lifetime, Jesus is recorded to have performed many miracles of healings, signs, and supernatural feats. Scripture records that He fed more than 5,000 people with only a few fishes and loaves, that He walked on water, that He calmed a violent storm, and that He raised people from the dead. Even though Jesus became very popular with the people, He never submitted Himself to be made king or sought worldly power.

Visiting the Jewish People

The prophet Daniel wrote that the Messiah would come to the Jewish people. In other words, the Messiah was not coming to just anyone—He was coming to His people in fulfillment of the prophecies. In the biblical accounts of His life, Jesus seems to make it a special point to go only to the Jewish people. He traveled through the regions of Israel preaching His message and teaching in the synagogues. He was so focused on carrying His message to the Jewish people that He is even reported to have avoided non-Jews.

On one particular occasion, He even admonished a gentile woman who sought His help. A Canaanite woman of Greek descent came to Jesus and begged Him for help, but Jesus did not even respond to her. Finally, when His disciples asked Jesus to send her away, Jesus told the woman that He had been sent to the lost sheep of Israel and had nothing to do with their "dogs." This event is recorded in Matthew 15:22–28. Scripture records other situations in which Greeks sought out Jesus, but it was clear from everything Jesus did that His message was for the Jewish people.

They Knew Their Prophecies

So Jesus came to the Jewish people. But did they understand the Old Testament prophets? How did they interpret the prophecies about the coming Messiah, the King of the Jews? Were they aware that this was the time of His coming?

The New Testament provides plenty of evidence that the prophecies regarding the coming Messiah were common knowledge at the time. As I mentioned earlier, the Roman imposed King of Israel, Herod, believed the prophecies about a coming King. The wise men who first came to Jerusalem seeking the child who was King of the Jews understood the prophecies. The priests and teachers of the law in Judea, whom Herod consulted, understood the prophecies and knew that the Messiah would come from Bethlehem and that He would be the one to shepherd the people of Israel. So before the birth of Jesus Christ, and during His life, many in Israel were aware of the prophecies about the Messiah.

The Prophet Says

"The crowd spoke up, 'We have heard from the Law that the Christ will remain forever ....'" (John 12:34)

The general knowledge about the Messianic prophecies is also evident in accounts of the crucifixion of Jesus. When Jesus was being beaten and flogged by the Roman Praetorian Guard, they mocked Him and called Him "King of the Jews." The Roman governor of Judea, Pontius Pilate, had a sign placed on the cross above His head that read, "This is Jesus, the King of the Jews."

And many recognized Jesus as the fulfillment of these prophecies. Everywhere Jesus went, crowds and people addressed Him as "the Son of David." When they wanted to be healed, they would call out to Him, "Lord, Son of David, have mercy on us." When Jesus rode into Jerusalem on the colt of a donkey as the prophet Zechariah had written, the crowd shouted to Him, saying, "Save us, Son of David," and "Blessed is He who comes in the name of the Lord."

There was also much confusion, however. The prophecies related to His First Coming and those describing the Second Coming are mixed together. Trying to reconcile the descriptions of the two separate events at one time caused doubt and confusion. On one occasion, we are told that when the crowd was trying to decide whether Jesus was the Messiah, they remembered that the Christ was to be King forever. They also had difficultly reconciling the fact that the Messiah was to come from Bethlehem but is also described as appearing in clouds from the sky. These two accounts are from the Gospel of John 12:34 and 7:27.

Expecting Company

So Jesus was coming to the Jewish people, and they knew of the prophecies about the Messiah. However, were they expecting Him to appear at this time, circa A.D. 32?

— Last Days Timeline —

Day 1	*Day 2*	*Day 3*	*Day 4*	*Day 5*	*Day 6*	*Day 7*
1,000 years	2,000 years	3,000 years	4,000 years	5,000 years	6,000 years	7,000 years
Adam	Noah	Moses	David	Christ	Church	Kingdom

First Coming
A.D. 32

At the time, John the Baptist was preaching repentance in the desert and baptizing people in the Jordan River. The people were waiting expectantly for the Christ, and some wondered if John might be the Christ. This is written in Luke 3:15. During this time, some Jews from Jerusalem sent people to ask John if he was the Christ. John denied that He was the Christ. In fact, he, too, was waiting for the Christ's appearance and sent his disciples to ask Jesus if He was the Messiah.

During the time that John the Baptist was preaching and baptizing, Jesus began to assemble His own disciples. Several of Jesus' disciples seemed to know that the Messiah's time was at hand. For example, in the Gospel of John Chapter 1, Andrew went to his brother Simon Peter and declared that Jesus was the Messiah. On another occasion, a Samaritan woman told Jesus, "I know the Messiah (called Christ) is coming."

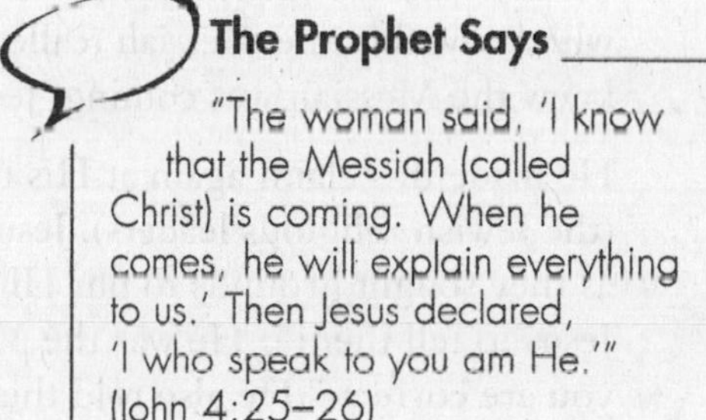

The Prophet Says
"The woman said, 'I know that the Messiah (called Christ) is coming. When he comes, he will explain everything to us.' Then Jesus declared, 'I who speak to you am He.'" (John 4:25–26)

Clearly, many of the Jewish people were aware of the general timing of the Messiah's coming, probably because of the information that the prophet Daniel had provided.

Who Did He Claim to Be?

Jesus fulfilled many of the Messianic prophecies, but many are still unfulfilled. But before we find out more about the remaining prophecies that will be fulfilled in Days 6 and 7, we should consider who Jesus Himself claims to be.

The Son of God

On one occasion, Jesus asked His disciples, "Who do the people say that I am?" At that time, Jesus also asked Simon Peter, "Who do you say I am?" When Peter said, "You are the Christ, the son of the living God," Jesus blessed Peter for his answer. Jesus also told Peter that this truth he had spoken was revealed by the Father, not something that could be given by man. Obviously, Jesus agreed with Peter's response. This exchange is recorded in Matthew 16:13–18.

Another time when Jesus was healing people and casting out demons, the Bible says the demons shouted at Jesus, saying, "You are the Son of God!" Jesus rebuked them and prevented them from speaking further because they knew He was the Messiah and He didn't want the demons proclaiming this. This is recorded in Luke 4:40–41. So even the demons, who are spiritual beings, are recorded as knowing who Jesus was.

Messiah Called the Christ

Though most of the time Jesus expected people to recognize Him by what He did, occasionally He identified Himself as the Christ. Remember the woman at the well who knew that the Messiah (called the Christ) was coming? When she said that she knew the Messiah was coming, Jesus told her that He was the Christ.

He made this claim again at His trial, before the chief priests and the whole Sanhedrin (the Jewish religious leaders). Jesus did not respond to their charges or defend himself as they sought grounds to put Him to death. However, when the high priest asked Jesus to tell them if He was the Messiah, the Son of the Living God, Jesus said, "Yes, you are correct." He also told them that in the future, He would be seen coming on the clouds of heaven. Not only did Jesus claim to be the Christ on this occasion, but He also quoted a prophecy about the Second Coming of the Messiah and told them He would be the one coming in His Father's glory. The trial exchange is recorded in the Gospels of Matthew Chapter 26 and Mark Chapter 14.

So far, we have seen that Jesus openly claimed to be the Son of God and the Messiah (called the Christ). Although He never called Himself the Son of David, He did affirm and receive the title on various occasions. Let's now look at some other claims Jesus made regarding His identity.

"I Am" of the Old Testament

Once when Jesus was having a debate with some Jews about God, Abraham, and the children of Abraham, Jesus claimed that He had existed before Abraham. Now, remember that Abraham had lived about 2,000 years earlier. In this exchange, Jesus referred to Himself as "I Am," which is recorded in the Old Testament as a title God used for Himself when speaking with Moses. The title "I Am" and its meaning were extremely well known to the Jewish people. They understood that, by using this title for Himself, Jesus was claiming to be God. They responded by picking up stones to kill Him, but He slipped away in the crowd.

> **The Prophet Says**
>
> John writes of an exchange between the Jews and Jesus. "'You are not yet fifty years old,' the Jews said to him, 'and you have seen Abraham!' 'I tell you the truth,' Jesus answered, 'before Abraham was born, I am!'" (John 8:57–59)

This was indeed an unusual claim by Jesus, but it was not the only one. In another exchange with some Jewish people, Jesus indicated that it was very important that they believed He was the one He claimed to be—a matter of life and death. He said, "Unless you believe that I am the one I claim to be, you will die in your sins." Many audiences understood who Jesus was claiming to be. On one occasion, He was told, "We are not stoning you for any of the things you did, but because you, a mere man, claim to be God." These accounts are written in John 8:24 and John 10:33.

Clearly, Jesus claimed to be God, the Messiah, and the one who would fulfill the prophecies of the Second Coming and appear in heavenly glory, coming on the clouds.

What About the Kingdom?

Now that you know more about who Jesus said He was, let's consider His primary topic: the Kingdom of God. Jesus taught about the current state of the Kingdom of God on earth and about the future kingdom. The future Kingdom of God, on the Last Day, or Day 7, is a major part of a discussion of the Last Days. However, you need to know a little more about the current Kingdom of God to understand the final one.

> **Prophetic Pitfalls**
>
> The Bible says that the Kingdom of God includes everything. From the biblical perspective, this means that everything that happens in the world happens in the Kingdom of God. However, this does not mean that everything that happens or exists pleases God or is considered good.

First, let's consider some Bible basics. According to the Bible, God created everything, and everything is His. Therefore, the Kingdom of God is made up of the heavens and the earth—the whole natural and spiritual creation. This means that, even though the Bible says that Satan is the current ruler of the earth, the earth is still part of the Kingdom of God. When Jesus taught about the Kingdom of God, He sometimes spoke about the kingdom on earth in its current state, and He sometimes spoke about it at a future time. You can usually tell which period He was talking about from the context.

Let's look at some of Jesus' teachings about the Kingdom of God, to help us understand the Last Days.

Kingdom in Parables

Jesus frequently taught the people about the Kingdom of God using parables, short stories that illustrate a principle. After using a parable, Jesus often took His disciples aside and explained it to them. He told them that the secrets of the kingdom were not for everyone, but that His followers would understand. In the parables, Jesus described the present state of the Kingdom of God on earth, the time during which the world would await the King's return.

On one occasion, Jesus told a parable of a man who planted good seed in the field. While everyone was asleep, the enemy came and planted weeds. When the wheat and the weeds grew, the servants came and asked whether the owner wanted the weeds pulled up. The owner told them to wait until the harvest; then the harvesters would separate the wheat from the weeds. The weeds would be burned in the fire, and the wheat would be taken into the barn.

Jesus explained the meaning of this parable to His disciples by saying that Jesus was the man who had planted the good seed in His field. The good seed represented the people of the Kingdom of God. The Devil planted the weeds, representing the people of the Devil. The angels were the harvesters, and the harvest would occur at the end of the age. This description of the earth after Jesus' First Coming shows a world inhabited by those of God and those not, awaiting separation at the time of Jesus' Second Coming.

The Prophet Says

Jesus said, "The one who sowed the good seed is the Son of Man. The field is the world, and the good seed stands for the sons of the kingdom. The weeds are the sons of the evil one, and the enemy who sows them is the devil. The harvest is the end of the age, and the harvesters are angels. As the weeds are pulled up and burned in the fire, so it will be at the end of the age." (Matthew 13:37–40)

Hidden Kingdom

Another time, Jesus compared the Kingdom of God to treasure that a man found hidden in a field. The man hid it and, in his great joy, sold everything and bought the field. Jesus did not specifically explain this parable, but the meaning is similar to that of the previous parable. Jesus is the man, and the field is the world. The treasure represents the people of the kingdom. Christ left His treasure hidden in the world but bought it with His sacrificial death.

Jesus also described the Kingdom of God as being like yeast that a woman mixed into a large amount of flour until the yeast worked its way all through the dough. The woman most likely represents the Devil because yeast in the Bible is always representative of evil and sin. Therefore, the parable illustrates that, by the end of the age, evil will have worked its way through the whole batch of flour.

Jesus also said that the Kingdom of Heaven is like a king who prepared a wedding feast for his son. He sent his servants to gather those who had been invited, but the invited guests paid no attention. Then the king sent more servants to gather his invited guests, but those invited still refused to come, and they beat and killed the king's servants. Finally, the king sent his army and destroyed the murderers and burned the city. After this, the king invited anyone His servants could find, and the wedding hall was filled with guests. This depicts many being invited to be one of God's chosen, until the end of the age and the return of the Son of God.

From each of these parables, we can see how the Kingdom of God on earth will be during Day 6, as the world waits for the end of this age and the Second Coming.

The Second Coming

During the last several days of Jesus' time on earth, His disciples came to Him and asked what would be the sign of His Second Coming and the end of the age. His response to their question is popularly called the Olivet Discourse because He was on the Mount of Olives. The Olivet Discourse forms the basis of our discussion of the signs of the times in the next two chapters, but an aspect of the Olivet Discourse touches on the Kingdom of God.

Waiting for the Groom

Jesus told the disciples another parable about what the Kingdom of God will be like just before Christ's Second Coming. In the New Testament, Jesus often described His relationship to His followers in terms of a marriage, with Jesus the groom and His followers His bride. A wedding banquet and marriage ceremony will take place when He is united with His followers at His Second Coming. With that perspective in mind, let's consider the parable of the 10 virgins.

Jesus said that just before His Second Coming, the Kingdom of God will be like 10 virgins waiting for the bridegroom. Half of them were wise, and the other half were foolish. The foolish virgins took their lamps but didn't take any oil. The wise virgins took extra oil along with their lamps. The bridegroom was a long time in coming, and all of the virgins fell asleep. At midnight the watchman called out, "The bridegroom is here," and they all awoke. The foolish virgins' lamps were going out, and they went looking for oil. The wise virgins were ready. They entered into the wedding banquet, and the door was shut. Later, the others came and asked the bridegroom to let them in. He told them that he did not know them, and he did not let them in.

> **The Prophet Says**
>
> Jesus said, "The bridegroom was a long time in coming, and they all became drowsy and fell asleep. At midnight the cry rang out: 'Here's the bridegroom! Come out to meet him!' Then all the virgins woke up …." (Matthew 25:5–7)

Oil in the New Testament frequently represents the Spirit of God. The foolish virgins think that they are followers of Christ and will be waiting for Him. However, they are not true followers and do not have the Spirit of God. Once again, this parable shows a separation of the people at the end of Day 6, with Christ's true followers going into the kingdom and others, some of whom thought they were His followers, being left out.

Here Comes the Judge

This is another parable in the Olivet Discourse about the Kingdom of God on Judgment Day. Judgment Day will occur at the very end of the age as the world goes from Day 6 to Day 7.

Jesus said that at this time, the Kingdom of God will be like a man who gave His servants some of His resources based on their abilities. To one He gave five talents of money, to another He gave two talents, and to another He gave one talent. After a long time, the master returned to settle accounts with His servants.

The servants who had been given five talents and two talents had doubled their talents. The master said, "Well done, good and faithful servants! You have been faithful with a few things, so I will put you in charge of many things and you will share in your master's joy."

However, the servant with the one talent believed His master was a hard man, and he hid his talent in the ground. The master said to him, "You wicked and lazy servant, because you thought I was a hard man and did nothing with your talent, you will be thrown outside the kingdom, where there will be weeping and grinding of teeth."

After sharing this parable, Jesus reminded His disciples that when He returns in heavenly glory with all His angels, the people will be separated as a shepherd separates the sheep. The Sons of God will be gathered into the new Kingdom of God on earth, and the sons of the Devil will be cast out into utter darkness.

Inherit the Kingdom

In addition to entering the Day 7 Kingdom, Jesus says His followers will inherit it. Inheriting the Kingdom of God seems to involve more than just entry into the kingdom: each follower will also receive a reward. Let's see how Jesus described inheriting the kingdom.

At one of Jesus' earliest preaching engagements, He gave what is called the Sermon on the Mount. Jesus spoke of the qualifications for inheriting the Kingdom of God. On another occasion, Jesus taught about the rewards to be given to those inheriting the kingdom. Jesus said that those who have sacrificed much will receive much, as well as eternal life. He also warned His followers that the order of things in the coming Day 7 kingdom will not be as they are in this present age. He said that many who are first in this age will be last in the kingdom, and many who are last in this age will be first in the Kingdom of God. We discuss this aspect of the Kingdom of God and the coming age in more detail in the guide's final chapters, when we discuss what the coming kingdom will be like.

Coming Quickly

We can glean one other important point from the parables of the 10 virgins and the talents. In both of these, Jesus implies that He will be gone a long time and then will return. Jesus has been gone for almost 2,000 years now, so it has obviously been a long time! However, this has been a topic of confusion because of the New Testament writers' expressed expectations for Christ's return. Also, in the Book of Revelation, Jesus is recorded as saying several times that He would be coming soon. Reconciling these passages with Jesus' teachings that He would be gone a long time has been difficult.

But hindsight is 20/20, so it is easier to understand. Some still say, "It's all Greek to me," which raises another good point. The Greek word in the original manuscripts translated as "soon" in many Bibles also has another meaning: "quickly." Therefore, it is just as correct to translate what Jesus said as "I am coming quickly," instead of "I am coming soon."

The difference between the two possible meanings is important. If I said to you this morning as I left the house, "I'll return soon," you would have certain expectations about when I would return. But if I said, "I'll return quickly," your expectation might be different. You may understand my statement to indicate how long I will be gone, or you may understand it to mean that I will drive fast on my way home.

Prophetic Pitfalls

In some Bible translations, Jesus is recorded as saying, "I am coming soon." However, the better translation is "I am coming quickly." Jesus did not mean that He would be back soon; He meant that when He returns, His return will take place quickly. For us, this means we must always stay alert and keep watch because when the prophecies start to be fulfilled, everything will happen quickly.

After almost 2,000 years, we should understand Jesus' statement, "I am coming quickly," as an indication of how quickly the Second Coming will occur. This is consistent with other Scriptures, which describe the Second Coming of the Messiah as an event that will come very fast once it starts. In the next few chapters, we discuss the signs leading up to the end of the age and His return. At this point, we know that when the Second Coming prophecies begin to be fulfilled, everything will happen quickly!

The Least You Need to Know

- Jesus of Nazareth fulfilled many of the Messianic prophecies during the time of His First Coming.
- The people of Israel knew about the Messianic prophecies and were expecting the Messiah to appear when He did.
- Jesus acknowledged that He was the Messiah and indicated that He would be fulfilling the prophecies about the Second Coming in the future.
- Jesus said His true followers would enter the new Day 7 Kingdom of God.
- Jesus said that he would be gone for a long time but that His return would be quick.

Part 2

Signs of the Times

They say, "Ignorance is bliss," but that is not what the Bible says. The Bible says not to be ignorant and uninformed about the Last Days.

As you go through this book, you will see that the Bible tells us many things that must happen before the world changes from this present age to the age to come. Scripture has recorded a great many signs that it says tell when the Kingdom of God is near. Several Old Testament prophets mentioned Last Days signs in their prophecies. The New Testament writers reiterate the prophecies of the Old Testament and explain other signs that indicate the end is near.

In Part 2, you will learn how to distinguish the signs of the times.

YOU SHOULD HAVE PAID ATTENTION IN SUNDAY SCHOOL.

Chapter 6

Returning Soon?

In This Chapter

- Uncertainty about the coming kingdom
- Waiting a long time for the kingdom
- How will we ever know when?
- Lessons from the past

In the last chapter, we learned how the First Coming of the Messiah fulfilled many of the Old Testament prophecies, and we talked about some of the things Jesus taught about the future Last Day, Day 7, the Kingdom of God. The Bible teaches that Jesus lived on earth in human form for approximately 33 years until His ascension into heaven in A.D. 32. As of this writing, that means Christ has been in heaven for 1,974 years, waiting for the appointed time of His return. As we know, with God, 1,974 years may be just short of 2 days, but by human standards, it's a long time.

In this chapter, we discuss why there are differing ideas about when the Kingdom of God will come on earth and what we can learn from them. We also discuss how people in the Bible interpreted prophecy, and some of the theories and interpretations people have developed during the long wait for Christ's return. Because Christ did not give a specific date and time, there has been a lot of speculation, and some people have interpreted the Bible to fit their own circumstances.

Jesus Didn't Say When

Jesus taught extensively about the coming Kingdom and His return. On many occasions, Jesus said that the Kingdom of God was near. He told His followers to watch for the coming kingdom and to be ready for its arrival. So convinced were His disciples that the Kingdom of God was at hand that they even anticipated what their roles would be in the kingdom. They expected the Kingdom of God to come at anytime. After all, the King was present—why wait?

> **The Prophet Says**
>
> "'Lord, are you at this time going to restore the kingdom to Israel?' He said to them: 'It is not for you to know the times or dates the Father has set by his own authority.'" (Acts 1:6–7)

However, Jesus indicated in several of His parables that He would be gone a long time before returning to establish His kingdom. As we have discussed, Jesus told His followers about many things that would happen before He returned to set up the kingdom. Jesus spent more than 3 years teaching about the kingdom and explaining about His return, but no one knew when the Kingdom of God would come on earth.

The Disciples Didn't Know When

Up to the moment in A.D. 32 when Christ left earth and ascended into the clouds from the Mount of Olives, His disciples were still trying to figure out when He was going to set up His kingdom. Just before His ascension, they asked Him, "Lord, are you at this time going to restore the kingdom to Israel?" Obviously, Christ's followers were confused.

— Last Days Timeline —

Day 1	*Day 2*	*Day 3*	*Day 4*	*Day 5*	*Day 6*	*Day 7*
1,000 years	2,000 years	3,000 years	4,000 years	5,000 years	6,000 years	7,000 years
Adam	Noah	Abraham	David	Christ		

↑ First Coming A.D. 32

Christ never directly told His followers the specific time when He would set up the kingdom. However, before Jesus ascended into heaven, He told His disciples that the Holy Spirit would come to them and remind them of everything He had said. Jesus said that the Holy Spirit would also tell them what was yet to come.

The New Testament Didn't Say When

The documents that make up the New Testament were all written within 60 years of Christ's ascension. The New Testament gospels (the first four books of the New Testament) recorded what Christ said about the coming kingdom. The New Testament letters (from Acts to Jude) conveyed a message of watchfulness, expectancy, and patience about the future kingdom. In the Book of Revelation (the last book of the New Testament), Jesus is recorded as saying He would return quickly or soon.

The authors and apostles of the New Testament told Christ's followers to watch for several things that had yet to occur as indicators of the Second Coming. The Apostle Paul said that the Antichrist would be revealed in the temple of God before the kingdom comes. The Apostle John also warned Christ's followers that they would face the Antichrist before the kingdom arrived.

> **The Prophet Says**
>
> "Don't let anyone deceive you in any way, for that day will not come until … the man of lawlessness is revealed, the man doomed to destruction. He will oppose and will exalt himself over everything that is called God or is worshiped, so that he sets himself up in God's temple, proclaiming himself to be God." (2 Thessalonians 2:3–4)

Though the message of the New Testament is watchfulness and patience, there's also a certain expectancy regarding the return of Christ. The Apostle Paul told the Corinthian church to press on as they "eagerly wait" for Jesus Christ to be revealed on the Day of the Lord. The Apostle Peter wrote that Christ's followers should look forward to the Day of the Lord and anticipate its coming.

The New Testament writings were copied and widely circulated among followers of Christ for hundreds of years. It is very likely that thousands and thousands of copies of the gospels, letters, and the Book of Revelation were in circulation during the first century following Christ's departure. By the end of the first century, all 27 of the New Testament books had been written. By the middle of the second century, most Christians had accepted the books of the New Testament as part of the Word of God.

However, the New Testament didn't say when the kingdom would come, and that opened the door for speculation and theories.

The Old Testament Didn't Say When

The Old Testament is also considered by Christians to be the Word of God. But although the Old Testament provides much information about the coming Kingdom of God and the Messiah, it doesn't provide a specific date and time, either. Interestingly, the Old Testament prophet Daniel received a prophecy (Daniel 9:25) that indicated how to calculate the precise time of the Messiah's First Coming, and in the same prophecy (Daniel 9:27) he provided signs indicating when the Kingdom of God would come. But Daniel does not tell us how to determine the precise time that the kingdom will come.

> **The Prophet Says**
>
> "He [Antichrist] will confirm a covenant with many for one 'seven.' In the middle of the 'seven' he will put an end to sacrifice and offering. And on a wing of the temple he will set up an abomination that causes desolation, until the end that is decreed is poured out on him." (Daniel 9:27)

Even though the Old Testament prophets provide many clues and signs to the approach of the kingdom, nowhere in the Old Testament are we told exactly when the Kingdom of God will come on earth.

That hasn't prevented people from trying to predict the time of Christ's return and His kingdom. Let's see some of the thinking from the last 1,900 years.

Waiting and Wondering

During the first century, the followers of Christ were zealously persecuted by the Jews in Jerusalem and parts of Asia. Jewish religious leaders did not believe that Jesus was the Messiah, and they were determined to defeat this new sect of His followers. On the heels of the persecution by the Jews came great persecution by the Roman government.

In A.D. 70, the Romans under General Titus conquered Israel, sacked Jerusalem, and destroyed the Jewish Temple. Many of the Jewish people who were not killed in that campaign were taken captive to Rome. Then Rome put down a final Jewish revolt in A.D. 135. This final defeat left Jerusalem desolate, and the Jews were dispersed throughout the nations. After their defeat and exile, the Jews were in no position to persecute the Christians.

As Christianity spread through the Roman Empire, the Roman government began to persecute the Christians. The Romans practiced emperor worship, which put Rome and Christianity in conflict. Christianity held that only God was to be worshipped, and Christians refused to worship the emperor. Christian persecution reached a peak under the Emperor Nero when a great fire burned much of Rome. Nero blamed the Christians, and the persecution intensified.

Because of this persecution, many Christians in the first century believed that Christ would return in their lifetime to save them and deliver them into the coming kingdom. During this time, the Apostle John was on the Island of Patmos, where he wrote the Book of Revelation. It was widely believed by Christians that the Book of Revelation was about the defeat of the Roman government and the coming Kingdom of God. The Roman government was seen as the kingdom of the Antichrist, and the Roman emperor as the Antichrist.

Coming Soon!

The first-century followers of Christ in Thessalonica were also persecuted by the Romans and believed that the end was near. However, the Thessalonians also observed that generation was succeeding generation, and the end had not yet come. Paul addressed their concerns and questions by telling them that certain things must happen first. (We discuss these things in the coming chapters.)

In the second century, Justin Martyr, an early Christian church leader, said that God was delaying the end of the world because Christianity was to become a world religion first. In A.D. 313, the Emperor Constantine made Christianity legal for the first time. Then in A.D. 391, Rome made the worship of other gods illegal and established Christianity as the state religion. At this time, Rome controlled most of the civilized world.

The conversion of the previously "evil" Roman Empire to Christianity presented a serious theological predicament for church leaders. Previously, the church had taught that when the evil empire was defeated, they would be delivered into the millennial Kingdom of God. But now that the Roman government had become the church's supporter and partner, a new theology was needed to explain the current situation. Many theologians theorized that the millennial kingdom was a metaphor for heaven. Instead of an earthly millennial kingdom, heaven now became the Christian's eternal reward.

Because Christianity was on the rise and the end had not come, many Christians also began to believe that the end would not happen in their lifetime. During the third century, some even believed that trying to determine when the end would come was an attempt to divine the future and contrary to Christ's teaching. For a while, attempts to determine the times and seasons of God's plan were discouraged.

Even so, in subsequent centuries, many continued to predict when the end would come, and some even set dates for its arrival. Each date came and went with no return and no kingdom. By the middle of the first millennium (A.D. 500), the importance of the Last Days and the end of the world had become less significant in Christian teachings.

A New Millennium (A.D. 1000)

Relatively few recorded predictions about the end of the age are found until near A.D. 1000. As the new millennium approached, a state of near hysteria about the end of the world seemed to overcome the European Christian world. By December A.D. 999, people seemed to be on their best behavior. They gave to the poor, and some traveled to Jerusalem to meet the Lord at His return. Buildings went without repair and crops were not planted. It was as though there was something magic about the date A.D. 1000. However, the millennium changed without incident.

Following the turn of the century, attention seemed to turn to A.D. 1033. Because Jesus was believed to have been crucified in A.D. 32 or 33, many speculated that He would return around A.D. 1033—1,000 years after his ascension. After *that* date passed, interest in predicting the end seemed to go through cycles based on world or regional events and on individual theories. During the second millennium (A.D. 1000 to 2000), predictions generally diminished until we neared the twentieth century.

The Prophet Says

"The bridegroom was a *long time* in coming, and they all became drowsy and fell asleep. At midnight the cry rang out: 'Here's the bridegroom! Come out to meet him!'" (Matthew 25:5–6)

The Twentieth Century (1900s)

Early in the twentieth century, an increased interest in prophecy and the Second Coming developed. In 1910, the earth passed through the tail of Halley's Comet and many believed this was a sign of the end. Charles Russell, who founded the Jehovah's Witnesses, predicted that the rapture would take place in 1910 and the end of the world would occur in 1914. He later changed his prediction, saying that Christ would return in 1914. The Jehovah's Witnesses, also known as the Watchtower Bible and Tract Society, have revised their predictions several times since then. Their latest prediction called for Christ's return in 1994. Like everyone else, their predictions have come and gone without fulfillment. Undeterred, "prophets" have continued to make predictions, sell books, and excite people about the end of the age and the return of Christ.

Israel Reborn (1948)

A huge theological obstacle has always challenged Christ's followers in their attempts to identify the hour of His return. This obstacle involves the nation of Israel.

Scripture states that the Jewish people will be in the land of Israel before Christ's return. However, Israel did not exist as a Jewish nation from the time of the exile, in A.D. 143, until 1948. Anyone interpreting Scripture at face value would need to conclude that the return of Christ was a *long* way off.

Some felt that it would be totally impossible for the Jewish people to ever occupy the Promised Land again. Remember that the Promised Land had been occupied by Arab tribes for over 1,000 years, and was surrounded by Arab nations and religions violently hostile to the Jews. Essentially, Israel becoming a Jewish state in the Promised Land was a mission impossible.

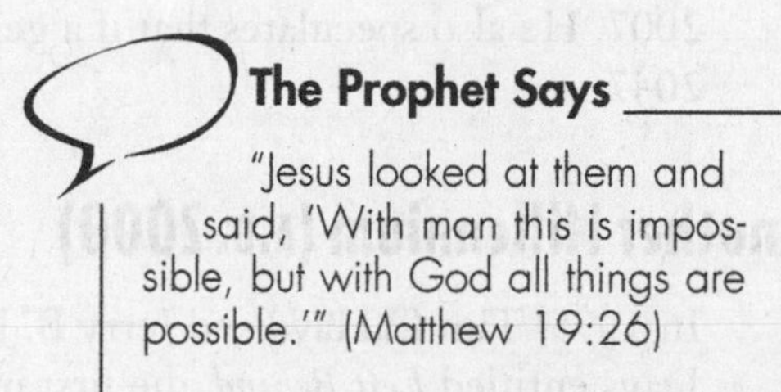

The Prophet Says

"Jesus looked at them and said, 'With man this is impossible, but with God all things are possible.'" (Matthew 19:26)

What seemed impossible in the world did not deter the Old Testament prophets. They said the people of God would return to their land in the Last Days. Then on May 14, 1948, David Ben-Gurion, Israel's first prime minister, announced to a great crowd in Tel Aviv that Israel was once more an independent Jewish state located in the region of the Promised Land.

Within hours of the declaration, the first of several wars ensued between the infant state of Israel and her Arab neighbors. Nineteen years later, in 1967, during the Six-Day War, Israel regained, for the first time, Jerusalem and the Temple Mount. The Temple Mount is the site of the first two Jewish Temples of God.

— Last Days Timeline —

Day 1	Day 2	Day 3	Day 4	Day 5	Day 6	Day 7
1,000 years	2,000 years	3,000 years	4,000 years	5,000 years	6,000 years	7,000 years
Adam	Noah	Abraham	David	Christ		

Israel a Nation
A.D. 1948

The successful rebirth of the Jewish nation of Israel seemed to awaken Christians to the Old Testament prophecies about the signs of the times. One example of the awakening was Hal Lindsey's 1970 best seller, *The Late Great Planet Earth.* Lindsey speculated that the time of the Second Coming of Christ and the rapture would be one generation (40 years) from Israel's rebirth in 1948. Many more books have been written capitalizing on this idea. A book by Edgar C. Whisenant was entitled *88 Reasons Why the Rapture Will Be in 1988*!

Lindsey later revised his 1988 prediction. By adding 40 years to 1967, when Israel regained Jerusalem and the Temple Mount, he indicated that the date could now be 2007. He also speculates that if a generation is longer, the rapture may even happen in 2047.

Another Millennium (A.D. 2000)

In 1995, Tim LaHaye and Jerry B. Jenkins authored a novel about the earth's Last Days entitled *Left Behind,* the first in a series of best-selling books depicting what could happen in the world based on the author's beliefs regarding the Last Days and the Second Coming of Christ. Like Hal Lindsey, Tim LaHaye and Jerry Jenkins promote the popular theory of a rapture before the Great Tribulation.

Today Christians are still waiting and wondering—waiting for the promises of the Bible to be fulfilled and wondering when and how God will accomplish His plan.

What Do We Know?

As the year A.D. 2000 approached, interest in the Second Coming of Christ was still widespread. If we do not know today, after almost 2,000 years, when the end will come, why have so many people erroneously believed that they did know the time of the end? To answer this question, we need to examine biblical history from another vantage point. The vantage point is how prophetic Scripture has been understood. Let's see what Scripture itself has to say about understanding prophecy.

From the Old Testament

In the Old Testament, we find some accounts of prophecies and their fulfillment. From these we can determine how biblical prophecy has been fulfilled and how biblical prophecy has been understood. Let's look at some examples to see what we can learn.

In the Book of Daniel (Daniel 9:2), we find that Daniel read the prophecies of Jeremiah and interpreted them literally. Seventy years meant 70 years, Babylon meant Babylon, and Jerusalem meant Jerusalem.

Another Old Testament prophecy and fulfillment is recorded in Ezekiel Chapter 26. Ezekiel prophesied in 590 B.C. that the city of Tyre would be totally destroyed by King Nebuchadnezzar of Babylon, and that Tyre would never again be rebuilt. About 17 years later, in 573 B.C., this prophecy was fulfilled when King Nebuchadnezzar of Babylon laid siege to Tyre and left her destroyed—just as it was written.

Both of these prophecies were fulfilled literally as written.

From the Old to New Testament

During the time depicted in the New Testament, many Old Testament prophecies were fulfilled, most of them specifically related to the First Coming of Jesus the Messiah. We have already discussed several of these, which were fulfilled in the life and times of Jesus, the Messiah. From these examples we learn more about how biblical prophecies are fulfilled.

According to the New Testament writings, virtually all of the numerous prophecies were fulfilled in the life of Jesus of Nazareth *as written*, in a literal way. That is not to say that the Bible does not also contain prophecies written as *allegories* that help in understanding the message of prophecy. However, to attempt to understand God's prophetic plan using allegory alone is a dangerous way to interpret Scripture. Allegories have no consistent rules of interpretation. Therefore, allegories that are not anchored to clear statements of Scripture allow theories and ideas to develop that are inconsistent with the biblical message.

For example, one theory uses Daniel's "70 sevens" prophecy (Daniel 9:24–27) as a prophetic allegory for God's plan for separating mankind into two groups. The theory indicates that the Jewish believers and the Christian believers comprise two different groups, each with their own eternal destiny. However, there are no statements in Scripture to support this theory. To the contrary, the Bible specifically states that the followers of God are one body that comprises all believers, regardless of national origin.

def•i•ni•tion

An **allegory** is a symbolic story that conveys a disguised message about something else. Parables are allegories that Jesus often used as He taught His followers. Jesus said He used parables to reveal truths to His followers while concealing it from others.

Armed with some examples from church history and lessons for interpreting prophecy from Scripture, what else can we learn from the 2,000-year history of mistaken predictions?

Learning from Mistakes

For nearly 2,000 years, every Christian scholar, teacher, and leader who has tried to predict when Christ will return has been wrong. That's a .000 batting average.

Part of this can be explained by failure to interpret prophecy literally, and part by attempts to force current events to mesh with prophecy. We discussed earlier in this chapter that some Christians began to read the Bible differently after Rome adopted Christianity. They theorized that the New Testament messages were allegories or metaphors about Christ's reign and the Kingdom of God, and were not to be taken literally.

Allegory: Not the Whole Story

Over time, theories and new theologies were developed to explain the reign of Christ and the Kingdom of God in terms of current circumstances. The church was, in a sense, already "on earth"—therefore, some reasoned that the Kingdom of God must have already come. By interpreting certain passages from Scripture allegorically, the idea developed that Christ will reign over the earth from God's throne in heaven through the Holy Spirit and the Word of God. The God of the Bible is sovereign over His whole creation; therefore, God must be currently reigning over the earth.

This theory regarding God's kingdom has lasted in one form or another for more than 1,000 years but has waxed and waned in popularity. It persists today; however, it comes in sharp contrast with some very straightforward statements of Scripture:

- "He will rule from sea to sea and from the River to the ends of the earth .... All kings will bow down to him and all nations will serve him." (Psalm 72:8–11)
- "... the Lord Almighty will reign on Mount Zion and in Jerusalem." (Isaiah 24:23)
- "The Lord will be king over the whole earth. On that day there will be one Lord, and his name the only name." (Zechariah 14:9)
- "They came to life and reigned with Christ a thousand years." (Revelation 20:4)

To have a proper understanding of what the Bible says, one must take the whole of it into consideration. We must find harmony with the whole of Scripture. According to the Bible, anything less than the whole truth can lead to error and deception. After all, if we just pick the parts that support our ideas, we could most likely prove anything using Bible verses. This principle can also guide our understanding as we consider other ways people have misinterpreted the message of Scripture.

Metaphor: Not the Whole Story

Let's consider again the example of how circumstances caused some to shift from a literal reading of biblical prophecies. From A.D. 143 to 1948, the Jewish people were not in possession of Israel. Without a nation of Israel, Christian theologians and scholars had two choices. They could drop their expectation that Christ would return anytime soon, or they could come up with an explanation of why "Israel" in prophetic Scripture did not really mean *Israel.*

Faced with these choices, many scholars chose to interpret prophetic Scripture metaphorically. They said that, under the New Testament theology, Israel was actually a metaphor for Christ's followers: His church. Therefore, any promises God had made to Israel or prophecies relating to the blessings and restoration of Israel in the Promised Land were now given to the church—a spiritual rather than a physical or geographical entity. It was no longer necessary to have the Jewish people in possession of the Promised Land before Christ could return and set up His kingdom.

Since the Bible often incorporates metaphors to communicate its message, this new application did not seem unusual. However, when theologians said that the church had replaced Israel, they did not include the prophecies about the condemnation and judgment of Israel. These, they said, belonged to Israel, the place. Their interpretation was inconsistent and incomplete, picking and choosing where to apply the metaphors.

So we can conclude that erroneous pronouncements are frequently made when people try to adapt Scripture to their current circumstances.

What Have We Learned?

When it comes to biblical prophecy, we cannot rule out the seemingly impossible, such as the return of the Jewish people to Israel, and we must consider the whole Bible in arriving at our understanding.

Finally, we must keep in mind that *all the events and signs* that the Bible says will occur must be fulfilled before the Bible's Day 7 will come. Attempting to discern the Bible's plan using only select circumstances and signs will only lead to confusion and error.

The next chapters of the book discuss all the major events and signs the Bible says will occur before the end of Day 6 and the beginning of Day 7. Then you will be able to determine for yourself when the Bible says the end will come by applying them to our current circumstances.

The Least You Need to Know

- No one knows precisely when the Kingdom of God will come on earth, but Christians have been trying unsuccessfully for almost 2,000 years.
- Prophetic Scripture has always been fulfilled literally, just as it was written. Expect future prophecy to be fulfilled in the same way.
- We cannot expect Christ to return until all the prophesies have been fulfilled.

Chapter 7

No, We're Not There Yet

In This Chapter

- What will happen in Days 5 and 6
- Deception is here, there, and everywhere
- No end to war is in sight
- Things will not get better soon

In the last chapter, we learned how the First Coming of the Messiah fulfilled many of the Old Testament prophecies, and we talked about some of the things Jesus taught about the future Last Day–Day 7 Kingdom of God. In this chapter, we discuss the things that Jesus said would happen in Days 5 and 6 of the Last Days, as the world approaches His return and the end of the age. Generally, these occurrences aren't tied to a specific time and will occur throughout Days 5 and 6.

Last Days Stuff

The Bible tells about some types of events that have happened in the past and that will occur in the future. In themselves, they do not signify that the end of the age is near. For example, the Apostle Paul wrote in his second letter to Timothy that in the Last Days, children will become more disobedient to their parents. Hardly something new or unusual! Now, if family behavioral statistics were to show a consistently increasing rate of child disobedience, this *could* indicate that the prophecy is being fulfilled. However, no matter how apocalyptic that temper tantrum seemed, our children's behavior doesn't reveal how close to the end of Day 6 we are getting.

In contrast, some signs given in the Bible will occur at a specific time in God's seven-day plan and indicate where in God's appointed times we are. Specific signs may give us a broad indication—in generations, say—or may pinpoint within years where we are in relation to the end of the age. For example, the prophet Micah wrote that the land of Israel will be abandoned until she is reclaimed by her offspring, the Israelites. The nation of Israel was established in May 1948, after being abandoned for almost 1,900 years, so this would be a sign indicating that the end is getting near—perhaps within a few generations. However, other signs do provide exact timing, and we discuss some of those in subsequent chapters.

— Last Days Timeline —

Day 1	*Day 2*	*Day 3*	*Day 4*	*Day 5*	*Day 6*	*Day 7*
1,000 years	2,000 years	3,000 years	4,000 years	5,000 years	6,000 years	7,000 years
Adam	Noah	Moses	David	Christ		Kingdom

Nation of Israel
May 14, 1948

Jesus expects His followers to know the signs of the times. On a couple occasions, He reprimanded the religious leaders for not knowing the signs. He said, "You know how to determine the weather by watching the sky, but you cannot tell the signs of the times." On another occasion, recorded in Luke 19:44, Jesus told them that *because* they hadn't recognized the time of His coming, Jerusalem and the temple would be destroyed. This prophecy was fulfilled just 38 years later, in A.D. 70: under the Roman general Titus, the army destroyed Jerusalem, and the temple was dismantled stone by stone.

An important fact about biblical prophecies is that there are more prophecies, both general and specific, about the approach of the end of Day 6 than about any other time mentioned in Scripture. Therefore, we begin with the general signs and progress to more specific signs in later chapters.

From Now Until Then

Once again, you may want to know where Jesus was and what was going on when Jesus spoke of many of the signs we discuss in this chapter. In A.D. 32, preparing for the Passover Feast, Jesus rode into Jerusalem on the colt of a donkey. This fulfilled several prophecies, as we discussed in Chapter 4. He came into Jerusalem after being with His friends, Mary, Martha, and Lazarus, in the town of Bethany.

The crowd on the road into Jerusalem was excited and full of expectation about what might happen. Rumors and reports were being widely circulated in the city and the Judean countryside about Jesus of Nazareth. Could this be the Messiah? Was He going to claim His kingdom? Contributing to the rumors and excitement were new stories of Jesus raising His friend Lazarus from the dead, after Lazarus had been in his tomb for four days.

Jewish leaders were very upset about the uproar; Jerusalem was under Roman control at the time, and they feared Roman reprisals. If the Jewish people had mass demonstrations because they thought this was the Messiah, the Romans would certainly put down the revolt with force and would blame the religious leaders for not keeping control. The religious leaders were even plotting how they might kill Jesus. Interestingly, the Bible indicates that the High Priest Caiaphas declared that it would be better if one man died for the people than the whole nation perish. The account of these events is recorded in the Gospel of John Chapters 11 and 12.

A Question of Timing

Following Jesus' arrival in Jerusalem, He spent some time in the Jewish temple speaking to the religious leaders. Jesus finished by telling them that the temple would be destroyed and that the people of Israel would not see Him again until they acknowledged Him as the Messiah.

Following this, Jesus and His disciples retired from the temple and crossed the Kidron Valley to the Mount of Olives. Here four of Jesus' disciples came to Him privately and asked, "Tell us, what will be the sign of your Second Coming and the end of the age?" Jesus' response is recorded in the Gospels of Matthew (in Chapter 24), Mark (in Chapter 13) and Luke (in Chapter 21). Jesus described many things that would happen before His Second Coming.

Don't Believe Everything You Think

Jesus began by telling them general things that would take place from that time until the end of the age. However, He began by warning them to be careful not to be deceived, that many would come who would use His name and deceive many unsuspecting people. He also told them that some people would even claim to be the Messiah (called the Christ). After the warnings about deceptive people, He told them that there will be talk of wars and rumors of wars, but that this is not a sign that the end is near. The end of the age will be later.

A careful examination of what Jesus said makes clear that each of the things He mentioned will happen, but none of them is a specific indication that the end of the age is at hand. Scripture does indicate that each of these things will continue to happen in increasing frequency and severity until the Second Coming at the end of Day 6. I list each of the things Jesus mentioned so we have a clear picture of this "stuff that'll happen."

Stuff that happens before Day 7:

1. Anyone may deceive you.
2. Those professing to be Christians will deceive many.
3. False Messiahs will try to deceive you.
4. You will hear of wars.
5. There will be rumors of coming wars.

Jesus cautioned His followers about these things and told them not to be alarmed that these are indications that the end is near.

> **The Prophet Says**
>
> Jesus said, "See, I have told you ahead of time. So if anyone tells you, 'There he is, out in the desert,' do not go out; or, 'Here he is, in the inner rooms,' do not believe it." (Matthew 24:25–26)

Once again, Jesus tried to prepare those willing to listen for the future. Let's examine what Scripture says about these types of occurrences and look at some historical examples so that we can learn from the past. In this way, we will be better prepared to recognize the specific signs of the times and the Last Days—and distinguish them from stuff that just happens.

Then Who Can You Trust?

The first thing that Jesus warns about is deception, a major theme of His Olivet Discourse. Jesus repeatedly describes the deception that will be perpetrated on His followers, following His death and continuing until Day 7. Jesus describes three sources of deception. He says deception will come from the world, from individuals claiming to be Christians, and from individuals claiming to be the Messiah.

First, let's look at what the Bible says about deception from the world. Scripture simply declares that anything that is not biblical truth is untrue, and anyone who claims something that is not true is involved in deception. The Bible contrasts the wisdom of God, which is His Word as revealed through Scripture, with the wisdom of the world, which is any other type of teaching. King David, writing in Psalm 12, warned of worldly deception in contrast to the flawless words of the Lord. King David said the words of God would protect people from those who would try to deceive them with words they wanted to hear. The Apostle Paul, writing to the Corinthian Church, declared that the wisdom of the world was not wisdom at all, and that it would result in destruction for those who followed it.

> **The Prophet Says**
>
> Jeremiah wrote, "'Beware of your friends; do not trust your brothers. For every brother is a deceiver, and every friend a slanderer. Friend deceives friend, and no one speaks the truth. They have taught their tongues to lie; they weary themselves with sinning. You live in the midst of deception; in their deceit they refuse to acknowledge me,' declares the Lord." (Jeremiah 9:4–6)

Jesus warns that anyone may be a deceiver. The prophet Jeremiah said to watch out because there is deception everywhere. Deception could come from individuals whom you wouldn't expect, such as your friends and family members, so the Bible teaches that everything should be tested against the written Word of God. Remember, deception is not necessarily intentional; those who deceive and those who are deceived may not know it.

In Sheep's Clothing

Jesus said that many will come in His name and that they will deceive many. He meant that many who claim to be His followers (Christians) will be involved in deceiving many people. Of course, it shouldn't seem strange that the very people who claim to be followers of Christ would be the ones, in pursuit of their own ends, to cause the greatest deception. This is exactly what the Scripture declares from the Old Testament through the New Testament.

The Old Testament prophets wrote very clearly about this. It occurred in their time, and they prophesied it happening in the Last Days, before Day 7. One Old Testament prophet, Jeremiah, said the leaders in Jerusalem, who were supposed to proclaim the Word of God, would be the ones to deceive the people and lead them astray. They would prophesy false hopes to the people, telling them what they wanted to hear.

The Prophet Says

The Apostle Paul wrote, "For such men are false apostles, deceitful workmen, masquerading as apostles of Christ. And no wonder, for Satan himself masquerades as an angel of light. It is not surprising, then, if his servants masquerade as servants of righteousness." (2 Corinthians 11:13–15)

Jeremiah also contrasted what these false prophets said with what God was really saying. He said they did not speak according to the Word of God, but spoke from their own minds and then claimed that what they said was from God. These deceivers were saying that no harm would come to the people, while God was saying that His wrath was about to be poured out on them. God did punish His people during Jeremiah's time, as we know: the Babylonians came and conquered Israel, and destroyed Jerusalem and Solomon's Temple.

We are also able to determine from Jeremiah's prophecy that this warning is about the Last Days. He declares that this will happen in the days to come when God is ready to accomplish His purpose, which we know happens at the beginning of Day 7. Jeremiah also warned about the sword, famine, and plague that were coming, the same warning we read from the prophet John in Revelation Chapter 6 (which we discuss in a future chapter). John says that a quarter of the earth will be killed by sword, famine, and plague during the Last Days before Day 7.

In the New Testament, there is another important warning concerning deception within the household of God. Paul wrote to the Corinthian Church warning about false leaders who would appear among the faithful. He informed them that the Devil disguises himself as an angel of light and that the Devil's servants also pretend to be leaders of the faith.

Deception has gone on in the past and, according to Scripture, will continue in the future. As we get closer to the end of Day 6, deceptions will become very powerful. The last deceptions will be those of the Antichrist and the False Prophet, and will take place at a specific time in God's timetable.

He Seemed Like a Nice Guy

The next type of deception Jesus warns about is that which will come from individuals who claim to be the Messiah or Christ. Many people over the last 2,000 years (2 days) have been taken in by such claims. No one can know how many false Christs there have been; no doubt some have been little-known figures ruling over small, inconspicuous groups.

During just the past several years, many false christs have appeared and reached mass-media attention. Often we hear of these individuals and their followers because of some tragedy, such as a mass suicide. From the perspective of the Last Days, these groups are interesting for at least two reasons. First, they appear just as Jesus prophesied. Second, as part of their deception, they claim to be fulfilling Last Days' prophecies concerning the Christ. The following is a partial list of some recent false christs:

- **Jim Jones, 1978: The Peoples Temple:** Asked his members to consider him the incarnation of Christ and of God
- **David Koresh, 1993: Branch Davidians:** Claimed to be Christ
- **Maitreya, 2006:** Claims to be the Christ who is prophesied to sit on the throne of David
- **Sun Myung Moon, 2006: Unification Church:** Says he is the Messiah of the Second Coming

The world has already experienced many false christs, and the end is still to come. However, one final false christ is prophesied to appear: the Antichrist. We discuss him in detail in subsequent chapters. The prophecies related to the future Antichrist are different from those of the other false christs, in that they are specific to an individual and will be fulfilled when the end is very close. In the meantime, the Bible tells us that we should expect other false christs to appear before the end of Day 6.

The Prophet Says

Jesus said, "For false christs and false prophets will appear and perform signs and miracles to deceive the elect—if that were possible. So be on your guard; I have told you everything ahead of time." (Mark 13:22–23)

Wars and Rumors of the End

The next thing Jesus tells His followers is that they will hear of wars. Certainly, wars have been a cause of alarm, and some wars have raised concerns about the end of the age.

This list of End Times predictions and recent wars from the Ontario Consultants on Religious Tolerance website may indicate that the world becomes concerned about the end of the age when we hear of wars and rumors of wars.

More Wars

1850: Ellen White, founder of the Seven Day Adventists, was born.

1891 or before: On February 14, 1835, Joseph Smith, the founder of the Mormon church, said that Jesus would return within 56 years.

1914: The Watchtower Society (or its members) predicted Christ's return.

1914 to 1919: World War I

1936: Herbert W. Armstrong, founder of the Worldwide Church of God, predicted that the Day of the Lord would happen sometime in 1936. He believed the Great Depression would lead to the end.

1939 to 1945: World War II

1948: The state of Israel was founded. Some Christians believed that this event was the final prerequisite for the Second Coming of Jesus. Various end-of-the-world predictions were made in the range of 1988 to 2048.

1950 to 1953: Korean War

1967: During the Six-Day War, the Israeli army captured all of Jerusalem. Many conservative Christians believed that the rapture would occur quickly.

1961 to 1971: Vietnam War

1975: This was a major Jehovah's Witness prediction date for the end.

1978: Chuck Smith, pastor of Calvary Chapel in Cost Mesa, California, predicted the rapture in 1981.

1981: Rev. Sun Myung Moon, founder of the Unification Church, predicted that the Kingdom of Heaven would be established in this year.

1982: Pat Robertson predicted a few years earlier that the world would end in the fall of 1982.

1986: Moses David of The Children of God faith group predicted that the Battle of Armageddon would take place in 1986.

1988: Hal Lindsey had predicted in his book *The Late, Great Planet Earth* that the Rapture was coming in 1988—one generation or 40 years after the creation of the state of Israel.

1991 and 2002: Iraq Wars I and II (ongoing)

1993: The Branch Davidians of Waco, TX, believed that they would be killed, resurrected, and transferred to heaven by April 22.

But Jesus said that wars in themselves are not to be seen as indications that the end is near. As we know, wars have been going on for a long time—and the prophet Daniel, among others in the Old Testament, tells us that wars will continue to the very end of the age.

More Rumors

The final thing Jesus warned His followers about was rumors of wars. These seem to be a perpetual thing—even during wars, there are rumors of other potential wars. The Cold War between the USSR and the USA certainly fueled the fire for rumors of war. Even now there are rumors of the U.S. going to war with any number of potential adversaries: China, Russia, Iran, North Korea, or Syria. Of course, as history reveals, any small conflict can escalate into even a world war.

Sometimes rumors of wars cause as much alarm as wars themselves. They certainly upset people and cause them to wonder about what will happen. Today we worry about any number of issues starting a hot war—nuclear proliferation, border disputes, control of oil reserves, and food shortages, to mention a few.

But in all these things, Jesus tells His followers not to be alarmed because these things must happen.

From Bad to Worse

Jesus is not the only one to describe things that will happen in the Last Days. The Apostle Paul provides a long list of things that he says will indicate that the world is in the Last Days. He says that there will be terrible times in Days 5 and 6 of the Last Days, with a general deterioration in personal behavior.

People always like to discuss and debate personal behavior as a sign of the times. Some say people are worse today than yesterday. Others say there has always been evil and sin in the world. However, the Bible seems clear that the closer we get to the end of Day 6, the more people will practice bad behavior. Paul described how people will be in the Last Days:

- Lovers of themselves
- Lovers of money
- Boastful and proud
- Abusive
- Disobedient to their parents
- Ungrateful and unholy
- Without love
- Unforgiving
- Slanderous
- Without self-control
- Brutal
- Not lovers of the good
- Treacherous
- Rash
- Conceited
- Lovers of pleasure instead of lovers of God
- Having a form of godliness but denying its power

Paul prophesied this condition of general evil in people as going from bad to worse as people become more deceived and participate in deception.

In the New Testament, James also warns people about the Last Days and provides some additional insight. James says that those who are rich in the world should be in despair about what they will experience in the Last Days. Not only will their wealth not help them, but it will actually be a cause of their downfall.

James goes on to warn them to pay attention to the way they are living and to recognize that they are not paying a fair wage to those who provide their food. God has heard the cries of people who harvest for them, and God is not happy with their behavior. Because they have accumulated wealth, fattened themselves, and lived in luxury and self-indulgence in the Last Days, their destruction at the judgment is certain.

The Least You Need to Know

- Jesus wants His followers to be prepared.
- Deception is a great threat to being prepared for the Last Days and the coming kingdom.
- Wars and concern about wars will continue to the very end of Day 6.
- In general, people will go from bad to worse until Day 7.

Chapter 8

Early Warning Signs

In This Chapter

- First signs that indicate the end is near
- Comparing current events to prophecy
- Birth pains lead to the coming kingdom
- The Four Horsemen of the Apocalypse ride

Many prophecies concern the approach of the end of the age. We can try to figure out where we are in God's seven-day plan by matching these prophecies to current events. From the information in this chapter, you will be able to recognize the early signs of the beginning of the delivery of the final Day 7 kingdom.

Indications of Things to Come

In the Olivet Discourse, Jesus tells His followers what signs will occur before His Second Coming and the end of the age. In the last chapter, we discussed things that will happen in the Last Days that aren't necessarily indications that the end is near. This chapter discusses the signs that will

The Prophet Says

Jesus said, "Nation will rise against nation, and kingdom against kingdom. There will be famines and earthquakes in various places. All these are the beginning of birth pains." (Matthew 24:7–8)

tell us that the end is not far off. Once again, Jesus' explanation of the signs is recorded in the Gospels of Matthew Chapter 24, Mark Chapter 13, and Luke Chapter 21.

Jesus said that ethnic group will rise against ethnic group, and kingdom will rise against kingdom. He also said that there will be great earthquakes, famines, pandemics, fearful events, and great signs from heaven, and that all of these are the beginning of the birth pains.

Birth Pains Deliver the Kingdom

As we discussed in previous chapters, Jesus often used familiar happenings from everyday life to communicate what He was saying. In this case, He used the analogy of a woman in labor as she prepares to give birth to describe the changes taking place in the world before Day 7. As a woman approaches the time of delivery and labor begins, the birth pains usually increase in frequency and severity. Therefore, Jesus is saying that these signs will increase in frequency and severity as the world approaches the end of Day 6 and His return.

The Old Testament prophets also talked about birth pains in relation to the coming Kingdom of God, imagery with which Jesus expects His followers to be familiar:

1. The birth pains indicate that the kingdom is not far off.
2. The kingdom will come as we go from Day 6 into Day 7.
3. The kingdom will come at Christ's return from heaven.

The Prophet Says

Isaiah wrote, "As a woman with child and about to give birth writhes and cries out in her pain, so were we in your presence, O Lord .… See, the Lord is coming out of his dwelling to punish the people of the earth for their sins." (Isaiah 26:17, 21)

So the birth pains lead to the delivery of the Kingdom of God.

As usual, the prophet Isaiah provides us with a very good description. In Isaiah Chapter 26, he describes the birth pains, the resurrection of the dead, and the Lord's earthly kingdom. These are all things that the Bible indicates will take place at the Second Coming, at the end of Day 6.

In this prophecy, Isaiah describes the nation of Israel struggling in her birth pains to give birth to the

Kingdom of God on earth. However, it is the Messiah who will deliver His kingdom when He returns from Heaven and gathers up His people in the resurrection.

Isaiah talks about a woman in childbirth who struggles and cries out in her pain as she tries unsuccessfully to give birth to her own salvation and bring the Kingdom of God to the people of the world. The woman is the city of Jerusalem and the nation of Israel. Isaiah indicates that at the time of Israel's birth pains the Lord Himself will bring about the delivery of the Kingdom of God. However, the delivery will not come until after a time of great distress which God will bring on the nation of Israel, because of her unbelief. Following this time of distress, the Lord will protect His people as He punishes the people of the earth for their sins. When the Lord appears from His dwelling place in heaven the dead will be raised and the people of God will shout for joy.

In another prophecy, Isaiah again refers to the city of Jerusalem as he describes the birth pains. Isaiah indicates that the nation of Israel will be born in a day and her Kingdom will come into being in a moment. Isaiah seems to say the birth pains will be short-lived because when they begin the Lord will bring delivery. When the Lord comes He will deliver His people and comfort them as a mother does her children, but He will punish His enemies with His wrath. Isaiah says the Lord will come with great fire and with the sword of the Lord He will execute judgment on all men. On that day many will be slain by the Lord when He appears from heaven in glory. Isaiah describes Israel's struggle, but it's the Lord's sudden return in judgment that delivers the Kingdom of God to the earth. When the Lord delivers the Kingdom, Isaiah says, great will be the rejoicing in Jerusalem, for the Kingdom of God will be one of great peace and abundance for the people of God. Those that mourned for Jerusalem will be glad for the Lord will bless her with the wealth of the nations.

The prophet Micah also envisioned the future time leading up to the birth of the Kingdom of God. Micah wrote that Israel would be abandoned until she goes into labor and gives birth, and the rest of the Israelites join together. As we know from history, Israel was abandoned for almost 1,900 years, until 1948, when she was once again established as a nation. Micah goes on to say that the Lord will arise and shepherd

The Prophet Says

"Therefore, Israel will be abandoned until the time when she who is in labor gives birth and the rest of his brothers return to join the Israelites. He will stand and shepherd his flock in the strength of the Lord, in the majesty of the name of the Lord his God. And they will live securely, for then his greatness will reach to the ends of the earth." (Micah 5:3–4)

His flock in "strength and majesty," and they will all live in peace that will extend to the ends of the earth.

Each of these prophecies describes the coming of the Lord and His kingdom in terms of birth pains and childbirth. Jerusalem is the pregnant woman preparing to give birth to the eternal kingdom of righteousness.

Now let's list the seven signs, or "birth pains" :

1. Ethnic group rising against ethnic group
2. Kingdom rising against kingdom
3. Great earthquakes
4. Famines
5. Pandemics
6. Fearful events
7. Great signs from heaven

Now that we have a clear picture of what the birth pains are, let's discuss them individually so we can understand more about them and consider whether they may be taking place in the world today.

The Natives Are Restless

In most English Bible translations, Jesus' first type of birth pain is translated as "nation will rise against nation" because the Greek word *ethnos* is translated as "nation." However, *ethnos* also means "tribe," or "people of the same custom or ethnic group." We will have a more complete understanding of this sign if we think of it as "ethnic group will rise against ethnic group."

The Prophet Says

Daniel said, "The end will come like a flood: War will continue until the end, and desolations have been decreed." (Daniel 9:26)

In the world today, we see more ethnic groups fighting against other ethnic groups. Tribes are currently fighting other tribes in many of Africa's conflicts. These tribal wars take place within and across national borders. We have also seen similar types of war in the former Yugoslavia between Croats, Serbs, and Albanians. In Iraq we see ethnic and religious groups fighting against each other.

The World at War

The next sign Jesus gave is "kingdom will rise against kingdom." Kingdoms are historically governed by kings, but today we generally refer to kingdoms as nations.

In the last 100 years, the world has seen two world wars, from 1914 to 1919 and from 1939 to 1945. The list of national wars in the last 100 years is very long, and many national wars are being fought today without formal declaration. Nationally supported terrorism could even be said to pit kingdom against kingdom. At any rate, all we need to do is turn on the TV or open the newspaper to see that this birth pain continues.

The Bible indicates that those birth pains will continue until the birth of the kingdom. War is a good example. From the prophets to the *Book of Revelation*, we are told of a final war that will take place at the very end of Day 6. We discuss the final war in more detail later; for now, just keep in mind that, according to the Bible, there will be no end of war in this age.

Prophetic Pitfalls

At the end of World War I, there was a feeling that it would be the war to end all wars and that through education and science, the world could exist in peace. However, the Bible clearly states that war will continue until the Messiah sits on His earthly throne.

def•i•ni•tion

The **Book of Revelation** is the last book in the Bible. It is the revelation of Jesus Christ for His followers to show them what will quickly take place. Jesus made the revelation known to His servant John through an angel.

The Shake, Rattle, and Roll

The third sign of the End Times is "great earthquakes." Now, if you weren't shaken by the previous two signs, you'd better fasten your seatbelt for this one. In the past year or so, the world has seen some of the largest earthquakes in recorded history. Just a few years ago, we heard of earthquakes of magnitudes 6 or 7 on the Richter scale, killing perhaps hundreds of people. Recently earthquakes have been recorded as high as 9 on the Richter scale and have killed hundreds of thousands of people. Not only does the severity of this particular type of birth pain seem to be increasing, but the frequency of earthquakes seems to be increasing as well. Earthquake data is readily available on the Internet; one good site is http://earthquake.usgs.gov/. For a quick review of major activity, this is a list of recent earthquakes and related death tolls:

- **December 26, 2003:** 6.6 magnitude, Southeastern Iran. About 31,000 people were killed.
- **December 26, 2004:** 9.0 magnitude, Northern Sumatra, Indonesia. More than 283,100 people were killed by resulting tsunami.
- **February 22, 2005:** 6.4 magnitude, Central Iran. Almost 1,000 people were killed.
- **March 28, 2005:** 8.7 magnitude, Northern Sumatra, Indonesia. More than 1,000 people were killed.
- **October 8, 2005:** 7.6 magnitude, Pakistan. At least 86,000 people were killed.
- **May 27, 2006:** 6.3 magnitude, Indonesia. Approximately 5,800 people were killed.

If earthquake activity follows the pattern of birth pains, we would expect them to increase in magnitude and frequency. Like wars, this is a type of birth pain that goes the distance. The Bible records in Revelation that an earthquake will occur at the same time Jesus returns to earth, more powerful than any in the world's history. The prophet Zechariah indicated that this final earthquake will happen when the Messiah stands on the Mount of Olives east of Jerusalem.

The Cupboard Is Bare

The next in the series of signs is "famines." Famines are disastrous, leading to the death of many thousands and leaving many thousands more sick and malnourished. Historical data on famines is more difficult to summarize because famines from drought and crop failures are often complicated by political and economic issues, as well as other natural and man-made disasters such as wars, earthquakes, and genocide. Nevertheless, some stand out in recent history.

The famine in Ethiopia in the late 1980s, in which over a million people died, is notable. In Sudan during the 1990s, more than two million people died as a result of war and famine-related effects. The near future appears ominous. Several areas of the world

The Prophet Says

John said, "I looked, and there before me was a pale horse! Its rider was named Death, and Hades was following close behind him. They were given power over a fourth of the earth to kill by sword, famine, and plague ...." (Revelation 6:8)

seem poised on the brink of famine-related disasters, with Africa leading the emergency list:

- **Ethiopia:** In the Somali region of Ethiopia, more than a million people are at risk due to pre-famine conditions resulting in part from the lack of rain during the past five years.
- **Somalia:** Rapidly deteriorating food production in southern Somalia has the potential for a major humanitarian emergency and more famine.
- **Kenya:** In the southeastern and coastal lowlands, there could be another humanitarian emergency if rains do not improve.
- **Zimbabwe:** Rapidly diminishing food supplies and worsening food production has more than 1.5 million people at risk and in need of famine relief.
- **Uganda:** Continuing war has put 1.4 million at risk of starvation, requiring more food and famine relief to avert disaster.

Clearly, the African continent's underdeveloped food production plus drought, war, and social upheaval are straining already stretched humanitarian resources. The conditions point to potential crises affecting and killing millions.

Pandemics and Pandemonium

The fifth type of birth pain that will occur from the beginning is "pestilences." In many Bibles, the Greek word *loimos* is translated as "pestilence." It also means plague, disease, epidemic, and pandemic. Pandemics have occurred regularly over the centuries. The last three influenza pandemics occurred in 1918, 1957, and 1968.

- The Spanish Flu of 1918 killed between 20 million and 40 million people. It was the most devastating pandemic recorded in world history.
- The Asian Flu of 1957 killed more than 2 million people worldwide.
- The Hong Kong Flu of 1968 killed 1 million people worldwide.
- The avian influenza is a current pandemic concern.

To date, the worst outbreak in the category of "pestilence" is HIV/AIDS. Although several medical treatments have been developed, it continues to threaten countries, continents, and civilizations. In Sub-Saharan Africa, which has a little more than 10 percent of the world's population, more than 60 percent of the population (almost 40 million people) is living with AIDS. In 2004, approximately 2.3 million people in the region died from AIDS-related causes. That same year, more than three million more people became infected with AIDS.

By the end of 2005, more than 25 million people had died from HIV/AIDS since 1981, and there is still no cure. Of all the people infected with the AIDS virus today, less than 1 in 6 is receiving AIDS drug treatment.

No Place to Hide

In the gospel of Luke, Jesus is recorded as saying that "fearful events" are one of the signs that will begin the birth pains. Many things fit into the category of "fearful events"—hurricanes, tornadoes, floods, tidal waves, tsunamis, and monsoons. With increasing evidence of global warming and the recent revelations that the Arctic ice cap is melting at an accelerating rate, the likelihood of ever-increasing fearful events goes up.

In 2005, three Category 5 hurricanes were recorded—Wilma, Katrina, and Rita. A Category 5 hurricane is the most powerful of hurricanes, with sustained winds more than 155 mph. 2004 and 2003 each had one Category 5 hurricane: Ivan and Isabel, respectively. More tropical storms were also recorded in 2005 than in any previous hurricane season. The frequency and intensity of hurricanes seem to be increasing. Whether they are or not, the Bible says "fearful events" will be a type of birth pain leading to the birth of the Day 7 kingdom.

The Prophet Says

Jesus said, "There will be great earthquakes, famines and pestilences in various places, and fearful events and great signs from heaven." (Luke 21:11)

Great Signs from Heaven

The last type of sign in the list of signs of the beginning of the birth pains is "great signs from heaven." This brings to mind many things, such as comets, solar eclipses, lunar eclipses, asteroids, and meteors.

About 1985, when Halley's Comet made its most recent pass by earth, many believed it was a sign of the End Times. In the last couple years, there has been talk of an asteroid that could hit the earth in 2029. Some speculate that the 2029 asteroid will just pass by.

The Bible records Jesus mentioning great signs from heaven two times. He mentioned them in Luke Chapter 21, when talking about the birth pains we are discussing, and when He was giving the Apostle John the Revelation. In Revelation Chapter 13, John is told that during the Last Days, there will be great signs coming down from heaven, signs that people will see.

We discuss these signs from heaven in more detail in subsequent chapters. However, for now you should know that the great signs from heaven mentioned in Revelation will occur during the last three and a half years of the present age, Day 6. The last three and a half years are called the Great Tribulation and its duration is indicated in several places in the prophecies of Daniel and Revelation. We will be discussing this period in great detail in subsequent chapters.

The Prophet Says

John saw the False Prophet, "and he performed great and miraculous signs, even causing fire to come down from heaven to earth in full view of men." (Revelation 13:13)

The Seals Reveal the Signs

Do the birth pains begin when we see the first of the signs, or do they begin when we see all seven types of signs occurring together?

I believe we must conclude that the signs are progressive, occurring in sequence, increasing in severity and frequency. In other words, the signs Jesus mentioned as being birth pains will begin with the first type of sign He mentioned and continue to the last, culminating at the end of Day 6. As we look back over the list of seven birth pain signs, it would seem that the world has already begun to experience them. However, before we conclude this, we should consider still more information in the Bible regarding these early warning signs.

In the Book of Revelation, John writes about a series of seven seals, seven trumpets, and seven bowls. Each of these series starts at a different time. However, they all conclude at the end of Day 6 with the Second Coming of the Messiah.

We discuss the trumpets and bowls in more detail in the coming chapters. For now, we concern ourselves with the seals because they are the first series of signs. Like the birth pains listed in the Olivet Discourse, they contain early warning signs that the end of the age is approaching. You should also know that the seven seals parallel the Olivet Discourse birth pains. Both start with people and nations in conflict and end with signs from the heavens.

Revealing Supernatural Signs

In the Olivet Discourse, Jesus identifies the same sequence of events and timetable that He reveals to John in the seven seals of Revelation. However, there is a big difference. When Jesus is speaking to His disciples on the Mount of Olives, He speaks to them from the perspective of how the birth pains will affect the earth. His description is of man-made and natural events, such as wars, earthquakes, and famines.

On the other hand, in the Book of Revelation, when Jesus reveals the seals and the horsemen to John, John has been brought up to heaven to receive visions of the future. John is able to see the supernatural side of the events as well as the natural side, so some of what he describes in Revelation will not be visible to people on earth. In several places in Scripture there is an interaction between the supernatural realm and the natural realm, and Revelation is a good example.

So John is in heaven and sees a scroll, like a rolled-up piece of parchment, before him. A scroll is an ancient book or document. On this scroll are seven seals that prevent the contents of the scroll from being read or seen. As each seal is broken open, we move closer to the time when the contents of the scroll can be read. As each seal is opened, John describes what he sees.

The Trouble with Heavenly Horsemen

When the first seal is opened, John sees a white horse and rider. This part of what John saw is most likely a supernatural vision. No one on earth will see a white horse and rider when this event takes place. However, the people on earth will be able to see the corresponding natural events.

This type of relationship between the supernatural and the natural is described in other places in the biblical record. For example, Chapter 1 of Zechariah says that riders and their horses in the supernatural realm are supernatural beings under the direction God, with assigned responsibilities on earth. Zechariah Chapter 6 says that different-colored horses are assigned certain areas of the earth. The white horse goes to the west, the red horse goes to the east, the black horse goes to the north, and the dappled or pale horse goes to the south. Zechariah's directions are from the location of Israel, which is always the case with the prophets of God. This information will prove helpful as we consider the horses and riders of Revelation.

From the Vantage Point of Israel
HORSES: White West, Black North, Red East, Pale South

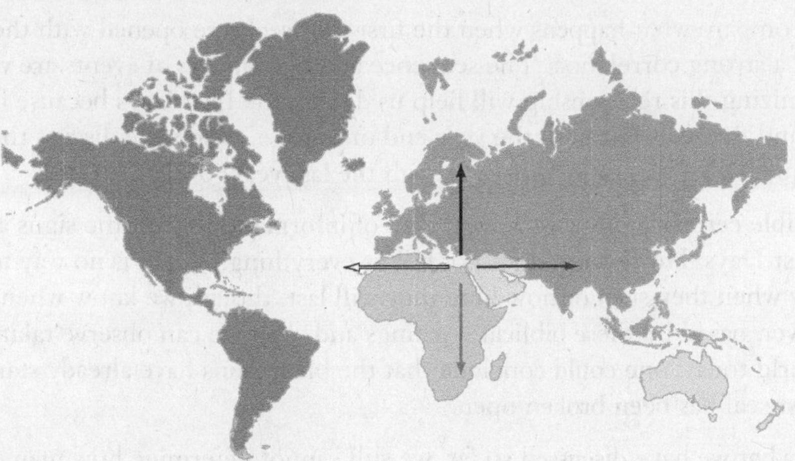

So when John writes about a horse and rider, he is describing something God is doing in the supernatural realm that corresponds to events that will happen on earth. Let's see what will happen as each of the seals is broken during Day 6 and the four horsemen of Revelation ride.

When the first seal is opened, a white horse and rider come out. The rider has a bow and rides out determined to conquer. Because the white horse has been assigned to the west, the west will be determined to conquer. Due west from Jerusalem crosses northern Africa and extends to the United States of America.

When the second seal is broken open, a red horse and rider come out. Its rider is given power and a large sword to take peace from the earth and to make men kill each other. The red horse has been assigned the east, so the east will have a powerful weapon or army and will take peace from the earth. Due east from Jerusalem crosses Jordan, Saudi Arabia, Iraq, Iran, Pakistan, and India, and extends to China.

When the third seal is opened, a black horse comes out. Its rider holds a pair of scales, and a quart of wheat and three quarts of barley sold for a day's wages. Because the black horse has been assigned the north, the north will cause great damage to grain production. True north of Jerusalem crosses Lebanon, Syria, Turkey, and extends to Russia.

When the fourth seal is opened, a pale horse and rider come out. They are given power over a fourth of the earth to kill by sword, famine, plague, and the wild beasts. Because the pale horse has been assigned the south, the south has power over a quarter of the earth to kill by sword, famine, and plague. South of Jerusalem is Africa.

The End Is Near

If we compare what happens when the first four seals are opened with the birth pains, we see a strong correlation. The sequence and description of events are very similar. Recognizing this relationship will help us discuss the Last Days because both the birth pains and the seals last until the very end of the age. Again, we discuss this more in subsequent chapters as we move through the last years of Day 6.

The Bible certainly provides a great deal of information about the signs and events of the Last Days. However, it does not tell us everything. There is no way to determine exactly when they start or how long they will last, though we know when they end. However, based on these biblical warnings and what we can observe taking place in the world today, one could conclude that the birth pains have already started and that the first seal has been broken open.

From what we have discussed so far, we still cannot determine how many years there will be from the beginning of the birth pains to the end of Day 6 and the beginning of the Kingdom of God. However, when we get into Chapter 11 of this book, we begin discussing other prophetic signs that are said to occur closer to the end of the age. As we examine and discuss the next signs, we will be able to determine approximately how much time will remain after the beginning of their fulfillment. As the world moves closer to the end of Day 6, the prophecies go from general to specific, and the time periods go from approximate to precise.

However, even if we examine the Scripture carefully and remain alert and watchful, we will never be able to zero in on the 24-hour day or the exact hour of the Messiah's appearance and the end of Day 6.

The Least You Need to Know

- The signs Jesus referred to as birth pains will start the countdown to the end of Day 6.
- Earthquakes and wars will get progressively worse as the world gets closer to the end of Day 6.
- Great signs from heaven will take place just before the return of the Messiah at the end of Day 6.
- The seals of Revelation correspond to the early birth pains mentioned in Matthew Chapter 24.

Chapter 9

Back to Israel's Future

In This Chapter

- Perspective of Israel's future from her past
- The lost Ark of the Covenant will be found
- The Third Jewish Temple will be built
- Why the Temple Barbeque has lost its savor

As the world moves closer to the end of the age (the end of Day 6) and approaches the biblical Last Day (Day 7), the ancient history of the Jewish people and their religious practices will gain attention because of amazing archeological discoveries. These discoveries will serve as a catalyst to a great awakening in Israel, encouraging the Jewish people to worship their God the way He prescribed in Old Testament Scripture.

A Great Awakening

In this chapter, we discuss some events that the Bible indicates will happen in Israel and Jerusalem in the Last Days as the world moves closer to the end of Day 6. The Bible says that events will begin to take place that are currently believed to be impossible. Because many of the biblical prophecies about Israel's future refer to things in Israel's past, we discuss some of her history.

As you may recall from Chapter 3, the first Temple of God was built in Jerusalem in the period when Israel had kings. Before the Israelites had a permanent temple for worship, they had a Tent of Meeting and the Tabernacle of God, which God had instructed them to make during the Exodus from Egypt.

The Tent of Meeting was about 150 feet by 75 feet and housed the tabernacle. The tabernacle was a tent of about 45 feet by 15 feet that consisted of two rooms. The first room was called the Holy Place and contained several golden articles of worship. The second room was the Most Holy Place and housed the Ark of the Covenant. The Ark of the Covenant was a gold-covered chest that contained the tablet with the Ten Commandments from God.

When the Israelites first entered the Promised Land, they set up camp and the Tabernacle at Gilgal. About 400 years later, in about 1000 B.C., shortly after David became king, he brought the *Ark of the Covenant* to the City of David and placed it in a tent that he had set up for the Ark. The City of David was previously the fortress of Zion, and David made it his residence in Jerusalem.

David's son, Solomon, built the first Temple of God in Jerusalem in about 950 B.C., and he had the Ark of the Covenant moved from the tabernacle in the City of David to the temple. Solomon's temple was ultimately destroyed in about 590 B.C. when the Babylonians captured Jerusalem. When Nebuchadnezzar, King of Babylon, conquered Jerusalem, he carried gold treasures and gold articles of the temple back to Babylon. However, the Bible is silent regarding what happened to the Ark of the Covenant and the sacred articles of worship.

def•i•ni•tion

The **Ark of the Covenant** is a gold-covered chest that contains the Ten Commandments of God. It has been lost since the time of Jeremiah the Prophet, 586 B.C. (Day 4), when Babylon destroyed Solomon's temple.

Since that time, the sacred articles of Jewish worship have not been seen. There remains much mystery and speculation about what happened to these incredible biblical treasures.

Even Hollywood seems to have been intrigued by the mystery . In the 1980s, a movie titled *Raiders of the Lost Ark*, starring Harrison Ford, was very popular and incorporated the discovery of the lost Ark of the Covenant as part of the movie's plot. But that was Hollywood, and we're interested in what the Bible says about the Last Days.

The Prophets Saw the Future

The Bible indicates that the Ark of the Covenant and the Tabernacle will be discovered before the end of Day 6. The Old Testament prophet Amos wrote about the future *Day of the Lord* and how it would be in Israel in the Last Days. Amos wrote around 800 B.C. at a time when Israel was still in the Promised Land and Solomon's temple still existed. Amos describes the trouble that would come upon Israel in the next 200 years, as well as the trouble that would precede the coming Day of the Lord, also called the Lord's Day. Jesus said that He is the Lord of the Sabbath. We know the Day of the Lord as Day 7, the ultimate Sabbath rest.

def•i•ni•tion

The **Day of the Lord** is at the end of Day 6, when Jesus Christ returns from heaven to gather His elect, punish the unbelieving world, and establishes the Kingdom of God on earth. The Day of the Lord is a significant event in God's prophetic plan. It is referred to by name 24 times in Scripture and is written about so often that the prophets abbreviated its name by referring to it as "the day" or "that day." Several times in Scripture it is called "the great and dreadful day" because it will be both a day of deliverance and a day of judgment.

Amos Saw the Ark

Amos wrote that, nearing the end of Day 6, the Israelites will be practicing temple worship. Temple worship, as described in the Bible, requires either the tabernacle, which the Israelites used until Solomon built the first temple, or the temple.

Now, as I said before, at the time Amos was prophesying, the tabernacle of David had not been used for about 150 years and Solomon's temple stood on the Temple Mount in Jerusalem. Solomon's temple would be destroyed during the Babylonian conquest of Israel about 200 years later. When the Babylonians destroyed Solomon's temple, not only was the temple destroyed and the Ark of the Covenant lost, but the tabernacle that King David had used for temple worship was also lost.

The Prophet Says

Amos wrote, "'In that day I will restore David's fallen tent. I will repair its broken places, restore its ruins, and build it as it used to be, so that they may possess the remnant of Edom and all the nations that bear my name,' declares the Lord, who will do these things." (Amos 9:11–12)

The tabernacle is very important because Amos prophesied that in the Last Days it would be restored just the way it used to be. He said that its broken places would be repaired and its ruins restored. The fact that Amos states that the tabernacle will be restored "as it was" indicates that the tabernacle will once again house the Ark of the Covenant. Therefore, as we get closer to the end of Day 6, the tabernacle of David and the Ark of the Covenant will be discovered and used again in the practice of temple worship.

The prophecy of Amos does not indicate where the tabernacle will be set up. The tabernacle of David was used for worship in several places: on the high place at Gibeon, Shiloh, the plain of Gigal, and in the City of David in Jerusalem.

Hosea Saw the Tabernacle

However, another Last Days prophet does tell us the location. This Old Testament prophet, Hosea, states that God will make the Israelites live in tents again. Hosea, like Amos, also sees the Israelites once again practicing temple worship using the tabernacle. In his prophecy, Hosea specifically mentions Gilgal and describes it as it would have been in ancient times when the Israelites were camping in an open field and using stone altars in the tabernacle.

If we consider fulfilled biblical prophecy, we find that much of it is hard to imagine before it is actually fulfilled. A good example in recent times is the restoration of the nation of Israel in 1948. Before that event, which was clearly prophesied, no one could have even imagined that it was possible. Even people who knew what the Bible prophesied said Israel could never be restored to the Promised Land. After all, the territory was occupied by many Arabs and surrounded by Muslim nations. Most said it could never happen. However, the prophet Amos, who tells us the Tabernacle of David will be restored, also says that God does nothing without revealing His plan to His servants the prophets.

> **The Prophet Says**
>
> Hosea says, "For the Israelites will live many days without king or prince, without sacrifice or sacred stones, without ephod or idol. Afterward the Israelites will return and seek the Lord their God and David their king. They will come trembling to the Lord and to his blessings in the last days." (Hosea 3:4–5)

Real Raiders of the Lost Ark

A few recent archeological reports may have some bearing on the lost Ark of the Covenant and the Tabernacle of David. Several years ago, an archeologist by the name of Ron Wyatt claimed he found the Ark of the Covenant outside the ancient walls of Jerusalem. Wyatt had been involved in many archeological excavations searching for biblical artifacts. In 1982, he claimed that he saw the Ark of the Covenant's mercy seat—its gold lid—inside a secret chamber. Wyatt claimed this secret chamber was prepared by the prophet Jeremiah as a hiding place for the Ark of the Covenant and other sacred articles. He said Jeremiah hid the Ark there before the Babylonian army destroyed the temple.

Wyatt later claimed that bureaucrats within the Israeli Antiquities Department insisted that the discovery be kept from Jewish fundamentalists. According to Wyatt, the bureaucrats felt that if the discovery were made known, some people would interpret it as a sign that it was time to build the Jewish Temple on the Temple Mount in Jerusalem. The Temple Mount is the historic site of Solomon's temple and the current site of the Muslim mosque, known as the Dome of the Rock. The Dome of the Rock would have to be taken down to make way for the Jewish Temple to be built. Because the Dome of the Rock is a sacred Muslim holy site, its removal from the Temple Mount would almost certainly instigate a broad war in the Middle East.

Wyatt died around 1999, several years after he claimed to have discovered the Ark of the Covenant, and no one has yet confirmed discovery of the Ark.

Another archeologist in search of the lost Ark and related antiquities is Dr. Vendyl Jones. Jones has been searching for the Ark for decades and has made some interesting discoveries that make him believe he is on the right trail to the Ark. Like Wyatt, he believes that the prophet Jeremiah was involved in hiding the Ark from the Babylonians before they came against Jerusalem in 586 B.C.

Jones has been working from the "Copper Scroll," an unusual document discovered with the Dead Sea Scrolls in 1952. This document is actually a scroll made of copper metal. All of the approximately 1,000 other scrolls discovered in the caves of Qumran were parchment. The Copper Scroll is also unusual because, unlike any of the other *Dead Sea Scrolls* discoveries, it appears to be an inventory of the treasures of Solomon's temple, including the Ark of the Covenant, the articles of worship, and the tabernacle from the time of the kings of Israel.

def•i•ni•tion

The **Dead Sea Scrolls** are a collection of almost 1,000 ancient (circa–200 B.C.) parchment scrolls and the Copper Scroll, which were discovered in the caves of Qumran from 1947 to 1956. Qumran is a mountainous desert area near the Dead Sea, about 13 miles east of Jerusalem.

In addition to the inventory, Jones believes the Copper Scroll is a treasure map that contains clues that will lead to the Ark's hiding place. Jones has been studying and interpreting this treasure map for many years. On one occasion, he discovered a jar of sacred oil that he believes is the same formula used in temple worship at the time of Solomon's temple. On another occasion, at the same location, his team discovered approximately 60 pounds of material that is reported to be ashes from a red heifer. Ashes from a red heifer are a biblical requirement for sacramentally cleansing the temple for worship. With these finds, Jones feels that he has located the true hiding place of the Ark of the Covenant and the ancient Jewish tabernacle.

At the time of this writing, Vendyl Jones and the Vendyl Jones Research Institute are raising funds for what Jones believes will be the final step to discovering the treasures of Solomon's temple, which have been lost for almost 2,600 years.

If the name Dr. Jones and the discovery of the lost Ark of the Covenant sound familiar, rumor has it that the idea for *Raiders of the Lost Ark*, with the lead character of Dr. Henry "Indiana" Jones Jr., was inspired by Dr. Vendyl Jones and his search for the lost Ark. Someone even said if you drop the *V* and the *l* from *Vendyl*, you get Endy Jones, very similar to Indy Jones. Coincidence?

Well, maybe. For our purposes, we should just keep in mind that the Bible indicates that the Ark and the tabernacle will be discovered, and it may be soon.

The Four Temples of God

When the Ark is discovered, it will almost certainly be interpreted by some to be a fulfillment of biblical prophecy. Even without the discovery of the Ark, many people have already been planning how and when the third Jewish temple will be built.

The second Jewish temple was built in about 525 B.C. King Herod completely refurbished it from the ground up, and it was standing at the time of the First Coming of the Messiah in A.D. 32. As we know, Herod's temple was completely destroyed in A.D. 70 by the army of the Roman General Titus.

The Bible has many prophecies that tell us about the third Jewish temple, the Last Days' (Day 6) Temple of God. However, there are biblical references to another Temple of God that will exist in Day 7.

The prophet Ezekiel, who lived at the time of Solomon's temple, is recorded in Scripture to have witnessed the glory of God departing from the temple before the Babylonians destroyed it. Ezekiel also recorded a very detailed prophecy describing a future Temple of God. To date, there has been no temple matching Ezekiel's description; therefore, this prophecy remains to be fulfilled.

— Last Days Timeline —

Day 1	Day 2	Day 3	Day 4	Day 5	Day 6	Day 7
1,000 years	2,000 years	3,000 years	4,000 years	5,000 years	6,000 years	7,000 years
Adam	Noah	Moses	David	Christ	Church	Kingdom
			First Temple	Second Temple	Third Temple	

Daniel Saw Future Temples

The prophet Daniel also received several prophecies about two future temples. At the time Daniel was prophesying, the first temple had been destroyed and no temple existed. Some of his prophecies mention the temple that existed at the time of the First Coming of the Messiah (Day 5, the second temple) and some mention the one that will exist at the time of the Second Coming of the Messiah (Day 6, the third temple). One prophecy, recorded in Daniel Chapter 9, actually mentions both, which allows us to date the time of the First Coming and gives two signs that point to the time of the Second Coming.

Let's take a look at this amazing prophecy, which speaks of the two temples and the coming of the Messiah. Daniel tells us about a decree that will signal the rebuilding of Jerusalem and the second Jewish temple. He says that from the time of this decree there will be 483 years until the Messiah comes (the First Coming). Daniel also prophesies that Jerusalem and the temple will be rebuilt in times of trouble, which they were. Jerusalem and the Day 5 temple were built during the time when Israel was dominated by foreign powers.

The Prophet Says

Daniel said, "His armed forces will rise up to desecrate the temple fortress and will abolish the daily sacrifice. Then they will set up the abomination that causes desolation. With flattery he will corrupt those who have violated the covenant, but the people who know their God will firmly resist him." (Daniel 11:31–32)

Daniel's prophecy also states that the Messiah will not remain after His First Coming, which was also fulfilled in A.D. 32 when Christ departed for Heaven, as recorded in Acts Chapter 1. Daniel also indicates that Jerusalem and the second temple would be destroyed by the people of a future ruler, which was fulfilled in A.D. 70.

Prophetic Pitfalls

Scripture never indicates when the third temple will be built. It may be built before the treaty is confirmed by the Antichrist, or it may be built afterward.

def•i•ni•tion

The **abomination that causes desolation** occurs when the Antichrist shows up in the Temple of God and proclaims himself to be God. This abominable act of blasphemy will set off a time of death and destruction that will cause the desolation of many. It's prophesied in the middle of Daniel's 70th Week, Daniel 9:27.

After referring to both the second temple and the First Coming of the Messiah, Daniel wrote about the end of the age, the end of Day 6. It reads as if he was talking about the birth pains that Jesus describes in the Olivet Discourse. Daniel said that war will continue until the end, that there will be much destruction, and that, in the end, conditions will worsen until everything breaks loose like a flood. Daniel said that the Antichrist will confirm a peace treaty with Israel that will last only seven years, and that the Antichrist will also set up the *abomination that causes desolation* in the third Temple of God. These events prophesied by Daniel will take place before the Second Coming of Christ. We will be discussing these things in detail in subsequent chapters.

Daniel finished his prophecy by indicating that the Antichrist will continue in power until the end of the age, when God will pour out his wrath and judgment upon him. We discuss the details of what happens when the wrath of God is poured out on the Antichrist and his followers later, when we discuss the seven bowls of God's wrath, described in Revelation Chapter 16.

Zechariah Saw Future Temples

The prophet Zechariah also prophesied about the third Temple of God. He wrote that the Lord God Almighty said, "I will raise up a man who will build the Temple of God, and many people who live far away will come and help build the temple." God said this will happen if His people diligently obey Him. God also said that His people will come to realize that God is behind this work.

Zechariah's prophecies about the future Temple of God present images of each of the future temples. After Zechariah's time, shortly before 400 B.C., the second temple construction had just begun. So from his vantage point, the second temple (built in Day 5), the third temple (which will be built in Day 6), and the final kingdom temple (which will be built in Day 7) were all in the future.

Malachi Saw a Future Temple

The last Old Testament prophet was Malachi. Like Daniel and Zechariah, his prophecies envisioned both comings of the Messiah. He also spoke of a future Temple of God in the Last Days. In Chapter 3 Malachi wrote that the Messiah will come suddenly to His temple. He also described several aspects of the day of the Messiah's appearing, saying that it will be a day difficult to endure, a day of judgment and a time when the Messiah will be like a refining fire. Malachi said that the Messiah will purify His people as fire refines silver and gold, and that after this, men will bring offerings to the Lord and they will be acceptable to Him.

This prophecy of Malachi depicts several aspects of the Second Coming of the Messiah. For one, it declares that He will come suddenly to His temple. You may recall from previous chapters that Jesus went to the temple in Jerusalem at His First Coming, but He did not do so suddenly. Jesus spent three years setting the stage for His arrival.

The Prophet Says

Malachi wrote, "'See, I will send my messenger, who will prepare the way before me. Then suddenly the Lord you are seeking will come to his temple; the messenger of the covenant, whom you desire, will come,' says the Lord Almighty. But who can endure the day of his coming? Who can stand when he appears?" (Malachi 3:1–2)

A Temple for the Messiah

We should understand by now that there is a huge difference between the First and Second Comings of the Messiah. For example, Scripture reveals that at the First Coming, Jesus came as a humble prophet and teacher to instruct His people and to make a sacrifice for their sin. However, at His Second Coming, Scripture portrays Him appearing suddenly in glory, coming out of heaven to earth and entering His temple. Even though the two Advents will be very different in circumstance, Scripture indicates that the same Jesus will return.

It wasn't just the Old Testament prophets who wrote of a Temple of God in the Last Days. Jesus spoke of the temple that would exist in the Last Days just before His return. In the Olivet Discourse, when He was telling His followers about the end of the age and His return, He spoke about the future abomination that causes desolation when the Antichrist goes into the Temple of God and declares himself to be God.

— Last Days Timeline —

Day 1	Day 2	Day 3	Day 4	Day 5	Day 6	Day 7
1,000 years	2,000 years	3,000 years	4,000 years	5,000 years	6,000 years	7,000 years
Adam	Noah	Moses	David	Christ	Church	Kingdom
				Second Temple First Coming	Third Temple Second Coming	

At this point, we can see that the Bible indicates that at some time in the future, the ancient articles of Jewish worship will be discovered. Their discovery will make Jewish temple worship possible. We also know that the third Jewish temple will exist at the time of the abomination that causes desolation, and at the time of the Second Coming of the Messiah at the end of Day 6. It's logical to assume that the Tabernacle of David will be set up before this temple is built, but Scripture doesn't say whether the tabernacle or the temple will come first.

On October 14, 2004, a group of 71 rabbis from across Israel convened in Tiberias, Israel. This was the first meeting of the Sanhedrin in 1,600 years. Historically the Sanhedrin is the highest Jewish legal tribunal in the land of Israel. The Sanhedrin existed at the time of the First Coming of the Messiah but ceased to exist when Jerusalem was destroyed in A.D. 70.

Rabbi Yeshai Baavad, one of the leaders of the newly formed Sanhedrin, said that the 71 rabbis received the special ordination in accordance with Maimonides' rulings (Jewish Law). One of the first orders of business was to start the process of planning for the next Jewish temple. It is interesting to ponder whether, without the articles of the tabernacle, this will be the "true" Third Temple.

Temple Worship Once Again

After the Tabernacle of David is set up, the Jewish people will once again be able to make sacrifices and offerings following Old Testament instructions. This practice will continue in the third Jewish temple, after it is built, until the Antichrist goes into the temple and orders that it be stopped.

The Bible records specific and detailed instructions regarding worship, which we simply refer to as "temple worship." Temple worship takes place at the seven annual feast celebrations, which we discussed in Chapter 3. All Jewish adult males were to observe three of the Feasts of God. The people would bring offerings made to the Lord, and the resulting feast celebrations were to be joyous occasions.

The Bible tells of one occurring when Solomon dedicated the first Jewish temple. Music was played, and there was great feasting. Part of the temple worship involved slaughtering the best livestock. The meat was then cooked over an open fire. Today we might picture the feasts being celebrated like a large, organized community barbeque, with fine meats grilled on an open fire and people fellowshipping together, sometimes for several days. This is what the God of the Bible prescribed.

The Prophet Says

"All the Levites who were musicians … [were] playing cymbals, harps, and lyres. They were accompanied by 120 priests sounding trumpets. The trumpeters and singers joined in unison, as with one voice, to give praise and thanks to the Lord. Accompanied by trumpets, cymbals, and other instruments, they raised their voices in praise to the Lord and sang: 'He is good; his love endures forever.' Then the temple of the Lord was filled with a cloud, and the priests could not perform their service because of the cloud, for the glory of the Lord filled the temple of God." (2 Chronicles 5:12–14)

A Place to Worship

Every religion in the world has its own form and practice for worshipping its god or gods in the way the people want. Since the Tabernacle and the Tent of Meeting were lost at the same time Solomon's temple was destroyed, the Jewish people have been unable to practice temple worship.

Since the second Jewish temple was destroyed in A.D. 70, the Jewish people haven't even had a temple! Therefore, the Jewish people today are not following their God's instructions about worship, which is a grave spiritual situation for the Jewish people. The Law of God indicates that blood from a temple sacrifice is required for the forgiveness of the people's sins. Essentially, without the blood of a temple sacrifice, there can be no forgiveness of sin.

The Prophet Says

"Moses said to Aaron, 'Come to the altar and sacrifice your sin offering and your burnt offering, and make atonement for yourself and the people; sacrifice the offering that is for the people and make atonement for them, as the Lord has commanded.' So Aaron came to the altar and slaughtered the calf as a sin offering for himself." (Leviticus 9:7–8)

So imagine a group of devoutly religious people with a long, deep historical tradition, unable for more than 1,900 years to worship their God as He has prescribed. Imagine the reaction and excitement of the Jewish people when they hear that the Tabernacle of King David and the Ark of the Covenant—articles designed by God and built by Moses during the Exodus—have been discovered.

When the Ark of the Covenant is discovered, the news will impact millions of people around the world. This discovery will be the greatest archeological find since the Dead Sea Scrolls—without doubt the greatest archeological find of all time. It's impossible to imagine the effect of this monumental discovery. Personally, I have a hard time imagining enough planes, boats, and trains to carry all the Jewish people to Israel and Jerusalem. Many will interpret these events as a sign that it is time to return to the Promised Land. The Jewish people have an expression, "Next year in Jerusalem." When the discovery is made, the expression will become, "This year in Jerusalem."

Christians, who derive their faith from Jewish roots, will also be very excited by the discovery of the Ark of the Covenant. This will cause a great awakening in the Jewish and Christian faiths, and very likely will alter the course of human history, moving it ever closer to the end of Day 6 and the beginning of the Sabbath rest, Day 7.

Something's Not Right

The Bible reveals one other thing about this time when Israel moves back to the future. It's about Jewish temple worship and the way God reacts to this practice in the future. This particular prophecy in Isaiah Chapter 66 depicts the circumstances that will be occurring in the third temple and in the city of Jerusalem just three and a half years before the end of Day 6 and the beginning of Day 7. Let's take a look at Isaiah's prophecy:

> *This is what the Lord says: "Heaven is my throne, and the earth is my footstool. Where is the house you will build for me? Where will my resting place be? Has not my hand made all these things, and so they came into being?" declares the Lord. "This is the one I esteem: he who is humble and contrite in spirit, and trembles at my word. But whoever sacrifices a bull is like one who kills a man, and whoever offers a lamb, like one who breaks a dog's neck; whoever makes a grain offering is like one who presents pig's blood, and whoever burns memorial incense, like one who worships an idol. They have chosen their own ways, and their souls delight in their abominations; so I also will choose harsh treatment for them and will bring upon them what they dread. For when I called, no one answered, when I spoke, no one listened. They did evil in my sight and chose what displeases me." (Isaiah 66:1-4)*

Clearly, God is not pleased with their practice of temple worship in the Last Days. In Chapter 3, we discussed that God reveals to His people what He plans to do through the annual feasts. The spring feasts, starting with Passover, clearly pointed God's people to the First Coming of the Messiah. Yet most of the religious leaders failed to recognize the signs and His coming.

When temple worship begins again, the religious leaders will once again celebrate the feasts of God, but they still will not have stopped to consider what they mean. Many will also fail to recognize that several of the feasts were fulfilled more than 1,900 years ago. That is why God will be so angry. His people still will not listen to His word and obey what He says. Because they will not stop to consider what the Feasts of God mean, they will be blindsided by the Second Coming of the Messiah.

—Timeline to the End of the Age—

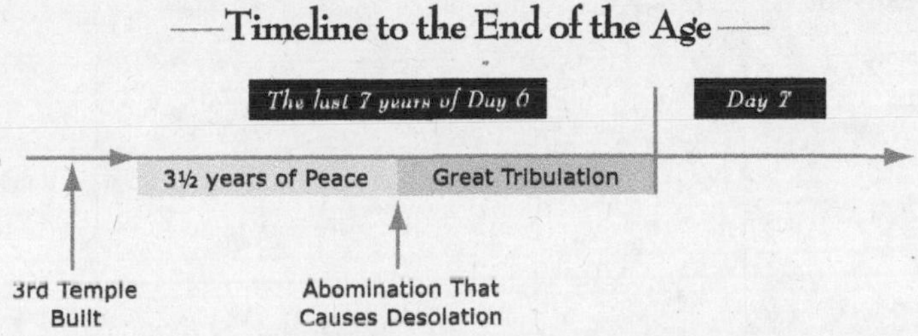

Nevertheless, as we have discussed, temple worship will continue in the Temple of God until the abomination that causes desolation, three and a half years from the end of Day 6.

The Least You Need to Know

- Just as Israel once practiced temple worship in the Tent of Meeting before the Tabernacle of David, she will again in Day 6.
- *Raiders of the Lost Ark* is much more than a Hollywood movie! The Ark of the Covenant will be discovered in Day 6.
- The third Jewish temple will be built on the Temple Mount before the Second Coming of the Messiah.
- During Day 6, temple worship will be practiced for the first time in more than 1,900 years—but God won't be happy about it this time.

Chapter 10

The Last Worldly Empire

In This Chapter

- The four world kingdoms of the prophet Daniel
- The fourth kingdom and the Antichrist
- The fourth kingdom comes from the Middle East
- A treaty with Israel before the end of Day 6

Many events and signs must take place before the end of Day 6. However, one often-overlooked prophetic event must happen before many of the other signs can occur. This event was first described by the prophet Daniel and later described by John in the Book of Revelation.

The event is the appearance of the Fourth Beast Kingdom and its rise to power. The Antichrist will come from this kingdom. In this chapter, we will see what the Bible tells us about this kingdom and the identity of the Antichrist.

Daniel's Four Kingdom Prophecies

Some biblical prophecies were fulfilled in the past. These fulfilled prophecies provide important insight into Scripture and help us understand how future prophecies will be fulfilled. In the case of the *Fourth Beast Kingdom*, this is very important because the Bible contains prophecies about three Beast Kingdoms that have already been fulfilled. These prophecies and their fulfillment will shed light on the future Fourth Beast Kingdom.

The Old Testament prophet Daniel provides many key prophecies to End Times events. The rise of the kingdom of the Antichrist is no exception. Daniel gives us a detailed, step-by-step picture of how the Fourth Beast Kingdom develops into a world power.

def•i•ni•tion

"The **Fourth Beast Kingdom** will rise to power during Day 6 and will rule over the whole world. This kingdom will initially have ten kings, and then the Antichrist will arise among the ten and overthrow three of the kings. After this, the kingdom will have seven heads and ten horns." (Daniel 7:23–24)

But before we dig into those prophecies, we discuss some background information and then consider the first three Beast Kingdoms that are described in Daniel's prophecies.

When Israel was conquered and Jerusalem destroyed in about 586 B.C., Daniel, a Jewish youth, was taken to Babylon. There he was trained and prepared to serve Nebuchadnezzar, the Babylonian king. While he served in Babylon, Daniel received prophecies from God about the Last Days. Many of the prophecies describe the times and events in Day 6 that lead up to the Second Coming of the Messiah and Kingdom of God on earth (Day 7).

The Prophet Says

Daniel describes the Second Coming as such: "In my vision at night I looked, and there before me was one like a son of man, coming with the clouds of heaven. … He was given authority, glory, and sovereign power; all peoples, nations, and men of every language worshiped him." (Daniel 7:13–14)

Daniel's prophecies always describe the coming Kingdom of God (on Day 7) as the absolute final kingdom on earth, after which there will be no others. This final kingdom of God is described as coming immediately after the destruction and defeat of the Fourth Beast Kingdom. Daniel also saw in prophetic visions and wrote that the Day 7 Kingdom of God will come about not by natural means, but supernaturally. Daniel describes the Son of Man "coming on the clouds" to deliver His kingdom on earth.

Daniel's Statue Prophecies

Now let's look at some of Daniel's prophecies that have been fulfilled. The first of Daniel's prophecies involved interpreting a dream that King Nebuchadnezzar received from God about four world kingdoms. By "world kingdoms," I mean kingdoms that dominate the world.

King Nebuchadnezzar was greatly troubled by the dream, and was so intent on getting a true interpretation that he devised a scheme that would ensure that his advisors did not deceive him. He told his astrologers that they would first have to tell him the dream, and then he would let them interpret it for him. He also told his advisors that if they did not tell him his dream and interpret it, they would all be put to death. None of the king's advisors could tell the king his dream, so he ordered them killed. When Daniel heard of this he went to the king and asked for time to interpret the dream. God showed Daniel the king's dream and gave him its interpretation. The vision spanned the history of the world from the Babylonian Empire to the end of the age, when the Kingdom of God will be established on earth.

The Prophet Says

Daniel saw, "In the time of those kings, the God of heaven will set up a kingdom that will never be destroyed, nor will it be left to another people. It will crush all those kingdoms and bring them to an end, but it will itself endure forever." (Daniel 2:44)

The dream involved a giant statue of a man, which represented four world kingdoms. In the dream, King Nebuchadnezzar of Babylon was the first kingdom, represented by the head of Gold. After Babylon, the dream revealed another kingdom that would arise, "one of silver." The second kingdom would be inferior to Nebuchadnezzar's Babylon. Next, the dream showed a third kingdom, "one of bronze," which would rule over the world.

Finally, the dream revealed a fourth kingdom that would be strong like iron and would crush and break all other kingdoms. The fourth kingdom was the feet of the statue, and its 10 toes were like iron mixed with clay. This means that this kingdom will be partially strong and partially brittle. The dream went on to show that this fourth kingdom will be divided, with a mixture of conflicting peoples. Finally, the dream depicted the God of heaven crushing all these kingdoms and setting up His kingdom to endure forever.

The interpretation that Daniel received from God revealed that there will be four world kingdoms that will rise on earth before God sets up His eternal kingdom. The four world kingdoms are identified as follows:

- First: Babylon, the kingdom of gold
- Second: The kingdom of silver

- Third: The kingdom of bronze
- Finally: The kingdom of iron and clay

Daniel received other prophecies while he served in Babylon, several of which provide additional details concerning the four world kingdoms. For example, when Belshazzar became king of Babylon, Daniel received another dream about the four world kingdoms. In this prophecy, Daniel once again saw that the fourth kingdom would be in power when God sets up His eternal kingdom on earth.

Daniel's Beast Prophecies

Now let's look at a more detailed vision recorded in Daniel Chapter 7. Daniel saw four great beasts, each different from the other, coming out of the sea. The first was like a lion, with the wings of an eagle. Its wings were torn off, and it stood on two feet like a man. Then there was a second beast that looked like a bear. It was raised up on its side and told to get up and eat its fill of flesh. A third beast looked like a leopard, with four wings on its back and four heads. It was given authority to rule.

Next, Daniel saw a fourth beast, terrifying and powerful, with large iron teeth, which crushed and devoured its victims. It was different from all the former beasts, and it had 10 horns. We are told that while Daniel was thinking about the 10 horns, a smaller horn came up among them, uprooting 3 of the first horns.

In this vision, Daniel saw the four world kingdoms as beasts:

- The first was like a lion.
- The second was like a bear.
- The third was like a leopard.
- The fourth starts with 10 horns and ends with 7.

So we know that out of this terrifying and powerful Fourth Beast Kingdom will come a leader who will subdue 3 of its initial 10 kings. This new leader is the Antichrist. We will see the use of the terms *lion*, *bear*, and *leopard* again when we discuss what Revelation Chapter 13 says about the Antichrist. Now you also understand that these kingdoms are called beast kingdoms because of the animal metaphors.

Both of Daniel's visions end with the Kingdom of God being established at the time of the Fourth Beast Kingdom. In the second vision, there is some more information about the Antichrist. Daniel saw the leader (the Antichrist) of the Fourth Beast Kingdom with eyes like a man's, speaking boastfully. As Daniel watched, thrones were set in place and God took His seat. God's clothing is described as being as white as snow, and we are told that the hair on His head was white like wool. We are also told that flaming fire was His throne, and a river flowed out from before Him. Daniel saw thousands attending God and 100 million stood before Him.

Then a court was seated, books were opened, and the Antichrist was slain, and its body destroyed and thrown into the blazing fire. Daniel also saw "one like a son of man, coming with the clouds of heaven." The Son of Man, Christ in His glory, was given power to rule over the whole earth. We are also told, as we discussed previously, that His kingdom is an everlasting kingdom that will never pass.

In summary, this "beast prophecy," like Daniel's earlier "statue prophecy," describes four world kingdoms coming to power before the Kingdom of God is established supernaturally on earth. Both prophecies also tell us that the fourth kingdom will be comprised of 10 kings.

Daniel's Stern-Faced King Prophecies

In Daniel's third prophecy, he tells us about a goat, a ram, and a stern-faced king. We also learn that the fourth kingdom and the stern-faced king come from the breakup of Alexander's kingdom of Greece. We are told that in Day 6 of the Last Days, when rebels have become completely wicked (terrorists), out of one of the four kingdoms a stern-faced king (the Antichrist) will arise. This stern-faced king will be a master of intrigue, and he will become very strong—but not by his own power. He will cause astounding devastation and he will be successful at whatever he does. He will consider himself superior and use deception to succeed. He will destroy the mighty men and the people of God. When the people feel secure, he will destroy many and take his stand against God. Then he will be destroyed—but not by human power.

As you know from King Nebuchadnezzar's dream and Daniel's statue prophecy, Babylon is the first kingdom. In another of Daniel's prophecies, recorded in Daniel Chapter 8, Daniel reveals the identity of the second and third kingdoms, and specifically tells us that his vision concerns the End Times. We are told that the second kingdom, represented by the two-horned ram, is Media-Persia; and the shaggy goat is Alexander the Great, the king of Greece.

The Four World Kingdoms of Daniel's Prophecies

Four World Kingdoms	Daniel's "Statue" Prophecy	Daniel's "Beasts" Prophecy	Daniel's "Stern-Faced King" Prophecy
First	Gold: Babylon	Lion	Babylon
Second	Silver	Bear	Ram: Media-Persia
Third	Bronze	Leopard	Goat: Greece
Fourth	Ten toes of iron and clay	Ten kings then seven	Stern-faced king

The Fourth Beast Kingdom

We now know the identity of the first three Beast Kingdoms—Babylon, Media-Persia, and Greece. We also have a great deal of information from Daniel that will help us identify the Fourth Beast Kingdom when it appears. Let's look again at Daniel's prophecies concerning the Fourth Beast Kingdom. As we discuss the Fourth Beast Kingdom, keep in mind that the Antichrist comes from this kingdom.

The Prophet Says

Daniel received this explanation: "The fourth beast is a fourth kingdom that will appear on earth. It will be different from all the other kingdoms and will devour the whole earth, trampling it down and crushing it. The 10 horns are 10 kings who will come from this kingdom. After them another king will arise, different from the earlier ones; he will subdue three kings." (Daniel 7:23–24)

In Daniel's "Statue Prophecy" vision, recall that he described the Fourth Beast Kingdom as composed of 10 toes, being very strong, and crushing all other kingdoms. He also said that it was a divided kingdom, with a mixture of people who will not remain united. In Daniel's "Beast Prophecy" vision, the Fourth Beast Kingdom is terrifying and powerful, crushing and devouring its victims. The kingdom begins with 10 kings and their kingdoms; then another king comes up and subdues 3. At that point, the Fourth Beast Kingdom of 10 nations is led by the Antichrist and six other kings.

We have already seen from the "Stern-Faced King Prophecy" that the Fourth Beast Kingdom will come from one of the areas of Alexander's kingdom of Greece. Let's see if the Bible gives us additional clues to where the Fourth Beast Kingdom will be located and which country the Antichrist will come from.

Countries of the Fourth Kingdom and Antichrist

A lot of speculation over the centuries has arisen regarding where the fourth kingdom, which the Antichrist will come from, will be. There have been theories about Europe, the United States, Israel, Germany, and the United Kingdom, and lately speculation that the Middle East might become the Fourth Beast Kingdom described by Daniel. Once again, since we get the "fourth kingdom" and "Antichrist" terminology from Scripture, let's look to the Bible for clues of the identity of the Fourth Beast Kingdom. As it turns out, as with many questions that the Bible raises, it also answers this one.

Daniel's Many Clues

Daniel provides several clues in his prophecies that point to the identity of the fourth kingdom. In his "Beast Prophecy," Daniel described Babylon like a lion, Media-Persia like a bear, and Greece like a leopard. When we read Revelation Chapter 13, we find that the Antichrist comes out of a kingdom with 7 heads and 10 horns, with characteristics like a lion, a bear, and a leopard.

Because we know that the lion, bear, and leopard identify Babylon, Media-Persia, and Greece, we can conclude that Revelation Chapter 13 points to somewhere in the Middle East, the area ruled by the first three kingdoms, as the location of the fourth kingdom.

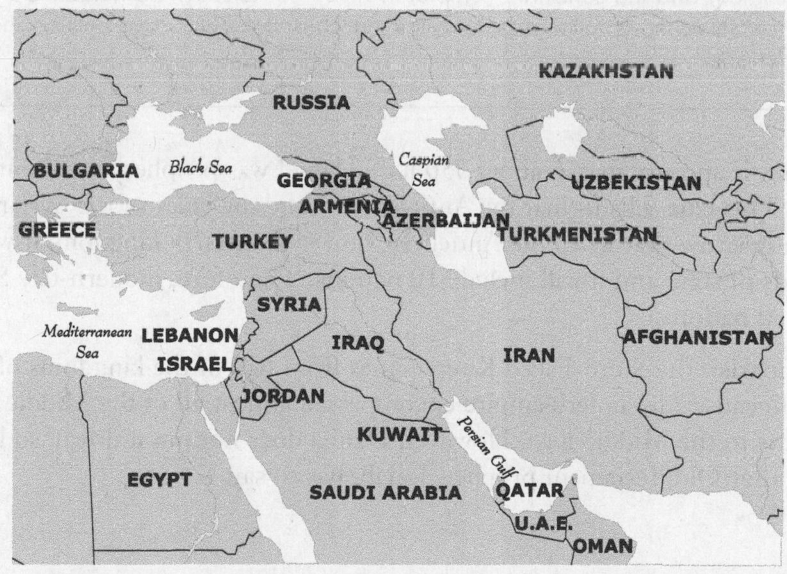

Daniel provides another clue in his "Seventy Sevens Prophecy" found in Daniel Chapter 9. He identifies a country over which the Antichrist will rule in verse 26 when he says, "The people of the ruler who will come will destroy the city and the sanctuary." First of all, the ruler who will come is the Antichrist. We know this because in the next verse Daniel tells us that this ruler will set up the abomination that causes desolation in the temple. Second, we can conclude that the people refer to those who destroyed the city and the sanctuary of Jerusalem. The Roman army destroyed the city of Jerusalem and the temple sanctuary in A.D. 70.

The Roman army that burned and destroyed the temple in A.D. 70 was heavily composed of conscripts from countries that Rome had previously conquered. According to the Jewish historian Josephus, Syrians made up a significant portion of the Roman army of General Titus. The Jewish historian Josephus wrote that Titus tried to preserve the temple as a trophy of his conquest. Titus was not pleased when the Syrians got caught up in the heat of battle, burned the temple, and looted its gold. The Syrians took so much gold from the Jewish temple that the price of gold in Syria dropped in half for some time following the fall of Jerusalem.

Prophetic Pitfalls

When Daniel prophesied about people who would come and destroy the city and the sanctuary, he was referring to the Syrians who made up a significant portion of the Roman army in question. The Roman people did not destroy the city of Jerusalem and the sanctuary (temple) in A.D. 70. Actually, the Roman General Titus tried to preserve the temple. Therefore, the Antichrist who will come will be the leader of the Syrians.

Therefore, it appears that in about 550 B.C., Daniel was prophesying about the people of Syria. This clue tells us that the Antichrist will be the ruler of the Syrian people. We already know that when the Antichrist is over the fourth kingdom, it will be led by 7 heads of state and it will include 10 nations. Therefore, modern-day Syria will be 1 of the 10 nations.

The Antichrist, the Stern-Faced King, comes from one of the kingdoms of Alexander's empire. Because Alexander's empire encompassed almost all of the Middle East, this clue points to the Middle East. However, Daniel does not pin it down, so let's look at what another Old Testament prophet, Isaiah, has to say.

The Assyrian Clues

In several prophecies, Isaiah describes how the Antichrist will come against Israel in the Last Days, Day 6. In these accounts, Isaiah refers to the Antichrist as the "Assyrian of the Assyrians." Isaiah portrays the Assyrian leader as the rod of God's anger and the club of His wrath. According to Isaiah, God will use the Assyrian against Israel to loot, plunder, and beat down the people for their sin and wickedness.

In another prophecy, Isaiah says that God will crush the Assyrian in the land of Israel and trample him down on Israel's mountains, delivering His people from tribulation. God says this is His plan for the nation of Israel and the whole world. What Isaiah describes in this prophecy is the final battle in Jerusalem at the end of Day 6. But we also know now that the Antichrist is an Assyrian, as the term was understood at the time of Isaiah, in 700 B.C.

The Prophet Says

"Therefore, Israel will be abandoned until the time when she who is in labor gives birth and the rest of his brothers return to join the Israelites. He will stand and shepherd his flock in the strength of the Lord, in the majesty of the name of the Lord his God. And they will live securely, for then His greatness will reach to the ends of the earth .... He will deliver us from the Assyrian when he invades our land and marches into our borders." (Micah 5:3–6)

The prophet Micah, who also prophesied around 700 B.C., talks about the Assyrian leader in the context of the final battle at Jerusalem. Therefore, we have a few clues that point to Assyria as the country of the Antichrist. Assyria, at the time of Isaiah and Micah, is basically modern-day Iraq.

So based on the prophecies of Daniel, Isaiah, and Micah, we conclude that the Antichrist will be an Iraqi. Now let's see what the Old Testament prophet Ezekiel can add.

The Gog and Magog Clue

Ezekiel prophesied about the armies of the Antichrist and described in some detail how the Antichrist would come against Jerusalem in the Last Days. Ezekiel refers to the Antichrist as "Gog, of the land of Magog." Ezekiel also describes Gog coming against Israel to loot and plunder in the Last Days. Ezekiel described Israel as a country of people recently gathered from many nations and at peace, secure in her borders. Similar to the other prophets, Ezekiel describes events that will take place just before and during the final battle on the Day of the Lord when the Messiah returns.

Ezekiel's clue to the country of the Antichrist is much like the clue we received from the prophets Isaiah and Micah. At the time of Ezekiel, the land of Magog was in the territory that is now northern Iraq and part of Iran.

So we are finding a certain consistency in the clues from the prophets. Each points to the Middle East, and several seem to zero in on the countries of Iraq and Iran. This information from Scripture should focus our attention on the Middle East as we watch for current events that match the Bible's description of the Last Days. The prophecies are so consistent that we can reject popular theories that the Fourth Beast Kingdom may be located somewhere else not pointed to in Scripture. All the clues point to the Middle East.

Based on Daniel's prophecies, we should watch to see if any of the Middle Eastern countries start to work cooperatively with each other, which they rarely do today. They do seem to share a common enemy in Israel and her allies. If they come together, we might expect to see a more formal group of Middle Eastern nations working together in perhaps a mutual defense pact. If we see 10 countries coming together and forming a strong alliance, we should realize where we are or may be in the prophetic timetable of the End Times.

—Timeline to the End of the Age—

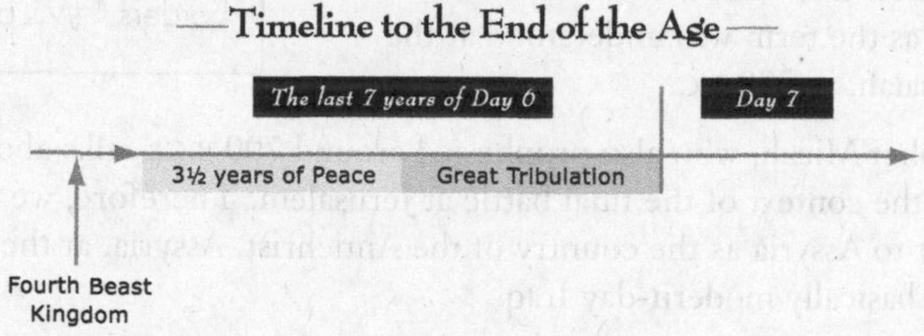

Of course, if a new leader replaces one of the original leaders and then defeats or otherwise subdues three of the original leaders, it would be hard to deny that events are the same as those described that will occur very close to the end of Day 6. Daniel told us that the leader who subdues the other three will be the Antichrist and that he will soon rule the whole world.

Keep in mind that because we have been told that the Antichrist is the "master of intrigue" and will "cause deceit to prosper," it's very likely that we will not be able to tell what he is going to do based on what he says. Therefore, at that point in Day 6, the best resource will be the Bible.

The Clues from the News

Because Scripture points to the Middle East as the location of the Fourth Beast Kingdom, let's consider what we find taking place in the Middle East as of 2006. We don't have to search to see the unstable and highly dangerous situation that currently exists in Iraq.

In addition, the major Middle Eastern countries that surround Iraq all appear to be in some kind of chaos of their own. Just the thought of a democratic Muslim nation in Iraq has many leaders deeply concerned about the prospects for their own kingdoms. Intelligence suggests that some of Iraq's neighboring kingdoms are so concerned about the threat to their dynasties that they are actively resisting a democratic Iraq with money and other resources.

Let's briefly discuss a few developments to get a feel for the issues that will be shaping the region's future.

Iran

For years Iran has been provoking worldwide concern about its nuclear ambitions. Now under a new administration, Iran appears to be almost openly pursuing the capacity to develop nuclear weapons. At the same time, the Iranian president, Mahmoud Ahmadinejad, has been making aggressive and provocative statements regarding the elimination of the Jewish state of Israel.

Ahmadinejad recently told senior clerics from all over Iran that the main mission of the Iranian government is to pave the way for a glorious reappearance of Imam Mahdi. Imam Mahdi is the Shia Muslim messiah predicted in Shiite Muslim writings to reappear in the End Times and rule the world for seven years before bringing about the Last Judgment and the end of the world. The Iranian president also indicated that Iran should become a mighty, advanced, model Islamic society, and that Iranians should "refrain from leaning toward any Western school of thought" and abstain from "luxurious lives" and other excesses.

Syria

As tensions increase in the Middle East, Iran and Syria seem to be strengthening their ties. A couple years ago, the two nations signed a mutual defense pact obligating themselves to defend each other against Israel in the case of an attack. The Syrian president, Bashar Al-Assad, recently backed Iran's right to develop nuclear power.

Israel

Recently, Israel's defense minister, Shaul Mofaz, weighed in on worldwide concerns about Iran and her nuclear ambitions by warning the Iranian people that Iran's president would bring disaster and suffering on them if he continued to call for the destruction of the Jewish state. In addition, he said Israel is preparing to defend itself if international diplomatic efforts fail to convince Iran to give up its nuclear program.

He went on to warn Iran's leadership about its current ideology of hatred, terror, and anti-Semitism, saying history reveals what happens to tyrants who have tried to annihilate the Jewish people and end up bringing destruction on their own people.

Certainly, Jewish and Muslim tensions have continued since Israel became a state nearly 60 years ago. Scripture and current events tell us that the situation is not likely to be resolved until the world reaches Day 7 and the Kingdom of God.

Israel and the Fourth Kingdom

In this chapter, we have discussed the fact that Israel's neighbors conquered the Jewish people and occupied the Promised Land in ancient times. Daniel wrote that Babylon dominated the land of Israel, followed by Media-Persia and Greece. This ancient history of tension and fighting between Israel and her neighbors has carried through to the twenty-first century. Indeed, it seems like we are going back to the future more as the world approaches the end of Day 6. The age-old animosity toward the Jewish people and her neighbors rages on.

However, in spite of this history of Middle Eastern tension between Israel and her Arab and Muslim neighbors, Scripture reveals that something very unusual will happen before we reach the end of Day 6.

Israel's Protector

When the Fourth Beast Kingdom appears out of the Middle East and the Antichrist comes to power, Israel will somehow be spared during the kingdom's rise to power and the Antichrist's world conquests. In addition, somewhere in the process, the Antichrist actually becomes Israel's protector, guaranteeing her security and peace.

The prophet Isaiah wrote that Israel would rely on the Assyrian (Antichrist) to protect her. Isaiah also revealed that the treaty guaranteeing Israel's protection, which will be confirmed by the Antichrist, will be short-lived and what Israel had feared will ultimately come to pass.

Ezekiel also described Israel as a people gathered from the nations to the mountains of Israel, which had long been desolate. He also said that Israel will be a nation recovered from war, whose people live in safety. As we know, Israel was desolate and abandoned for about 1,900 years before she was resettled by the Jewish people starting in 1948. Even today, Jewish people continue to migrate to Israel from many nations. Like Isaiah, Ezekiel tells us this security will not last because Gog (the Antichrist) will invade their land to destroy them.

Peace with the Beast

Daniel said the Antichrist will confirm a covenant or treaty with Israel for seven years. Then after the first three and a half years, he will halt temple sacrifice and offering when he sets himself up in the temple and declares that he is God.

In these prophecies, we see that the peace and security of Israel last just three and a half years before the Antichrist breaks the covenant and tries to destroy God's people. This period of punishment continues until the Messiah returns to deliver His people and usher in the Kingdom of God on Day 7. We discuss the things to come in more detail in the next few chapters.

The Least You Need to Know

- When the Fourth Beast Kingdom appears, it will lead to the end of Day 6.
- The Antichrist will rise to world power from the Fourth Beast Kingdom.
- The Bible indicates that the Fourth Beast Kingdom will form in the Middle East and that the Antichrist will come from Iraq or possibly Iran.
- Events in the Middle East seem poised to fulfill biblical prophecy.

Part 3

The Great Tribulation, Sound the Trumpets

In this part of the guide to the Last Days, we discuss the time called the Great Tribulation. The events that will take place during the Great Tribulation will be unmistakable. The events of the Great Tribulation last only three and a half years.

During the Great Tribulation, the nation of Israel will experience its worst persecution in history. Israel's persecution will come at the hands of a world leader whom the Bible refers to as the Antichrist. Also during this time, the world will be introduced to another sinister character called the False Prophet. The Bible says that these two will dominate the whole world for a few years, before their time runs out.

WILL THE *REAL* FALSE PROPHET PLEASE STAND UP.

Part

The Great Tribulation, Sound the Trumpets

In this part of the guide to the Last Days, we discuss the time called the Great Tribulation. The events that will take place during the Great Tribulation will be unmistakable. The events of the Great Tribulation last only three and a half years.

During the Great Tribulation, the nation of Israel will experience its worst persecution in history. Israel's persecution will come at the hands of a world leader whom the Bible refers to as the Antichrist. Also during this time, the world will be introduced to another sinister character called the False Prophet. The Bible says that these two will dominate the whole world for a few years before their time runs out.

Chapter 11

All Hell Breaks Loose

In This Chapter

- Jerusalem is set for the kill
- The Antichrist takes center stage in the temple
- Get out of Jerusalem while the gettin' is good
- Who are these prophets?

We are about to take a tour through future events in Jerusalem and Israel, events that will begin with the abomination that causes desolation, after which a period of death and destruction will be perpetrated on anyone who will not worship the Antichrist. This murderous period of three and a half years, the Great Tribulation, will be unprecedented in the history of the world, and never equaled again.

The Great Tribulation will begin in the Jewish Temple in Jerusalem and spread quickly throughout Israel. You will definitely want to schedule any trips to the Holy Land before this happens or postpone your trip until after the end of the age. As a matter of fact, if you're not inclined to worship the Antichrist, you might want to lay low for three and a half years.

The Stage Is Set

Many changes will have taken place in Israel leading up to this moment. Several peace treaties between Israel and her neighbors will have been signed, but each will have quickly succumbed again to mistrust, hatred, and violence. But then a new and very powerful leader will appear in the Middle East, someone who desires peace in the region. He will confirm a treaty with Israel and guarantee compliance with the force of his armies. Almost as soon as the treaty is confirmed, everyone in the region will feel secure and at peace. Israel had been at war or on the brink of war since becoming a nation in 1948. Now, for the first time, Israel will be at peace, a peace guaranteed by her Assyrian protector and his forces.

— **Last Days Timeline** —

Day 1	*Day 2*	*Day 3*	*Day 4*	*Day 5*	*Day 6*	*Day 7*
1,000 years	2,000 years	3,000 years	4,000 years	5,000 years	6,000 years	7,000 years
Adam	Noah	Moses	David	Christ	Church	Kingdom

You Are Here (↑ Day 6, Church)

Israel will also be experiencing a resurgence of Jewish culture that will envelop the nation and impact nearly the whole world. The third Jewish temple will be built on the Temple Mount, side by side with the Dome of the Rock, a Muslim holy site. Before the rebuilding of the temple, the Ark of the Covenant and the treasures of Solomon's temple will have been found. The discovery of the Ark will trigger the reestablishment of temple worship, in the Tabernacle of David, by the newly formed Sanhedrin. Within a few years, the third Jewish temple will be constructed on the Temple Mount, and animal sacrifices and offerings will be once again practiced regularly in the Jewish temple.

> **The Prophet Says**
>
> The Apostle Paul said, "While people are saying, 'Peace and safety,' destruction will come on them suddenly, as labor pains on a pregnant woman, and they will not escape." (1 Thessalonians 5:3)

This peaceful time is the calm before the storm. All hell is about to break loose in the holiest city on earth. An ominous event will change the world and set all the nations on a collision course with the end of the age. The prophets described several details about this turning point so we know what to watch for to be prepared.

Jerusalem Surrounded

Of all the signs and warnings that the Bible provides about the end of the age, recognizing the abomination that causes desolation and understanding its significance is the most crucial. You must understand how to recognize this sign and what it means. It's the opening of the door to the Great Tribulation, first for Jerusalem and Israel, and then for the rest of the world. The Bible speaks of this event many times to ensure that we've been warned. Let's just say that, at the end of the age, God will clearly be in a position to say, "I told you so."

Just before the abomination itself, Jerusalem will be surrounded by the armies of the Antichrist. Several of the prophets, including Jesus, Daniel, Isaiah, and Ezekiel, describe the state of affairs and how the armies of the Antichrist will set up Jerusalem for the coming disaster. Jesus told His disciples that a sign leading to this key biblical event will be that Jerusalem will become surrounded by armies. The prophet Daniel also wrote that the armed forces of the Antichrist will defile the temple and do away with temple sacrifices and offerings before they do the deed.

Prophetic Pitfalls

Often partial fulfillments of prophecy occur before the final or complete fulfillment. Partial fulfillments can often reveal something to help us identify the real deal. If any part of a prophecy remains unfulfilled after the event, we must continue to watch for the final fulfillment.

—Timeline to the End of the Age—

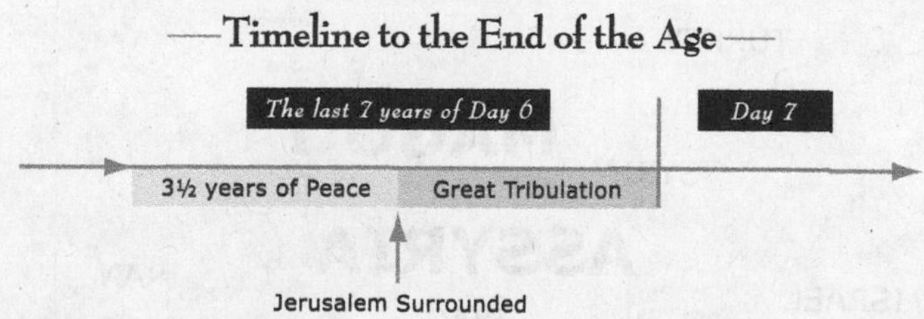

Roman Armies

You should be aware that several biblical prophecies are known to have dual or even multiple components. Jesus' prophecy about Jerusalem being surrounded by armies was partially fulfilled in A.D. 70 when the Roman army under General Titus came against Israel. The army surrounded Jerusalem and besieged it for more than a year. Jerusalem fell and the second Jewish temple was destroyed when the Assyrian soldiers burned the sanctuary. Another of Jesus' prophecies was totally fulfilled at that time. After the Assyrian soldiers burned the temple, they took it apart stone by stone to retrieve the gold that had melted into the stonework. Though the temple was destroyed, Titus never set himself up in the temple claiming that he was God. Therefore, the prophecy of the abomination that causes desolation remains as a future event.

Armies of the Antichrist

It appears from the prophecies of Daniel that the Antichrist and his armies will be returning from a campaign in the south when on this occasion they will stop at Jerusalem. We have discussed in a previous chapter that the Antichrist comes from the ancient area of Assyria and Magog which today is occupied by Iran and Iraq. We have also discussed previously that several other nations are aligned with the Antichrist. Therefore, it is likely that on this occasion the forces of the Antichrist will be formidable.

However, in spite of the ominous size of his force, Israel and Jerusalem will not be expecting trouble. There will be no cause for alarm because he will be Israel's protector, and his armies will have assured the peace and safety of Jerusalem for the past three and a half years.

Antichrist on Stage

With his armies stationed around Jerusalem, the Antichrist will enter the holy city. The Antichrist probably will have passed through Jerusalem from time to time since he confirmed the peace treaty between Israel and her Arab neighbors.

The Antichrist and his army will set up the abomination that causes desolation. The abomination is the blasphemy by the Antichrist when he stands in God's temple and claims to be God. This results in the destruction and desolation of many.

> **The Prophet Says**
>
> The Apostle Paul wrote this about the Antichrist: "He will oppose and will exalt himself over everything that is called God or is worshiped, so that he sets himself up in God's temple, proclaiming himself to be God." (2 Thessalonians 2:4)

On this particular visit, the Jewish priests will be actively involved in preparing the prescribed sacrifices and offerings on the altar in the temple court. They will be celebrating one of Israel's seven annual holy feast days.

Perhaps with several members of his entourage, Israel's protector will ask to visit the temple. Although this is an unusual request, concessions most likely will be made to grant him access. After all, without him and the peace he has guaranteed, this feast day in the temple would not be possible. Several priests will escort him and his party into the temple court.

Once in the temple court, the Antichrist may direct the sacrifice and offering to stop as he steps forward and declares that he is Almighty God. We know that he will denounce the God of the Bible and speak against His name and those in heaven. He then will demand that everyone show allegiance to him in worship.

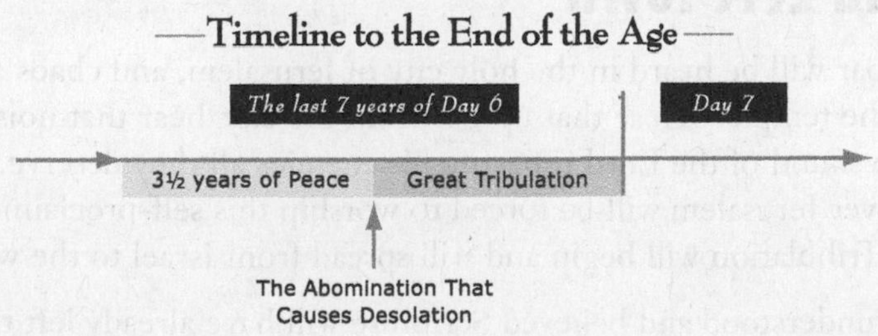

Death to Those Who Oppose Me

When the Antichrist makes his proclamation and demands to be worshiped, it's possible that some zealous priests will attack him for his blasphemous indignation. The priests might even attempt to kill him. Scripture does indicate that the Antichrist will die of a fatal head wound. Based on all prophesied events relating to the Antichrist, this event provides the opportunity, the motive, and the means for the crime. Whether or not this is the moment he is killed, it is certain that when he perpetrates this blasphemy in God's Temple, he will meet with great and violent opposition from the Jewish priests.

Unfortunately, when the Antichrist is killed, he does not stay dead. The Bible indicates that his fatal wound will be miraculously healed and he will return to life. Again, this will likely all occur at the time of the abomination that causes desolation. I will explain more about this in Chapter 11.

When the Antichrist rises from the dead, he will not be pleased with his reception by the religious order. He will immediately direct his forces to kill and subdue the priests and anyone in Jerusalem who will not worship him.

The Prophet Says

Jesus warned, "When you see 'the abomination that causes desolation' standing where it does not belong—let the reader understand—then let those who are in Judea flee to the mountains .... Because those will be days of distress unequaled from the beginning, when God created the world, until now—and never to be equaled again." (Mark 13:14–20)

I Wish I Had Left Town

A huge uproar will be heard in the holy city of Jerusalem, and chaos and noise will pour from the temple. "Hear that uproar from the city, hear that noise from the temple! It is the sound of the Lord repaying his enemies all they deserve." (Isaiah 66:6) People all over Jerusalem will be forced to worship this self-proclaimed God or perish. The Great Tribulation will begin and will spread from Israel to the whole world.

Those who understood and believed Scripture will have already left the city for the mountains. They watched as the birth pains occurred, and were alert to the implications of this peace treaty as well as other fulfilled prophecies. They suspected that this occasion could be the time of the abomination that causes desolation, and took precautions. Many of those remaining in Jerusalem will be killed in the genocide against Jews and Christians.

Flee Fast or Die

When Jesus warned His disciples about this event, He made very clear that time will be of the essence for those in Jerusalem and Judea. No one should go back to their house or stop for anything. The retribution will be severe and swift. He indicated that this time will be so terrible that people should pray for nothing to hinder their escape to the mountains. No one would want to be slowed by winter conditions, the Sabbath (when transportation systems are down), or even the complications of pregnancy. At this moment, quick escape will be a matter of life and death. Jesus referred to this period as the Great Tribulation.

The Prophet Says

Daniel wrote, "At that time Michael, the great prince who protects your people, will arise. There will be a time of distress such as has not happened from the beginning of nations until then." (Daniel 12:1)

Be Prepared to Persevere

Jesus says that the Great Tribulation will be so bad that if the Antichrist was permitted to continue his campaign unchecked, no one would survive. However, Christ will return immediately after the three and a half years of the Great Tribulation and destroy the Antichrist. The Antichrist's days are shortened for the sake of Christ's followers.

Prophetic Pitfalls

Jesus said, "If those days had not been cut short, no one would survive, but for the sake of the elect those days will be shortened." (Matthew 24:22) Don't assume that the three and a half years of Great Tribulation will be cut short. Jesus meant that if this period was not stopped at the end of the three and a half years, no one would survive.

Here is a list of places where the Bible indicates that the Great Tribulation will last three and a half years. Keep in mind that the Bible's prophetic calendar has twelve 30-day months, which is equivalent to a 360-day year:

1. **Daniel 7:25:** "time [year] times [2 years] and half a time [half a year]"
2. **Daniel 12:7:** "time times and half a time"
3. **Revelation 12:14:** "time times and half a time"
4. **Revelation 13:5:** "forty-two months"
5. **Revelation 11:3:** "1,260 days"
6. **Revelation 12:6:** "1,260 days"
7. **Daniel 9:27:** "in the middle of the seven"

I'll Be in the Mountains

When Jesus tells His followers to head for the hills, He is not suggesting a weekend getaway. Those who mange to escape won't be coming back to Jerusalem or Judea anytime soon. He wants them to understand the times and be prepared to persevere for the duration. This will be a time of testing throughout Israel. Jesus will prepare a place in the desert for His people, where they will be taken care of for 1,260 days.

The Bible describes the consequences of the Antichrist's system of control the way you might imagine life under a brutal totalitarian dictator. Stalin was bad—this guy will be much worse. This will be a time of life-and-death issues like never before in the history of the world. Some guy has just entered into the temple of God and declared that he is God. He suffers a fatal head wound and rises from the dead. He will have you killed if you do not worship him and pledge allegiance to him. Plus, he was raised from the dead and he says he's God. What are you going to believe? Only God can do that, right?

Jesus indicates that people will turn on each other, brother will betray brother to the death, parents will betray their children, and children will rebel against their parents and have them killed. He says that all men will hate His followers and warns them to hang on until the end. Jesus doesn't want his followers to be caught off guard.

Who Are These Guys?

At the time of the abomination that causes desolation, two men will appear in Jerusalem prophesying in the name of the Lord. They will be easy to recognize because their wardrobe won't likely be in the latest style and their behavior will be a dead giveaway.

They will be wearing sackcloth, the traditional dress of John the Baptist. They will prophecy for 1,260 days, the duration of the Great Tribulation. By the power of God, they will withstand any attack of the Antichrist and his forces as they deliver their message of warning to the world. They will have the power to kill anyone who tries to harm them. The world will be tormented by their message and the plagues they dish out.

When their testimony is finished, they will be killed by the *False Prophet.* (You'll read more about the False Prophet in Chapter 14.) Their bodies will lie in the streets of Jerusalem for three and a half days, and the world will rejoice and celebrate their demise by exchanging gifts. At the end of the three and a half days, the world will be terrorized when they return to life. At that time, they will be summoned into the clouds by a voice from heaven.

There are numerous theories about the identity of the two Great Tribulation prophets. My theory is that they will be Moses and Elijah. First, because the miraculous signs they do are characteristic of Moses and Elijah. In Egypt, Moses was responsible for various types of plagues, as are these prophets. Elijah was responsible for withholding rain for three and a half years, as are these prophets. Plus, during the time of the First Coming, Jesus gave a preview of His Second Coming in glory to a few of his disciples. When Jesus took His disciples up on the mount where He was transfigured, Jesus appeared with Moses and Elijah. I believe this was a sneak preview of the Second Coming and most likely identifies the two prophets who will prophecy up until the last trumpet when Christ returns.

def•i•ni•tion

The **False Prophet** is the second beast of Revelation Chapter 13. He comes out of the earth and deceives the whole world by performing miraculous signs, causing the inhabitants of the earth to worship the first beast. He and the first beast are thrown into the lake of fire at the end of the Great Tribulation.

What 144,000?

While I'm pointing out things you should look for during the Great Tribulation, I should also let you know what you will *not* see. You will not see 144,000 Jewish evangelists proclaiming the coming Messiah. Several theories have developed over the years about the identity of the 144,000 mentioned in Revelation Chapter 7. However, all we really know is that they are servants of God and come from all the tribes of Israel.

Considering the state of affairs in Israel during the Great Tribulation, if 144,000 Jewish evangelists appeared, they would be quickly killed. As we know from the two witnesses, supernatural power from God will be required to preach against the Antichrist and survive. Anyone who refuses to worship the Antichrist will certainly be killed. The most plausible theory explaining the 144,000 is that this number is spiritually symbolic and represents all believers. So, if you don't see a group of this number anywhere during the Great Tribulation, don't be concerned—they're in good hands.

The Least You Need to Know

- When you see armies surrounding Jerusalem, get out of Jerusalem and Judea, and head for the hills without delay.
- The abomination that causes desolation will confirm the identity of the Antichrist.
- After the abomination that causes desolation, stay out of Jerusalem and anywhere else under the control of the Antichrist for his control will spread to the whole world.
- Whatever you do, don't challenge the two witnesses who will be prophesying in Jerusalem during the Great Tribulation.

Chapter 12

Blow the Trumpet in Zion

In This Chapter

- The first trumpets sound the alarm
- The Antichrist revealed and 666 solved
- The rise of the Antichrist
- The Antichrist's rap sheet

In the Book of Revelation, we read of a vision into the future in which John sees seven angels sounding seven trumpets. As each of the first angels sounds his trumpet of warning, apocalyptic events take place on earth. In this chapter, we explore the events that take place as the first three trumpets are sounded. When the seventh angel sounds the last trumpet, the Kingdom of God arrives on earth.

In addition to learning about the apocalyptic events associated with the first three trumpets, we will solve one of the most fascinating mysteries in the Bible. I'll show you the Bible's solution to the 666 mystery, and how and when we will be able to confirm the Antichrist's identity.

Three Trumpets Sound Warning

Trumpets are sounded in the Bible as warnings, calls to assembly, and calls to arms. The Book of Revelation tells of seven trumpets. The first six are warnings, and the last is a call to assembly. These calls also represent the fulfillment of the Feast of Trumpets, which we covered in Chapter 2. The Feast of Trumpets is the first of the three fall harvest feasts.

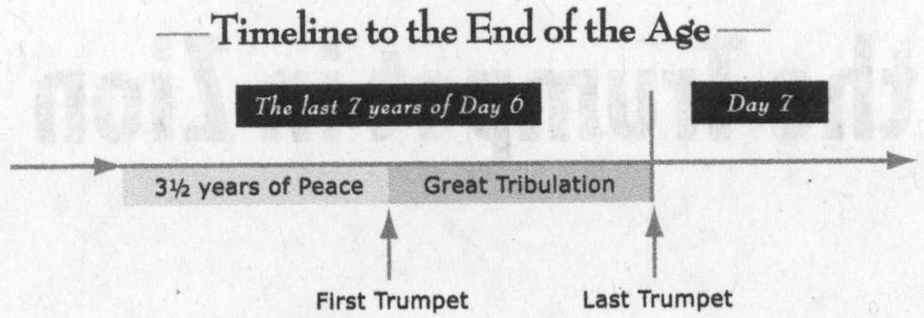

The first trumpet will sound its warning at the beginning of the Great Tribulation. As recorded in Revelation 11:15, the last trumpet will sound the call to assembly at the coming of the Kingdom of God on earth, immediately after the Great Tribulation. John says that as soon as the seventh angel sounds the last trumpet, loud voices from heaven will proclaim that the kingdom of this world has become the Kingdom of God and that Christ will reign forever and ever.

World on Fire

Differing opinions arise about when the seven trumpets of Revelation will begin to sound. The trumpets most likely begin with the start of the Great Tribulation. When the first angel sounds his trumpet, hail and fire will be hurled down on the earth and a third of the earth will be burned up—including trees, plants, and grass. When the second angel sounds his trumpet, something like a huge mountain, all ablaze, will be thrown into the sea. A third of the sea creatures and the ships will be destroyed. When the third angel sounds his trumpet, a great star, blazing like a torch, will fall from the sky on the rivers and springs of water. A third of the waters will turn bitter, causing many people to die.

Let's summarize what we know about the first three trumpets:

- First trumpet: The earth, trees, and grass burn.
- Second trumpet: The sea, sea creatures, and ships burn.
- Third trumpet: The rivers, springs, and waters turn bitter.

Now let me show you another event from Revelation that will also bring great devastation to the earth and sea. When Satan is thrown out of heaven to earth with all his angels, an announcement will be heard from heaven. Everyone in heaven will rejoice because Satan, who has been accusing God's people since the beginning of time, has now been cast out. Now, Satan is restricted to earth, and he is furious because he knows his time is short. He immediately begins to cause devastation with the earth and sea. From heaven we hear, "Woe to the earth and sea."

The Prophet Says

"The first angel sounded his trumpet, and there came hail and fire mixed with blood, and it was hurled down upon the earth. A third of the earth was burned up, a third of the trees were burned up, and all the green grass was burned up." (Revelation 8:7)

Because the destruction following the first three trumpets and the destruction caused by Satan and his angels is similar, the timing is very likely the same. Now if we can determine when Satan and his angels are thrown to the earth, we will know when the first three trumpets will sound their warnings.

Down and Out

Fortunately, Revelation Chapter 12 tells us how long Satan and his angels will have on earth from the time they are cast out of heaven. Satan's time is short, and he goes after the people of Israel, but God prepares a safe place for them in the desert where they can be taken care of for "a time, times and half a time" which is three and a half years. Apparently, this place in the desert is out of Satan's reach and allows for the protection of the people of God for the duration of the Great Tribulation. We are told again in a third account that when Israel flees to the safe haven in the desert, she will be protected for 1,260 days, or three and a half years. From these three references, we can determine that Satan will have only three and a half years to wreak havoc on earth, from when he is thrown down from heaven.

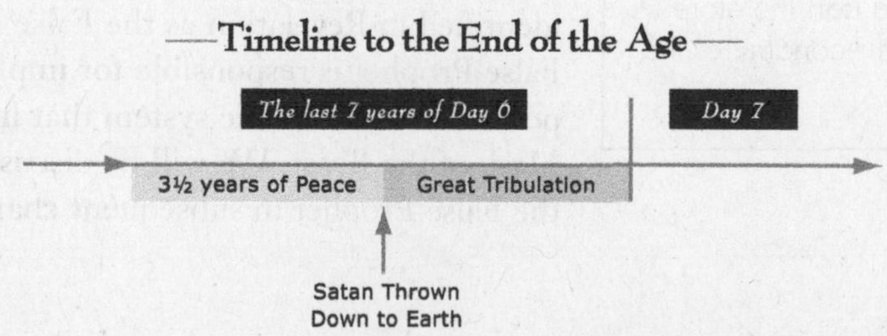

Prophetic Pitfalls

Some have mistakenly assumed that Satan has already been thrown down to earth because Jesus said, "I saw Satan fall like lightning from heaven." (Luke 10:18) However, Jesus didn't say when He saw Satan fall and Scripture is full of prophetic visions. Jesus does reveal when Satan is thrown out of heaven to earth in John's vision.

Because Satan's time runs out when Christ returns at the end of the Great Tribulation, we can count back from that point to determine when Satan is thrown from heaven. Counting back three and a half years from the end of the age brings us to the start of the Great Tribulation. So we know that Satan is thrown down from heaven to earth at the beginning of the Great Tribulation, and that means the first trumpets also sound at the beginning of the Great Tribulation.

So the trumpets described in the Book of Revelation will start at the beginning of the Great Tribulation, and the final and seventh trumpet will signal the return of Christ to earth.

Mystery 666 Solved

The Book of Revelation contains several Last Days mysteries. These mysteries are in the Bible to provide important information about the Last Days to those who believe and care to know. One of these mysteries has become so famous that the whole world seems to know that the number 666 is somehow connected to the identity of the future world leader known as the Antichrist.

def•i•ni•tion

The **Mark of the Beast** is a mark people will be required to have during the Great Tribulation to practice commerce. The mark is the name of the Antichrist or the number of his name. Having the mark indicates that the wearer supports or gives allegiance to the Antichrist and can therefore participate in the economy of the Antichrist.

The mystery of the number 666 is only described in the Book of Revelation. Not only is the number 666 a way to identify the Antichrist, it also seems to be connected to the *Mark of the Beast*. The Mark of the Beast is a mark that most people will receive on their hand or forehead during the Great Tribulation. The Mark of the Beast or the Mark of the Antichrist will only be used during the Great Tribulation when the Antichrist rules the entire world. When the Antichrist is in power, he will have a partner in crime, identified in Revelation as the False Prophet. The False Prophet is responsible for implementing the political and economic system that incorporates the Mark of the Beast. We will be discussing more about the False Prophet in subsequent chapters.

There are basically two mysteries related to the number 666. First, how does the number 666 help us identify the Antichrist? Second, what will the Mark of the Beast be like? Let's discuss how 666 can help identify the Antichrist.

For centuries, people have been trying to figure out how the identity of the Antichrist can be discovered using the number 666. They have used number-letter correlations with the Greek and Hebrew alphabets, the Bible Code, computer models, and political profiling, to mention just a few.

In the late 1700s, John Wesley, recognized as the founder of Methodism, wrote *Expository Notes on the Whole Bible*. In it he indicated that any man who acknowledged the Papacy as proceeding from God had the name of the beast as a mark and, therefore, the number of his name. Wesley also indicated that it would be the second beast who will enforce the receiving of this mark under the severest of penalties.

Some have speculated that President Richard M. Nixon was the Antichrist. Mikael Gorbachev was an interesting candidate, with the mark on his forehead that looked like a wound. In 1988, Robert W. Faid wrote *Gorbachev! Has the Real Antichrist Come?* In it he wrote, "It appears that there will be three separate things or marks which will qualify a man to buy or sell. The first is called the 'Mark of the Beast.' If indeed the antichrist is the leader of the Soviet Union, then the mark may well be the Red Star—the universal communist symbol. This may be a simple tattoo of the communist Red Star." Today, still others suggest that George W. Bush is the Antichrist.

In spite of all the energy and creativity that people have poured into solving this mystery over the centuries, they are still no closer to solving it.

Know Who to Ask

Wisdom comes from God, as does the answer to His mystery. If God wants you to be able to find the answer, He will provide the means of discovering the solution in His Word. Let's read the passage containing the mystery of 666.

> *[The False Prophet] also forced everyone, small and great, rich and poor, free and slave, to receive a mark on his right hand or on his forehead, so that no one could buy or sell unless he had the mark, which is the name of the beast or the number of his name. This calls for wisdom. If anyone has insight, let him calculate the number of the beast [the Antichrist], for it is man's number. His number is 666. (Revelation 13:16–18)*

In 2 Thessalonians Chapter 2, Paul stated that the *Day of the Lord* will not come until after the Antichrist is revealed. The Antichrist will exalt himself and oppose God and anyone who is worshiped, setting himself up in the temple of God and declaring that he himself is God. Therefore, we know that the Antichrist will be revealed at the abomination that causes desolation.

Know What to Ask

We will be able to identify the Antichrist at the abomination that causes desolation, but can't we do better than that? Paul states that the Antichrist will be revealed when he proclaims that he himself is God, and Daniel places the event in the middle of the last seven years. We know that this will take place three and a half years before the end of the age. Therefore, if the Bible states that the Antichrist will be revealed at that time, he cannot be revealed before that time.

Now let me explain how the number 666 relates to the identity of the Antichrist. Remember from Chapter 11 that sacrifices and offerings will be offered in the third Jewish temple at the time the Antichrist is to be revealed. Let's review the sequence of events leading up to the abomination that causes desolation:

1. Jerusalem is surrounded by the armies of the Antichrist.
2. Sacrifice and offerings are being prepared in the temple.
3. The Antichrist enters the Temple.
4. The Antichrist stops the sacrifice and offering.
5. The Antichrist declares that he is God and demands to be worshiped.
6. All hell breaks loose in the temple and Jerusalem.

Now imagine yourself watching this unfold from God's perspective in heaven, and read what He has to say about it. In Isaiah Chapter 66, God declares that heaven is His throne and the earth is His footstool.

> *Why have you built a house for Me? Do you imagine I need a place to rest? Is there anything I haven't created and brought into being? What I really desire is a humble and contrite spirit, someone who has a fear of My Word. But anyone who sacrifices a bull is like someone who kills a man, and anyone who sacrifices a lamb is like one who breaks a dog's neck. Anyone who makes a grain offering is like one who presents a pig's blood, and whoever burns memorial incense is like one who worships an idol. These people have chosen their own way, they delight in their religious practices, so I have decided to punish them and bring against them what they fear the most. Because when I called, no one answered; when I spoke, no one listened. They did evil in my sight and chose what displeases me. Hear what I say, you who tremble at My Word.*

Finally, in Isaiah 66:6, God says, "Hear the uproar from Jerusalem, hear the noise from the temple! It is the punishment and repayment I have planned for those who chose their own way and didn't heed my Word." God is very upset with these people. Why is He so upset? Aren't they merely doing what He told them to do in the first place?

Yes and no. It's true that God did prescribe His feasts and temple worship for His people. But remember from Chapter 3 that God prescribed His feasts to reveal His appointed times to His people. He is so angry and ready to severely punish His people because they did not recognize the fulfillment of His appointed times. God wanted them to understand the feasts so they would recognize what He was doing, not just to follow a list of religious rituals. His people missed the first four Feasts of God, which Jesus Christ fulfilled at His First Coming. Furthermore, based on this prophecy, it appears that they are about to miss the impending fulfillment of the last three harvest Feasts of God and Christ's Second Coming.

Man's Number

Isaiah's prophecy captures the chaos and uproar that occurs in the temple and Jerusalem resulting from the abomination that causes desolation. So what is the connection between the number 666 and the identity of the Antichrist? If you noticed that Verse 6 of Isaiah Chapter 66, or the number 666, depicts the situation following the abomination that causes desolation, then you have solved the mystery.

Now that you see the connection between Isaiah 66:6 and the Antichrist, another detail should further convince you that this 666 is the 666 that is being described in Revelation Chapter 13. Let's read it again: "If anyone has insight, let him calculate the number of the beast, for it is man's number. His number is 666."

When the Bible was originally written, there were no numbers for chapter and verse. Humans put the numbers in the biblical record hundreds of years later to organize Scripture so that we would have a method of referencing text from the Word of God. That's right, 666 is man's number. God didn't put it there. But, of course, God knew the number that would be on this verse before man put his number on it, just as God knows exactly what is going to happen in the Last Days.

Mark of the Antichrist

The Bible indicates that the Mark of the Beast will be the name of the Antichrist or the number of his name and that the mark will be placed on the hand or the forehead of the persons who receive it. We also know that the mark will be required to buy or sell. For hundreds and hundreds of years it was thought that the mark could be some kind of brand, as one brands cattle, or a tattoo. This interpretation of what the mark would be like continued to be prevalent until modern times.

Some of the last theologians to hold to these ideas were Clarence Larkin and Hal Lindsey. In *Dispensational Truth* (1918), Larkin wrote that, "The 'Mark' will be branded or burnt on. It will probably be the 'NUMBER OF THE BEAST' or '666.'" In *The Late Great Planet Earth* (1970), Lindsey wrote. "Everyone will be given a tattoo or mark on either his forehead or forehand, only if he swears allegiance to the Dictator as being God. Symbolically, this mark will be 666."

However, with the advent of modern electronic technology, the theories regarding the mark have exploded just as the technologies themselves have exploded. With each new technology, new theories of what the mark will be spring up. From the 1920s with the advent of gasoline credit cards to the 1950s with credit cards like Diner's Club, people began to speculate that credit cards would be the vehicle for the mark.

In 1980 Hal Lindsey wrote *The 1980's: Countdown to Armageddon*. In just 10 years, he was updating his theory regarding the mark. In his new book he wrote, "Those worshippers will each be assigned a trade number. Without that number, no one will be permitted to buy or sell anything …. The only safeguard would be to tattoo the number on your skin with an ink that could be seen only in a special light …. The anti-Christ, with the help of his False Prophet, will require that a number representing his name become part of your own banking number to make it valid."

Of course technology did not stop there, nor did the theories about what the mark could be. One of the next technologies was that of the barcode, which provided new possibilities for the mark. In 1982, Mary Stewart Relfe published *The New Money System,* in which she wrote, "The Prophet John identified this Cashless System of Commerce 1,900 years ago as one in which business would be transacted with a 'Mark' and a Number; the Mark will obviously be a Bar Code; the Number will be '666'…."

Then came computer chips and the possibilities they provide. In 1988, Texe Marrs explored several technologies in his theories about the mark when he wrote *Mystery Mark of the New Age*. Marrs asked, "Could a microchip be programmed with the number of the Beast and be inserted under a person's skin? And what of the bar code? Could the laser be used to 'brand' people with the Mark?" In 1991, Peter Lalonde wrote *One World Under Anti-Christ*. Lalonde said, "The microchips currently used in 'smart cards' could easily fulfill the definition of 'the mark' which will be issued under the Antichrist regime."

If our technological society survives what is in store for the world ahead, then it may be possible that a combination of these technologies will be incorporated into the application of the Mark of the Beast. However, if the technologies do not survive to the end of the age, then perhaps some of the original theories will be the fulfillment of this prophecy. Time will tell.

Rise of the Antichrist

The Great Tribulation is the period in which the Antichrist dominates and deceives the whole world. It will be a horrific time on earth. Those who used the motto "No Fear" will be rethinking their philosophy of life. The Antichrist will quickly strengthen his grip on what we once called the civilized world. For those who are able to survive during these years, it may be helpful to know something more about the Antichrist.

Start Small

The Antichrist will probably begin like many other overachievers and will rise from humble beginnings. My guess is, he will be born in the Middle East and raised in some oppressive regime. Certainly, he will possess superior intellectual abilities and will be well educated, perhaps fluent in several languages. He very likely will become heavily involved in rebuilding the political and socioeconomic infrastructure of his country as the Middle East begins its climb to power. Rising quickly in stature, he may become vice president and then succeed to president through a democratic election.

The prophet Daniel wrote about the Fourth Beast Kingdom and the rise to power of the Antichrist. He described him as starting small and then coming up among the first 10 kings of the kingdom. It appears that the Antichrist will take the position of one of the original 10 leaders and then defeat 3 of the other 10, leaving the Fourth Beast Kingdom with 7 heads.

Think Big

At the time the Antichrist becomes president, his country will be a member of the 10 nations that form the Fourth Beast Kingdom. The 10 countries will work together politically, economically, and militarily to advance their agenda in the Middle East and beyond. They will become very powerful on many fronts due to the extreme wealth they receive from their abundant oil reserves. The Fourth Beast Kingdom will also become a considerable military force in the region. It will have strong economic and military alliances with China, Russia, and her former satellite states.

As soon as the Antichrist takes his seat within the Fourth Beast Kingdom, he will make his presence felt. Aggressively consolidating his power, he will eliminate three of the other heads of the Fourth Beast Kingdom. Then the kingdom will be led by seven heads of state, with the Antichrist at the helm.

The Antichrist and His MO

The descriptions that Scripture provides of the Antichrist come from two perspectives. A few describe him before the abomination that causes desolation. However, most describe him after he has declared himself to be God in the Temple of God. Expect to see a marked difference in the Antichrist's behavior before and after the abomination that causes desolation. If you are expecting a certain behavior from the Antichrist early in his career and don't see it, you may drop your guard prematurely. The peacemaker who guarantees the peace treaty between Israel and her neighbors is the same man who, three and a half years later, will kill anyone who does not worship him.

A Rose Is Still a Rose

As you read about the Antichrist from Scripture, it will be important that you know the names that the prophets used when they wrote about him. The following is a list of prophets with a reference to a sample verse and the names each used when referring to the Antichrist.

- **John:** 1 John 2:18, "Antichrist"; Revelation 13:1, "The Beast"
- **Paul:** 2 Thess. 2:3, "Man of lawlessness"
- **Christ:** Mark 13:14, "The Abomination that causes desolation"
- **Daniel:** Daniel 7:11, "The Beast"; Daniel 9:26, "The ruler who will come"; Daniel 11:36, "The king"
- **Isaiah:** Isaiah 10:5, "The Assyrian"; Isaiah 10:12, "King of Assyria"
- **Ezekiel:** Ezekiel 38:3, "Gog, chief prince"

The God, the Bad, and the Ugly

The Bible provides numerous descriptions of this End Times leader and his method of operation. John tells us that he is a stranger to the truth and that he will deny that Jesus the Christ came in the flesh. The prophet Daniel wrote clearly about the behavior of the Antichrist, whom he called the beast. Daniel's description provides various characteristics and the modus operandi that will help us recognize the Antichrist and know what to expect:

- He will speak against the Most High.
- He will wage war against the saints.
- He will try to change God's set times and the laws.
- He is a stern-faced king.
- He is a master of intrigue.
- He will cause astounding devastation.
- He will succeed in whatever he does.
- He will destroy the mighty men and the holy people.
- He will cause deceit to prosper.
- He will consider himself superior.
- He will take his stand against Christ.
- He will corrupt with flattery.
- He will do as he pleases.
- He will exalt and magnify himself above God.
- He will say unheard-of things against God.
- He will show no regard for Christ.
- He will honor a god of fortresses.
- He will attack the mightiest fortresses.
- He will greatly honor those who acknowledge him.

Like Daniel, John in Revelation Chapter 13 provided good descriptions of the Antichrist, whom he also refers to as the beast. John describes him as receiving a fatal head wound that will be healed. John says the whole world will be astonished when the beast miraculously rises from the dead, and they will follow and worship him.

People will ask, "Who is like the beast? Who can make war against the beast?" The Antichrist will speak boastfully and blaspheme God and all those in heaven. He will receive power to make war against the followers of Christ and persecute them for the three and a half years of the Great Tribulation.

John also describes great division in the world. On one hand, the whole world will follow and worship the Antichrist. Those who will not submit to him will be killed by the sword or put into prison. John warns the followers of Christ to faithfully and patiently persevere to the end.

From Daniel and John, we are able to learn much about who the Antichrist is and what he will be doing during the Great Tribulation. So stay alert and keep watch.

The Least You Need to Know

- The first three trumpets of Revelation start their warning blasts at the beginning of the Great Tribulation, and a third of the earth and sea is destroyed.
- The 666 mystery reveals that the identity of the Antichrist will not be confirmed until the abomination that causes desolation.
- You should expect a dramatic change in the Antichrist's behavior from before and after the abomination that causes desolation, a real "Dr. Jekyll and Mr. Hyde" transformation.
- Remember, the Antichrist is a liar. Even though he is capable of amazing things—even rising from the dead—he is one of the bad guys. Don't trust anything he says or does.

Chapter 13

The Power Behind the Antichrist

In This Chapter

- Who restrains the power of lawlessness
- What the Devil has to do with it
- Last Days supernatural activity

Now let's introduce a very special End Times player you should know about. He has been taking care of business for God since things got started. He's what you might call God's "strongman" or "sergeant-at-arms." Some people may know him for his title role as the Restrainer in the Apostle Paul's second letter to the Thessalonians. This chapter gives you the scoop on my hero, the Restrainer of the secret power of lawlessness.

You will also learn more about the Devil. What would the End Times be without the Devil? No, you won't find him in a red suit with horns and a pointed tail—but if you know what to look for during the Last Days, you will be able to recognize his handiwork in several scenes before the closing curtain.

This chapter also tells you more about the spectacular supernatural activity in the Last Days, provided direct from the heavenly realm. Seriously, being able to identify the supernatural activities and determine who is behind it will help you understand what's going on and keep you from being deceived by it.

The Restrainer

In the last few chapters, you have learned a great deal about the Antichrist and how and when to recognize him. As big as the Antichrist will be in the Last Days, he would be nothing without his supporting cast. This includes several key players whose work we need to recognize.

Being able to determine who is behind certain signs and wonders of the Last Days will help us know whether we should believe them. The deception will be very great, and we will be tempted to believe some things that we should not.

As we have already seen, the Apostle Paul provided important information regarding the Last Days and the Antichrist when he wrote to the Thessalonians. In his second letter, Paul instructed the people to watch for the man of lawlessness (the Antichrist) to be revealed. Paul also wrote about two other characters who have parts to play at the time of the abomination that causes desolation.

Paul clearly identified the Antichrist. However, to identify the other two players, we have to do some investigation in other parts of the Bible. One being is the secret power of lawlessness; Paul also wrote of someone who holds back the secret power of lawlessness. He said that this *Restrainer* will continue to hold back the secret power of lawlessness until the appointed time, when he will be taken out of the way and the man of lawlessness—the Antichrist—will be revealed.

def•i•ni•tion

The **Restrainer**—Michael the Archangel, the great prince of the spiritual world, protects the people of God by restraining Satan. Satan will attempt to kill all God's people during the Great Tribulation, when he is no longer held back.

The Apostle John has given us the information we need to identify the secret power of lawlessness. In 1 John Chapter 3, he explains that everyone who sins breaks the law and that sin is lawlessness. John goes on to tell us that those who commit sin are being led by the Devil, and that the Devil has been sinning from the beginning of time.

John connects lawlessness to sin; whoever does what is sinful is of the Devil. Therefore, Satan is the power of lawlessness being held back.

Identifying the third player is more challenging. However, the Bible again provides the information needed. Previously, we figured out that the Antichrist will be revealed three and a half years before the end of the age. Asking ourselves the right question will lead us to the correct identity of the Restrainer.

What else will be happening at this time? In Chapter 12, we learned that Satan will be thrown out of heaven to earth three and a half years before the end of the age. Therefore, the Antichrist will be revealed at the same time that Satan is thrown out of heaven.

In John's futuristic vision as recorded in Revelation 12:7–8, John sees a war in heaven between the Archangel Michael (the great prince who protects the people of God) and his angels, and Satan and his angels. Michael and his angels are stronger, and they throw Satan and his angels out of heaven to the earth. This scenario clearly points to Michael as the Restrainer, as does other evidence in the Bible. Michael the Archangel is presented in Scripture as one of the two highest ranking angels in the heavenly Kingdom of God. Michael is presented as a powerful warrior. The other archangel is Gabriel, who is presented as the messenger from the throne of God in heaven. Gabriel was the one who gave the prophet Daniel prophecies and announced the birth of the Messiah to the Virgin Mary.

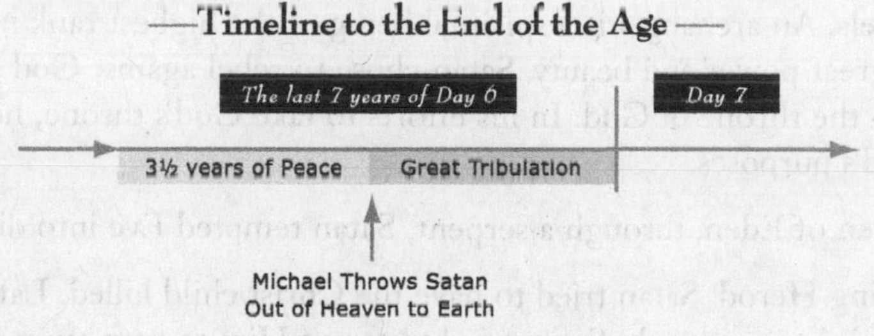

Michael is described in Daniel Chapter 10 as the chief prince, who protects the people and supports God's messengers when they are confronted by countervailing spiritual powers. The prophet Daniel recorded that Michael is on the scene just before the Great Tribulation. In Daniel 12:1, he says that Michael will arise to take action at a time of distress in such a way that has not happened from the beginning of nations.

The Hebrew word translated as "arise" also means to present oneself for service. This helps explain what we were seeing in John's vision about Michael and Satan. When the appointed time comes, God will tell Michael to throw the bum out. Michael will step up to the plate and, with his angels, will throw Satan and Satan's angels out of heaven to earth.

There are prophecies in Scripture which speak of Satan being thrown down from heaven to earth. Jesus once said that He saw Satan fall from Heaven. However, these appear to be prophetic statements, because the only place in the Bible which identifies the time that he is banished from heaven is in Revelation Chapter 12. The Bible also indicates that Satan still, today, has access to heaven and earth. But, when Satan is thrown down to earth in the future, he will be restricted to the earth.

Turning back to the New Testament, Jude informs us that Michael contends with Satan. The evidence is overwhelming that Michael is the Restrainer.

Prophetic Pitfalls

Since the Apostle Paul mentioned the Restrainer, in Second Thessalonians, some people have been uncertain about the identity of the Restrainer. However, the Bible provides all the necessary information. Michael, the great prince and protector of God's people, is the one who is restraining Satan, the secret power of lawlessness.

The Devil's in the Details

Now let's take a look at the hidden nemesis called Satan, or the Devil. Satan is one of the archangels. An archangel is a spiritual being of the highest rank in God's creation, possessing great power and beauty. Satan chose to rebel against God and attempted to ascend to the throne of God. In his efforts to take God's throne, he has violently resisted God's purposes.

In the Garden of Eden, through a serpent, Satan tempted Eve into disobeying God.

Through King Herod, Satan tried to have the Christ child killed. Later, when Jesus began His ministry on earth, Satan tried to tempt Him to turn away from His mission. Throughout this age, from Adam to the present day, the Devil has sought to thwart God's plan and to destroy the people of God.

Satan has also been at work making accusations against God's people, taking full advantage of his access to the throne and presence of God. An Old Testament account tells of Satan accusing Job of being one of God's people only because of the easy life he has. We learn that Satan travels in the company of angels and that he roams the earth. In the Book of Job, God holds up his servant Job to Satan and says that no one else is like Job: righteous and upright in all that he does, fearing God and rejecting evil. Satan is unconvinced and claims that Job will surely curse God if He removes the hedge of protection around Job and his family. Job remains faithful to God as Satan destroys his family and all of his property. Though we like to claim "the Devil made me do it," it is possible to stand true to God in the face of tests and temptations.

You may have noticed that Satan must get permission to take any action against God's people. Jesus even mentioned on one occasion that Satan had asked to sift Simon Peter like wheat, meaning to test him to the max. For now, Satan must be granted permission to touch God's people, but that will not always be the case. From Revelation, we know that Satan will continue in this role of accuser and tempter of God's people, right up to the time he is thrown out of heaven.

The Prophet Says

John saw, "The great dragon was hurled down—that ancient serpent called the devil, or Satan, who leads the whole world astray. He was hurled to the earth, and his angels with him." (Revelation 12:9)

We now have an idea of what has been going on behind the scenes between Satan and God. However, we need to consider something else as we prepare ourselves to cope with the End Times events. Satan will no longer be held back once he is thrown out of heaven and allowed to operate on earth unrestrained. This means that beginning at the abomination that causes desolation and throughout the Great Tribulation, Satan will be confined to the earth and will be unrestrained. To put it mildly, it will be hell on earth for God's people. The Bible describes this period of the Great Tribulation in many ways, including referring to it as the time of the fury and wrath of Satan.

As the Last Days tick by and Satan's time begins to run out, he will redouble his efforts. Many of the events and circumstances occurring on the earth in the Last Days will have Satan's fingerprints on them. I will show you from Scripture what is revealed about Satan's efforts in the Last Days, and how he will try to stop God's plan and take the throne from Christ for himself.

The Devil Made Me Do It

In the last years of the End Times, the Antichrist will accomplish amazing political, economic, and military achievements. He will have this success at a time in history when the world will be violently divided, with countries fighting against each other over diverse agendas. Achieving unity on a national scale will seem unimaginable; unity on a global scale would be out of the question. Yet, in spite of this, the Antichrist will rise to world power and bring everyone under his system. From the moment he takes over world leadership, he will implement a rigid theocracy, with himself as God. As he solidifies his power, those who appose him will be eliminated.

How will this be possible? Could any one man accomplish all this without some very powerful support? Of course not, but the Antichrist receives great power from Satan. Satan will give the Antichrist his power, his throne, and great authority. And when Satan is thrown down to earth, he will give the Antichrist his supernatural power.

The Prophet Says

John saw in his vision, "One of the heads of the beast seemed to have had a fatal wound, but the fatal wound had been healed. The whole world was astonished and followed the beast [Antichrist]. Men worshiped the dragon [Satan] because he had given authority to the beast, and they also worshiped the beast and asked, 'Who is like the beast?'" (Revelation 13:3–4)

The means of this transfer of power is not described in scripture. However, we do know that the Antichrist is killed at some point because he is said to have suffered a fatal wound that is healed. My theory is that the Antichrist will be killed at the time of the abomination that causes desolation, and that Satan will transfer his supernatural power to the Antichrist and raise him from the dead a superman.

Forecast: 100 Percent Chance of Supernatural Activity

When Jesus warned his disciples about the events of this period as recorded in Matthew 24:21–24, He tells of this coming supernatural phenomena. False christs and prophets will appear and perform great signs and miracles to deceive everyone, even Christ's followers. Jesus knew that the signs and miracles performed by the Antichrist would be very convincing, so He repeatedly warns His followers so that it won't be possible to trick them.

The Bible contains many warnings about great deception that will be perpetrated on the world in the Last Days. Deception is the major theme of Jesus' discourse to His disciples regarding His return and the end of the age. Based on the number of warnings from Jesus and the apostles about supernatural signs and miracles, it's apparent that they were concerned about this type of deception.

It's one of the frailties of the human condition to be deceived by what we see even when it goes against our beliefs. The sailors and pirates of old had an expression that they used to keep themselves from being deceived: "Don't believe anything you hear, and believe only half of what you see." It would be good to keep this motto in mind as we head into the Last Days and the end of the age.

Now let's look at some of the specific signs and miracles that we should expect in the Last Days.

Visible Signs

The first miracle, and potentially one of the most dramatic, occurs when the Antichrist rises from the dead. We do not know the specific details of how and when this happens, but according to Scripture, this satanic resurrection deceives the whole unbelieving world into believing that the Antichrist is God. We are told in Revelation Chapter 13 that his fatal wound will be healed. The astonished world will follow and worship the risen Antichrist.

My theory about when and how this miracle will happen was briefly described in Chapter 11. Because of the biblical circumstances that coincide at one time, I imagine that this event will take place at the abomination that causes desolation. When the Antichrist goes into the temple and claims to be almighty God, the priests will kill him. But, as Scripture says, he will be healed and rise again. As you saw previously, Satan will be behind this miracle of raising the Antichrist. The world will be astonished by this sign and will follow the Antichrist until the end of the age.

One of my favorite signs, from Revelation Chapter 13, will be performed by the False Prophet. The False Prophet is a powerful leader who works with the Antichrist, during the Great Tribulation, to firmly establish the kingdom of the Antichrist. For some reason, I imagine that this miracle will be covered by all the major news networks. The False Prophet will cause fire to come down from heaven to earth in full view of men. Most people will be unaware that Satan is behind this spectacular event and will believe that what they see is a sign from God.

We might think that the spectacular sight of fire coming down from heaven in full view of men could have some scientific explanation. With today's space and laser technologies, we could imagine that the False Prophet has some of these things at his disposal and will pull off a gigantic magic trick. It's also possible to imagine that he could artificially create lightning. However, a careful read of the Scripture indicates that this will be a miracle, unexplainable through human methods. None of the world's experts will be able to explain how this could have been done, and the world will be deceived into thinking that this must be from God, when it is not.

The Prophet Says

The False Prophet: "And he performed great and miraculous signs, even causing fire to come down from heaven to earth in full view of men." (Revelation 13:13)

Another miraculous sign, also performed by the False Prophet, is a bit harder to imagine, but it should be easy enough to recognize when it happens. The False Prophet will erect an image in honor of the Antichrist, who had been killed by the sword yet lived. The False Prophet will empower the image of the Antichrist to speak. All who refuse to worship the image will be killed. This will be truly extraordinary and, I imagine, very convincing.

The picture I get in my mind is that of an animated statue erected in the temple in Jerusalem. This statue of the Antichrist will probably become a substitute for the Jewish temple worship practiced in the temple before the Antichrist's claim of deity. People of the world will likely worship the Antichrist through this image of him.

Only those who expect these signs and understand who is behind these great performances will not be deceived.

The supernatural events mentioned earlier will be visible in the natural world. Others of the Last Days supernatural events will likely be visible only in the spiritual realm. The spiritual realm is that part of creation in which angels and demons operate. The natural realm is the part of creation in which we operate.

In Revelation 16:13–14, John tells of three evil spirits that look like frogs coming out of the mouths of the Antichrist and the False Prophet. He says they are demon spirits that perform miraculous signs and go out to the kings of the world to gather them for battle on the Great Day of the Lord.

Most likely, this behind-the-scenes occurrence will be visible only in the spiritual realm.

Godly Signs

But don't think for a minute that the unholy trio of Satan, the Antichrist, and the False Prophet will be the only ones empowering spectacular signs and miracles. While the trio is using supernatural powers to deceive the world, God and his servants will not be sitting idly by.

God will give power to His two witnesses, and they will prophesy for three and a half years, clothed in sackcloth. Anyone who tries to harm them will be consumed by fire that will come from their mouths. They will also have power to stop the rain during the three and a half years, and to strike the earth with every kind of plague whenever they want.

Clearly, there will be many unexplainable occurrences, the likes of which have not been seen on earth for some time. God knew that if He told us who would be doing what, we could hang on until the end if we stay alert and keep watch.

The Least You Need to Know

- Michael, the Restrainer, will throw Satan and his angels out of heaven at the time of the abomination that causes desolation, which is three and a half years from the end of the age.
- When Satan is thrown down to the earth, he will be unrestrained and he will give his power and authority to the Antichrist.
- During the Great Tribulation, there will be an unprecedented level of supernatural activity.

Chapter 14

New World Order

In This Chapter

- A global paradigm shift
- Mystery Babylon the Great
- Mystery solved, seven kingdoms revealed
- Mystery solved, False Prophet revealed

As we approach the end of Day 6 in God's plan, the world is about to experience a sudden and violent change. To say that this change will bring about a New World Order is a colossal understatement. Superpowers that we are familiar with will disappear and be replaced by some very scary characters. One or two of these characters will literally be out of this world.

This Changing World

So far, we have discussed the events relating to the rise of the Antichrist. You have learned that the Antichrist rises out of the Fourth Beast Kingdom and successfully dominates the world until the end of the age. If the Antichrist is to achieve world domination, the world as we know it must go through a dramatic, even catastrophic, change.

Imagine what will be required for the world to change from what we have today to a world system under the Antichrist. To put this in perspective, let's compare some of today's realities to what we have learned about the future world that will be run by the Antichrist.

Present:

- One superpower based in the West.
- This superpower dominates much of the world through its global economic influence and military strength.

Future:

- One superpower based in the Middle East.
- The superpower dominates the entire world by forcing compliance with its economic and political systems.

For this dramatic shift in global realities to occur peacefully, there would have to be gradual transformation over several generations. Based on the pattern of world history and human behavior, it's more likely that our world paradigm will change as a result of violent struggle and world war.

A Stern-Faced King

Since we are deriving our understanding from how the Bible describes the Last Days, let's examine what Scripture has to say about this future global change.

As usual, the prophet Daniel provides some key clues to how this future world change will take place. In one of his visions, Daniel sees a stern-faced king, the Antichrist, rising out of one of the four kingdoms left after Alexander the Great's empire was broken up. Daniel says this will occur at a time in world history when rebels have become completely wicked. Perhaps he was seeing in his vision the rebels of today whom we call terrorists. Daniel sees that this world leader, a master of intrigue and deception, will become very powerful with the support of another.

We saw in the last chapter that the Antichrist receives support, power, and authority from Satan. This may be the support that Daniel saw, or the support may come from a worldly ally. We cannot be certain which of these Daniel saw. However, the result of the support is that the Antichrist will cause astounding devastation and will destroy the existing superpowers. He also envisioned that the stern-faced king will consider himself superior to all others, standing against Christ and killing the people of God. Finally, at the end of this vision, Daniel sees the stern-faced king destroyed—but not by human power.

The Prophet Says

Daniel describes completely wicked rebels in the Last Days. "In the latter part of their reign, when rebels have become completely wicked, a stern-faced king, a master of intrigue, will arise. He will become very strong, but not by his own power. He will cause astounding devastation and will succeed in whatever he does. He will destroy the mighty men and the holy people." (Daniel 8:23–24)

King of Deception

Daniel recorded several visions regarding the Antichrist and his rise to world dominance. In another vision, in Daniel Chapter 11, Daniel sees that the Antichrist, through intrigue and deception, is able to invade a rich kingdom at a time when its people feel secure. Because of an agreement made with the Antichrist, the superpower will be completely destroyed by the Antichrist's forces. The Antichrist will distribute the wealth, plunder, and loot among his allies.

In each of his visions, Daniel sees the Antichrist successfully attacking and destroying the most powerful forces. Based on these futuristic visions, we can pretty much rule out a gradual global shift in world power. Daniel's prophecies clearly indicate that the change from our present reality will happen suddenly, over a relatively short period. This coming worldwide upheaval is another reason Christ warns His followers to stay alert and keep watch.

Mystery Babylon the Great

Daniel was not the only prophet to receive visions of the Antichrist and the Fourth Beast Kingdom attacking and overcoming the mightiest military power. In the Book of Revelation, John also sees a vision of the Fourth Beast Kingdom destroying the world's great superpower. His vision provides a great deal of information about the two End Time superpowers.

One of the two superpowers is already familiar to us. We know it as the Fourth Beast Kingdom. The other superpower is referred to as "Mystery Babylon the Great, the

def•i•ni•tion

Mystery Babylon the Great, or **Mystery Babylon,** is a Last Days superpower that will hold a position of great influence over the world until it is destroyed by the Antichrist and the Fourth Beast Kingdom, according to Revelation Chapters 17 and 18.

Mother of Prostitutes and of the Abominations of the earth." I refer to this country as *Mystery Babylon.*

The identity of Mystery Babylon is another one of God's Last Days mysteries, and figuring it out is critically important if we hope to recognize where we are in the timing of God's plan and be prepared for what is yet to come. Solving this particular mystery is also important because God commands His followers to come out of Mystery Babylon. Therefore, those interested in following God's instructions will want to do their best to determine her identity.

Let's begin our understanding of the prophecies about Mystery Babylon by examining the information we are given about each of the two superpowers mentioned. First, let's consider the Fourth Beast Kingdom.

This kingdom will dominate the whole world until the end of the age. As we learned earlier from the reading in Daniel, the Fourth Beast Kingdom will devour the whole earth, trampling it and crushing it. The Fourth Beast Kingdom will begin with 10 kings; then the Antichrist will arise among the 10 and defeat 3 of them. After he defeats 3 of the 10 kings, the Antichrist will be the leader of the Fourth Beast Kingdom. At that time, the kingdom of 10 nations will have 7 heads. In Revelation Chapter 17, we find that a nation is referred to as a horn.

In Revelation, this kingdom is referred to as having "7 heads and 10 horns." Therefore, whenever we read about 7 heads and 10 horns, we should realize that it is the Fourth Beast Kingdom with the Antichrist at the helm.

The Prophet Says

John hears of her demise. "A second angel followed and said, 'Fallen! Fallen is Babylon the Great, which made all the nations drink the maddening wine of her adulteries.'" (Revelation 14:8)

Now let's turn to the superpower called Mystery Babylon. Daniel gives us a few clues about this final kingdom. He states that the Antichrist and his kingdom will sweep aside an overwhelming army, destroying the mighty men and successfully attacking the mightiest fortresses. In Revelation Chapters 17 and 18, John completes the picture. All we have to do is understand John's vision.

Keep in mind, as we consider Mystery Babylon, that this prophecy has been in existence for almost 19 centuries. Many people have tried to figure it out based on the information available at the time. For example, St. Augustine (circa A.D. 400) believed that Mystery Babylon was the Roman Catholic Church. While that may have seemed reasonable at the time, the Roman Catholic Church doesn't fit the description today.

The identity of Mystery Babylon will be known only when a country appears that fulfills each aspect of the detailed description recorded in Revelation. The prophet Daniel was actually told in one of his prophecies that these mysteries will remain sealed until the time of the end. If, however, we are in the time of the end, the identity of Mystery Babylon will be revealed—now!

In John's vision, he sees Mystery Babylon "sitting on many waters," which we are told represent peoples, multitudes, nations, and languages. It is also seen sitting on a beast that has "7 heads and 10 horns." Therefore, we know that Mystery Babylon will sit on the Fourth Beast Kingdom. In the context of this prophecy, "sitting on something" signifies a position of dominance, just as a rider is dominant over his mount. Since Mystery Babylon will dominate the Fourth Beast Kingdom, peoples, multitudes, nations, and languages, it is clearly a superpower.

Prophetic Pitfalls

Over the centuries, students and scholars have tried unsuccessfully to figure out the identity of Mystery Babylon as described in Revelation Chapters 17 and 18. However, it will be identified only when it exists.

John's vision of Mystery Babylon does not stop with a description of who it dominates. He also shows how it lives, what it does, and how it is viewed by the world. Each piece of information will help us identify this nation. Many aspects of John's visions are easily understood; a few are less apparent.

Super Power Corrupts

John says, "The woman was drunk with the blood of the saints, the blood of those who bore testimony to Jesus." (Revelation 17:6) Understanding this description may require careful examination. In Scripture, blood usually signifies life. Therefore, this may mean that the woman was somehow responsible for the deaths of many. This offers some interesting challenges, but it appears that Mystery Babylon plays a role in the death of many Christians, since it is drunk with their blood.

When John saw Mystery Babylon, he was greatly astonished because it had become a home for demons, every evil spirit and every detestable bird. John's description indicates that the country he was seeing was full of corruption, greed, sexual immorality, and general lawlessness. Apparently, John was astonished because he didn't expect that it would turn out this way. Perhaps it had a more godly beginning, one with great promise.

Super Consumer

All the nations had become intoxicated with the wine of its adulteries. All the kings and merchants of the earth had participated in its adulteries and grown rich from its excessive consumption. John's vision indicates that the inhabitants of the earth greatly desired what it had; its wealth, its lifestyle, its stuff, its freedom, or something else. Whatever it was, the rest of the world wanted it.

One thing is quite clear: this nation has a lot of stuff. We are told that the merchants of the world became wealthy from the excessive luxuries that it purchased from them. Its great consumption of goods from other countries is a significant theme of John's vision. John even listed many of the items that Mystery Babylon purchases from the merchants of the world:

> "… cargoes of gold, silver, precious stones, and pearls; fine linen, purple, silk, and scarlet cloth; every sort of citron wood, and articles of every kind made of ivory, costly wood, bronze, iron, and marble; cargoes of cinnamon and spice, of incense, myrrh and frankincense, of wine and olive oil, of fine flour and wheat; cattle and sheep; horses and carriages; and bodies and souls of men." (Revelation 18:12–13)

In the vision, it is seen leading all the nations astray by its magic spell.

> **The Prophet Says**
>
> John hears a warning regarding Mystery Babylon. "Then I heard another voice from heaven say: 'Come out of her, my people, so that you will not share in her sins, so that you will not receive any of her plagues; for her sins are piled up to heaven, and God has remembered her crimes.'" (Revelation 18:4–5)

In summary, Mystery Babylon is a superpower and is a great consumer nation with significant wealth. It is a nation that has become corrupt, allowing all kinds of detestable and vile behavior. But somehow it makes all its stuff look so good that the whole world is chasing after what it has.

God is going to use the Antichrist and the Fourth Beast Kingdom to punish Mystery Babylon. Because its sins are so great, it will never recover from its punishment. Its destruction by the Fourth Beast Kingdom is vividly depicted in John's vision. John says the beast and the 10 horns will hate Mystery Babylon and bring it to ruin, destroying it with fire. God has put it into their hearts to accomplish his purpose. Because they are so determined to destroy this country, the 10 nations agree to give the Antichrist their power to rule. This will continue until God's plan is fulfilled. Mystery Babylon will be destroyed by fire in one day, in one hour. Its destruction will be complete and lasting. We know this because we are told that its wealth and its way of life will never be found in it again.

God shows us its coming punishment in John's prophecy. He says that it will be paid back double for all the evil it has done, a double portion. For as much glory and luxury as it took upon itself, it receives back double in torture and grief. In just one hour, it will be overcome by fire, plague, and death. It will be so terrible and quick that there will be no question that it is being judged by a mighty and angry God.

The World Mourns the Loss

The destruction of Mystery Babylon will be sudden, and when it comes there will be reactions of terror and mourning worldwide at the loss of such great wealth and power. The kings of the earth who participated in its sin and shared in its luxury will weep and mourn when they see the smoke of its burning. They will be terrified and standing far off will weep and cry: "Woe! Woe, O great city, O Babylon, city of power! In one hour your doom has come?" One reason they will weep and mourn is that their livelihood has been cut off. There will be no one to buy their cargoes and luxuries. The great consumer and all its wealth will be gone forever, never to be recovered. John says every sea captain and all who made their living by the sea will also stand far off and weep and mourn for their great loss.

Another aspect to this prophecy about Mystery Babylon requires some explanation. Scripture says, "The woman you saw is the great city that rules over the kings of the earth." (Revelation 17:18) However, it is obvious that a city alone could not possess the power and wealth required to have all the characteristics of the Mystery Babylon that is described. Therefore, Mystery Babylon is a city, but not only a city. It is a city that represents the spirit and nature of the country to which it belongs.

The Party's Over

Now that we know how Mystery Babylon is described and what is going to happen to it, one big question remains to be answered. When will the destruction of Mystery Babylon take place? After years examining Scripture for the answer to this question, I have found no direct indications of the timing of this catastrophic event. However, numerous circumstantial clues and evidence connect the destruction of Mystery Babylon to the time of the Great Tribulation. However, it also seems logical that Mystery Babylon would need to be overthrown before the Antichrist reaches world dominance. As you watch for yourself, there will be a point when the things will be clear and you can move beyond speculation.

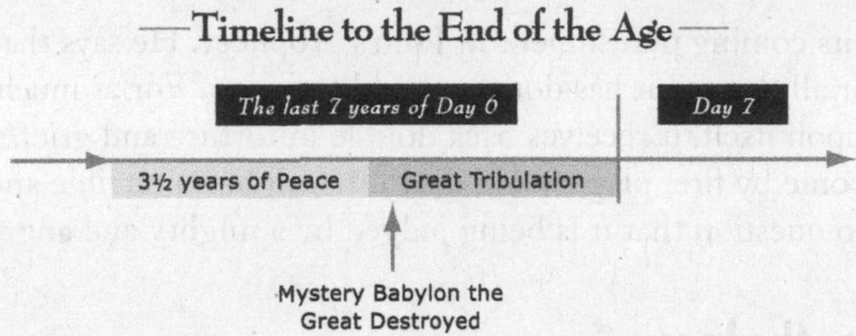

Now that you know a great deal more than you did about Mystery Babylon, don't forget that God placed a command in this prophecy. "Come out of her, my people, so that you will not share in her sins, so that you will not receive any of her plagues; for her sins are piled up to heaven, and God has remembered her crimes." (Revelation 18:4–5)

Kingdom with 7 heads and 10 Horns

We have covered a great deal already, but don't put the guide down quite yet. There is still another mystery to solve that will be important if you hope to be prepared for what lies ahead. The next mystery is also from Revelation Chapter 17, and it's about the identity of the beast with 7 heads and 10 horns and his kingdom.

God says that the world will be astonished when they see this beast, but the followers of Christ will not. The followers of Christ will not be astonished either because they know who this beast is and they will be prepared for him. Let's look further into the mystery of the beast with 7 heads and 10 horns to see if we can figure out what it is.

The Mystery

John tells us that the beast that has the 7 heads and 10 horns once was, now is not, and will come up out of the Abyss and go to his destruction. The seven heads are seven mountains or kingdoms on which Mystery Babylon sits. They are also seven kings. Five have fallen, one is, and the other has not yet come—but when he does come, he must remain for a little while. The beast who once was and now is not, is an eighth king. He belongs to the seven and is going to his destruction.

This mystery appears so complex that initially it seems to defy solution. From time to time, over the years I have tried unsuccessfully to put the pieces together. Then just a few years ago, I realized that God is actually saying that He is explaining the mystery. Because He is explaining the mystery, the solution must exist in the Bible. Plus, the prophecy states that wisdom will be required to solve it. Because wisdom comes from God, we should be able to examine Scripture and find the solution to the mystery of the beast that has the 7 heads and 10 horns. So where do we start?

The Prophet Says

God explains the mystery. "Then the angel said to me: 'Why are you astonished? I will explain to you the mystery of the woman and of the beast she rides, which has the 7 heads and 10 horns.'" (Revelation 17:7)

Let's start by identifying the kingdoms that appear in the prophecy. Then we will solve the mystery and identify the beast.

The Mystery Kingdoms

In Revelation 17:9, we are told about seven kingdoms. The kingdoms are described this way: the 7 heads are seven mountains on which Mystery Babylon sits. They are also seven kings. Five have fallen, one is, and the other has not yet come—but when he does come, he must remain for a little while.

We are told that the 7 heads are seven mountains. In biblical prophecy, *mountain* is almost always a reference to a "kingdom." In Isaiah Chapter 13, the prophet writes, "Listen, noise on the mountains, like that of a great multitude! Listen, a commotion in the kingdoms, like nations massing together! The Lord Almighty is mustering an army for war."

The prophet Jeremiah wrote about a mountain as a kingdom: "God said, 'I am against you, destroying mountain, you who destroy the whole earth. I will stretch out my hand against you and make you a burned-out mountain.'" (Jeremiah 51:24–25)

Finally, the prophet Micah, in Chapter 6, records what God says. "Arise, plead your case before the mountains; let the hills hear what you have to say. Hear, O mountains, the Lord's accusation; listen, you everlasting foundations of the earth. For the Lord has a case against his people; he is lodging a charge against Israel."

Clearly, these three examples show how the God of the Bible uses the term *mountains* when He is referring to kingdoms and peoples.

The Seven Kingdoms

Therefore, the mystery should read like this. The seven kingdoms are also seven kings. Five have fallen, the sixth is, and the seventh has not yet come.

> **The Prophet Says**
>
> Jeremiah identifies the first king and kingdom. "Israel is a scattered flock that lions have chased away. The first to devour him was the king of Assyria; the last to crush his bones was Nebuchadnezzar, king of Babylon." (Jeremiah 50:17)

At the time John was given the revelation, in about A.D. 90, Rome was the kingdom in power; therefore, Rome is the kingdom that "is." What does Scripture say about the five that have fallen? Because there is a strong prophetic connection between Revelation Chapters 17–18 and Jeremiah Chapters 50–51, let's look in Jeremiah. In Jeremiah Chapter 50, we find a prophecy regarding kingdoms and kings that have oppressed Israel. In this prophecy, God says that Israel is a scattered flock that lions have chased away. He also says that the first one to devour her was the king of Assyria, and the last was the king of Babylon.

According to Jeremiah's prophecy, the king of Assyria is the first kingdom; the king of Babylon was next.

Daniel picks up where Jeremiah left off. Starting with Babylon, he identifies it and the next three kings and kingdoms.

> "You [Babylon], O king, are the king of kings." (Daniel 2:37)
>
> "The two-horned ram that you saw represents the kings of Media and Persia. The shaggy goat is the king of Greece, and the large horn between his eyes is the first king." (Daniel 8:20)

Therefore, the five kings and kingdoms that have fallen are Assyria, Babylon, Media, Persia, and Greece.

The Final Kingdom

The final kingdom, yet to come, is the future kingdom described by Daniel as the Fourth Beast Kingdom. We have previously discussed, from both Daniel and in Revelation, descriptions of a kingdom comprised of 10 nations and with 7 leaders. We also know that when this kingdom has 7 heads, the Antichrist will be its king.

The Prophet Says

Daniel says, "The fourth beast is a fourth kingdom that will appear on earth. It will be different from all the other kingdoms and will devour the whole earth, trampling it down and crushing it. The ten horns are ten kings who will come from this kingdom. After them another king will arise, different from the earlier ones; he will subdue three kings." (Daniel 7:23–24)

Therefore, the final Beast Kingdom of Daniel Chapter 7 is also the seventh kingdom of Revelation Chapter 17, which is yet to come.

1. Fallen = Assyria
2. Fallen = Babylon
3. Fallen = Media
4. Fallen = Persia
5. Fallen = Greece
6. One is = Rome
7. Yet to come = Fourth Beast Kingdom

The Mystery King

Now that we have identified the seven kingdoms of the mystery and the Antichrist as the seventh king, let's figure out the identity of the mystery beast. We know that the Antichrist will be the seventh king because he will be the future leader of this seventh kingdom.

In Revelation Chapter 17, John said that the beast once was, now is not, and will come up out of the *Abyss* and go to his destruction. He is also an eighth king. He belongs to the seven.

This beast is destined for destruction. Scripture reveals that there will be two beast kings destined for destruction at Christ's

def•i•ni•tion

The **Abyss** is located either on or in the earth, where God secures demons and fallen angels. Satan will be locked and sealed in the Abyss at Christ's return and will remain there for a thousand years.

return. One is the Antichrist, who will be destroyed, but not by human power. This is prophesied in Daniel 8:25. The second one is the False Prophet, who is destroyed with the Antichrist when the two are thrown into the fiery lake of burning sulfur. This is set out in Revelation 19:20. Therefore, this mystery beast who is the eighth king must be either the Antichrist or the False Prophet.

We are told that this beast comes up out of the Abyss. Where is the Abyss? In Revelation Chapter 13, we are told many things about the Antichrist and the False Prophet, including where they come from. The Antichrist comes out of the sea. This means that he rises out of the sea of peoples and nations. The False Prophet, on the other hand, comes out of the earth. This is most likely a literal statement because there is no apparent figurative interpretation for it in the Bible.

King of the Abyss

In Revelation Chapter 9, we are told about the king of the Abyss. In this spectacular vision, John sees a star that falls from the sky to the earth. After the star opens the Abyss, smoke will rise from it. Demons then will come out of the Abyss and torment the people of the earth for five months. The demons, however, will not be allowed to harm any of the people of God. The king over the demons will be the angel of the Abyss, whose name in Hebrew is Abaddon and, in Greek, Apollyon.

The Hebrew name Abaddon means a destroying angel; the Greek name Apollyon also means destroyer. By telling us the name of this king, God is providing the means we need to identify this angel king, the False Prophet, as the Destroyer. The Destroyer is described in the Old Testament as an angel or supernatural being who kills and carries out destruction under the authority and instructions of God.

The Prophet Says

Jeremiah sees the Destroyer coming against Babylon. "The Lord will destroy Babylon; he will silence her noisy din. Waves of enemies will rage like great waters; the roar of their voices will resound. A destroyer will come against Babylon; her warriors will be captured, and their bows will be broken. For the Lord is a God of retribution; he will repay in full." (Jeremiah 51:55–56)

The False Prophet

The Abyss, as we discovered from Revelation Chapter 9, is located on the earth. We know this because it will be opened by a star that falls to the earth. Let's review what we know so far about the beast we are trying to identify.

- He goes to his destruction.
- He comes out of the Abyss.
- He is the destroying angel of the Bible.
- He is the False Prophet of the Last Days.

Identifying the False Prophet as the Destroyer also fits perfectly with another piece of the mystery in Revelation 17:8. The prophecy states that he once was, now is not, and will come.

John received this vision in about A.D. 90. At that time, the Destroyer had been present in the past but was not present at the time of the vision. He will come out of the Abyss sometime during the Great Tribulation and then go to his destruction when Christ returns at the end of the Great Tribulation.

Because the False Prophet is also the destroying angel of the Bible, it makes sense that the False Prophet will be able to perform great signs and miracles. The False Prophet is not human; he is a supernatural being.

The Eighth King

So how is the False Prophet an eighth king who also belongs to the seven? Once again, Scripture provides the answer.

Let's review Revelation Chapter 13. We find that the False Prophet was seen coming out of the earth. He exercised all the authority of the first beast, and made the earth and its inhabitants worship the first beast, whose fatal wound had been healed. He also performed great and miraculous signs, even causing fire to come down from heaven to earth in full view of men.

The Prophet Says

John explains the mystery. "The beast who once was, and now is not, is an eighth king. He belongs to the seven and is going to his destruction." (Revelation 17:11)

Notice that the False Prophet "exercised all the authority of the first beast." Therefore, when the False Prophet assumes all the authority of the first beast (Antichrist), he will be the next leader of the Fourth Beast Kingdom with its 7 heads and 10 horns. He will become an eighth king because he follows the seventh king. Also, the False Prophet will belong to the seven because he will be one of the seven.

Therefore, the False Prophet is the beast that has the 7 heads and 10 horns. Scripture has revealed who the seven kingdoms are and the identity of the mystery beast with 7 heads and 10 horns.

The Least You Need to Know

- Realize that the closer we get to the End of the Age, the more rapidly the world will change.
- You absolutely must be able to identify the world superpower referred to in Scripture as Mystery Babylon if you want to escape its fate.
- Be able to identify the superpowers of the Last Days and who will be on top at the end.
- Because you know who the False Prophet is, you can expect to see spectacular stuff performed.

Chapter 15

The Revelation Timelines

In This Chapter

- Warnings to the church in the Seven Letters
- Events occurring during the Seven Seals
- Events occurring during the Seven Trumpets
- Warnings and announcements from three angels
- Plagues occurring during the Seven Bowls

In this chapter, we discuss several series or sequences of events described in the Book of Revelation. These sequences start at different times at the end of Day 6, but they all conclude with the start of the Day of the Lord (Day 7) and the Second Coming of Jesus Christ. We go over the descriptions of these events and their timing so that you can see how they relate to the end of Day 6.

Seven Letters of Revelation

The first series, seven letters written of in the Book of Revelation, are addressed to the seven angels of the seven churches of God. Unlike the other series in Revelation, the seven letters do not fit into a Last Days timeline. The letters contain specific encouragement and warnings from Christ to the seven churches, as well as a timeless message to all who await His return.

Warning of Tribulation

Several of these letters from Christ address circumstances and events that will take place in the last few years of Day 6. For example, in the letter to the angel of the church of Smyrna, He warns His followers not to be afraid of what they will suffer at the hands of the Devil, and He cautions them to stand firm even if they are put in prison or killed. Jesus also tells them to remain faithful to the end and promises to give them eternal life. This warning and encouragement to persevere during the time of Great Tribulation echoes what Jesus told His followers during His Olivet Discourse.

The Prophet Says

Jesus warns His followers, "Wake up! Strengthen what remains and is about to die, for I have not found your deeds complete in the sight of my God. Remember, therefore, what you have received and heard; obey it, and repent. But if you do not wake up, I will come like a thief, and you will not know at what time I will come to you." (Revelation 3:3–4)

In the letter to the angel of the church in Thyatira, He tells His followers to hold on to their faith until He returns. This letter promises that Jesus will give them authority over the nations when He establishes His kingdom if they do hold on until the end.

Assurance to Overcomers

In the letter to the angel of the church in Philadelphia, Jesus warns His followers to remember what they have received and obey it. The letter warns them to wake up so that His return will not surprise them. He says that if they do not wake up, they will be unprepared to overcome the Great Tribulation that is ahead, and His Second Coming will catch them off guard. He closes this letter with the assurance that anyone who overcomes will be acknowledged when His kingdom comes.

In the letter to the sixth angel, Jesus promises that He will protect those who are faithful to His Word and endure patiently the time of Great Tribulation. Jesus also warns them that the Great Tribulation will be a time of testing and trial for those who live on the earth.

We will see shortly what Jesus meant when He said He will protect His followers during the Great Tribulation. For now, we can see how Jesus is consistent in His warnings and encouragement to His followers.

The Prophet Says

Jesus promises His followers, "Since you have kept my command to endure patiently, I will also keep you from the hour of trial that is going to come upon the whole world to test those who live on the earth. I am coming soon. Hold on to what you have, so that no one will take your crown." (Revelation 3:10–11)

Seven Seals of Revelation

The Book of Revelation provides one of Scripture's most complete accounts of the end of Day 6. As we have already discussed, John had been called up to heaven in the spirit when he received the Revelation from Jesus Christ. John saw into the future, and what John recorded from his visions includes both supernatural events and natural events. The Bible describes a connection between the supernatural (heavenly) creation and the natural (worldly) creation, telling us that when things take place in the natural, observable world, there are corresponding happenings in the supernatural. You will see this as we discuss the various events written of by John.

Several sequences of events are described in the Book of Revelation. These include the Seven Seals, the Seven Trumpets, the three angelic announcements, and the Seven Bowls. We discussed briefly the first four seals and the first three trumpets in previous chapters. However, because these series provide important information, we now look at all the events in each series, starting with the Seven Seals.

First Four Seals

You may recall from Chapter 6 how the Last Days "birth pains" are related to Christ opening the first four seals of Revelation. The first seal is broken open, and a white horse (West) and rider go out, determined to conquer. When the second seal is opened, the red horse (East) and rider take peace from the earth and cause men to kill each other. When the third seal is opened, a black horse (North) and rider cause devastation to grain production so that a day's supply of wheat and barley will sell for a day's wages. When the fourth seal is broken open, a pale horse (South) and rider will come out. They have power over a quarter of the earth to kill by sword, famine, plague, and wild beast.

This accounts for the first four seals and corresponds to the first of the birth pains. Now let's see what will happen when the fifth, sixth, and seventh seals are broken open.

When the fifth seal was opened, John saw a vision in heaven of people who had been killed because of their faith in God. They were asking God how much longer they would have to wait until He would judge the world. John saw that these people will be given white robes and told to wait until the full number of their fellow servants of God will be killed. This vision of martyred servants in heaven seems to have no specific relationship to End Time events on earth. Therefore, we cannot use this vision as a reference point in the Last Days timeline. However, because this vision is of martyred servants of God and we know that there will be many martyred servants during the Great Tribulation, we can reasonably place the fifth seal as being opened during the Great Tribulation.

The Sixth Seal

The sixth seal, on the other hand, is very easy to pinpoint in relation to events prophesied to occur at the end of Day 6. Several things that take place in John's vision of the opening of the sixth seal are described in Old Testament prophecies and by Jesus during the Olivet Discourse. Each of these things takes place at the time of the Second Coming of the Messiah, at the very end of Day 6.

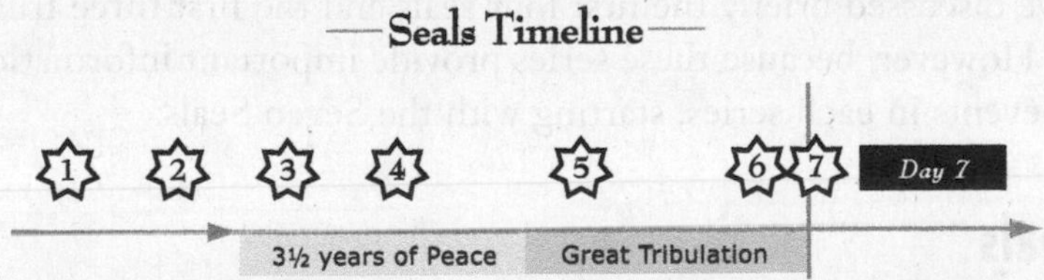

When the sixth seal is opened, there will be a great earthquake. A great earthquake is also mentioned in other places in Revelation as taking place in Jerusalem at the time of the Second Coming, when the Kingdom of God is established on earth. In Isaiah

Chapter 29, the Old Testament prophet told us about this same earthquake when he described the Lord as coming with an earthquake, great noise, thunder, windstorm, and fire.

In Ezekiel Chapters 38 and 39, Ezekiel recorded a vision of the Day of the Lord describing how the people of the world will tremble at the coming of the Lord when His fiery wrath is poured out. In this vision of that day, he also told of a great earthquake that will take place in Israel.

The Prophet Says

Zechariah describes the Second Coming like this: "On that day his feet will stand on the Mount of Olives, east of Jerusalem, and the Mount of Olives will be split in two from east to west, forming a great valley, with half of the mountain moving north and half moving south .... Then the Lord my God will come, and all the holy ones with him." (Zechariah 14:4–5)

Also, when the sixth seal is opened, the sun, moon, and stars will go dark. The heavens and the earth will be shaken, and the islands and mountains will be moved from their foundations. The sign of the sun, moon, and stars is mentioned several times by the prophets in connection to the Day of the Lord and His coming. The prophet Joel specifically tells us that the sign of the sun, moon, and stars will take place just before the great and dreadful day of the Lord.

At this same time, John says that the rulers of the earth, people in high positions, generals, the rich and mighty, and every slave and free man will hide in caves and in the rocks of the mountains. They will try to hide from the returning Christ and the day of His wrath.

Isaiah also wrote about these things happening, saying that mankind will hide in the rocks of the ground from fear of the Lord on the day when He appears in splendor and majesty.

The Fateful Seal

However, though we are at the end of Day 6, John saw one more seal to be opened before the contents of the scroll could be seen or read. Scripture does not reveal what

> **The Prophet Says**
>
> John wrote, "When he opened the seventh seal, there was silence in heaven for about half an hour." (Revelation 8:1)

this scroll contains; however, it is clear that there is one scroll that will be opened at the time of the Second Coming.

Now let's look back to some things we covered in Chapter 4. We discussed the parable in which Jesus compared His angels' coming to a harvest that would separate the sons of God from the sons of the Devil. Possibly, for the angels to know who to gather at the harvest, the "book of life" will have to be opened. In the English Bible, *scroll* and *book* are used interchangeably when translating from the Hebrew and Greek. Therefore, when you read about the "book of life" in Scripture, it is the same as if it said "scroll of life."

We know that the "book of life" contains the names of the followers of Christ. Whether or not this is the scroll that is being opened in John's vision remains to be seen. However, according to Scripture, the timing of the harvest and the opening of the scroll are coincidental.

We do know that the Seven Seals, like the birth pains, begin as warnings of the Kingdom of God to come, and continue until the delivery of the kingdom at the end of Day 6 and the beginning of Day 7.

Seven Warning Trumpets

The second sequence of events is the blowing of the Seven Trumpets. We discussed the first trumpets in Chapter 10 and determined that the first trumpets begin to sound their warnings at the beginning of the Great Tribulation, when Satan is thrown out of heaven to earth by Michael the archangel. Whereas the seals of Revelation are early warning signs of the end, the trumpets of Revelation are the final warnings.

Let's review the first four trumpets. When the first trumpet warning sounds, a third of the earth, a third of the trees, and all the green grass will be burned up. When the second trumpet sounds, a third of the living creatures in the sea will die and a third of the ships will be destroyed. When the third trumpet sounds, a third of the waters will turn bitter and many people will die as a result. When the fourth trumpet sounds, a third of the sun, moon, and stars will turn dark. It is written that a third of the day will be without light, and a third of the night will be without the light of the moon and stars.

Three Trumpets of Woe!

After the first four trumpet blasts, John tells us that he heard a loud voice that said, "Woe! Woe! Woe to the inhabitants of the earth, because of the other three trumpet blasts which are about to be sounded!" It appears that things are going to get considerably worse for the people of the world as the last three trumpets are sounded. Let's take a look.

When the fifth trumpet sounds, a star, which will have already fallen from the sky to the earth, will be given the key to the Abyss. When the Abyss opens, smoke will rise from it like the smoke of a huge furnace, and it will darken the sun and sky. Out of the smoke will come locusts, and they will be given power to torture the people of the world for five months with a sting like that of a scorpion. The locusts will not be able to touch anyone who has the seal of God on his or her forehead. Jesus will be protecting His followers as He had promised. People will wish they were dead but they will not die.

The locusts that will come out of the smoke of the Abyss are most likely demons. I say this because demons and fallen angels are kept in the Abyss. In the Gospel of Luke, it is recorded that on one occasion demons begged Jesus not to order them into the Abyss. The king over the demon locusts will be the angel of the Abyss, whose name is "Destroyer." We learned in Chapter 12 that the guide who comes up out of the Abyss is also the False Prophet of Revelation Chapter 13.

The Prophet Says

John said, "They had as king over them the angel of the Abyss, whose name in Hebrew is Abaddon (Destroyer), and in Greek, Apollyon (Destroyer). The first woe is past; two other woes are yet to come." (Revelation 9:11–12)

The Last Call Trumpet

When the sixth trumpet sounds, the four angels who had been bound at the Euphrates River for this appointed time will be released to kill a third of mankind. The number of the mounted troops will be 200 million. This vision also appears to depict supernatural beings. However, Scripture reveals that these supernatural descriptions often have counterparts in the natural world. For example, this vision of supernatural angels will correspond to things that will be taking place in the natural world. Most likely, various armies, led by the Antichrist, will be crossing the Euphrates River at this later part of the Great Tribulation.

—The Seven Trumpet Timeline—

This supernatural vision, written of in Revelation Chapter 9, takes place at the end of the Great Tribulation and at the end of Day 6. It parallels the account of the nations of the world gathering for the final battle in Jerusalem, which is recorded in Revelation Chapter 16. Scripture indicates that the sixth trumpet call of Revelation is the last call for the people of the world to repent and turn to God.

At The Last Trumpet

When the last trumpet sounds, the world will have reached the end of Day 6 and the beginning of Day 7. At the seventh trumpet, we are told that the kingdom of the world has become the Kingdom of God and that Christ will reign on earth forever. We know from our previous discussion of the Feast of Trumpets that the final trumpet blast signals the assembly of God's people at the beginning of the Harvest Feasts of God.

So the seven trumpets begin and end the Great Tribulation, and the last trumpet signals the end of the Great Tribulation and the arrival of the Messiah to establish His Kingdom on Day 7. Now let's see what else we can learn about the Last Day from the angels.

Three Angelic Announcements

In Revelation Chapter 14, we are told that three angels proclaim three messages to the people of the earth. Like the seals and trumpets, the angels are seen by John from heaven and are supernatural visions. But again like the seals and trumpets, these events will correspond to natural events taking place on earth at the same time.

—The Three Announcement Timeline—

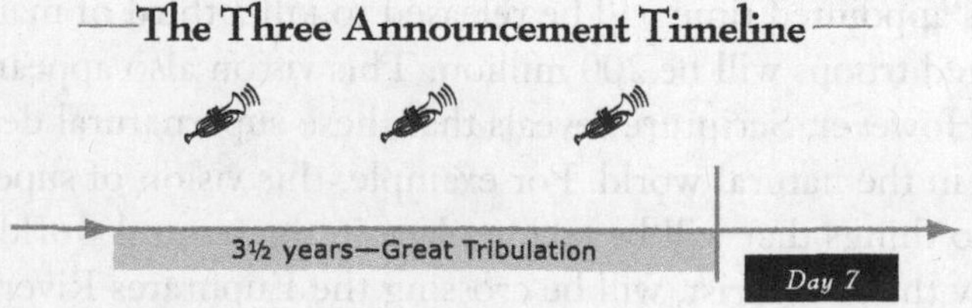

Based on the content of the three warnings given by the angels, we can place the proclamations as occurring during the Great Tribulation. As we discussed previously in Chapter 9, there will be two prophets of God prophesying in Jerusalem during the Great Tribulation; I imagine that the two prophets will communicate the angels' messages to the world. Now let's see what the angels' messages are.

John tells us that he saw an angel flying in midair. This angel had the eternal Gospel to proclaim to everyone on earth. The angel said in a loud voice, "Fear God and give him glory, because the hour of his judgment has come. Worship him who made the heavens, the earth, the sea, and the springs of water." Well, Jesus told His followers in the Olivet Discourse that the Gospel will be proclaimed to the whole world and then the end will come. From what follows this angel's proclamation, it appears that this is how Jesus' prophecy may be fulfilled.

Then John tells us that he saw a second angel. The second angel announced the destruction of Mystery Babylon the Great, a place that had enticed all the nations to participate in the intoxicating fruit of her labor. This seems to indicate that Mystery Babylon is destroyed just before or during the Great Tribulation, but it is impossible to be certain based on what we are given in Scripture.

The Prophet Says

Jesus told His followers, "… this Gospel of the kingdom will be preached in the whole world as a testimony to all nations, and then the end will come." (Matthew 24.14)

John saw a third angel who warned everyone in a loud voice about the consequences of worshipping the beast or receiving the "mark of the beast." The angel said that anyone who did these things would be subject to the wrath of God and would be tormented with burning sulfur forever, with no rest day or night.

The third angel did have words of encouragement for some. The followers of God were told that the Great Tribulation would call for patient endurance and faithfulness on their part. They were told that those who died during this time because of their faithfulness to God would be blessed and that they would rest from their labor. This prophecy reinforces other statements of Scripture that indicate that those who put their faith in God will enter the Sabbath rest on Day 7.

Following the three angelic proclamations, John saw one whom he described as looking like the "son of man" coming on a cloud in glory with a sharp sickle in His hand. This vision matches other prophets' descriptions of the Second Coming of the Messiah at the end of Day 6, when the gathering of God's people will be accomplished.

So we now know that, in addition to the opening of the seals and the blowing of the trumpets, three angels will make announcements sometime during the three and a half years of the Great Tribulation, and then Jesus Christ will appear. Now let's turn to the final sequence.

Seven Bowls of God's Wrath

The final sequence of events in the Book of Revelation is the pouring out of the Seven Bowls of God's Wrath. According to Scripture, this series is God's final judgment and wrath on an unbelieving and disobedient world. The bowls of Revelation start very late in the Great Tribulation.

Prophets of Doom

According to Scripture, this final wrath of God is poured out on the earth in connection with the coming Day of the Lord. In a couple Old Testament prophecies about this time, the prophets seem to indicate that this period could be as short as one 24-hour day.

Zechariah says that Jesus will come with all His holy ones and that the Day of the Lord will be a unique day without daytime or nighttime. We are told that this will be a day known to God when the Spirit of God will go out from Jerusalem year round. Zechariah goes on to say that on that day Jesus will be king over the whole earth, and His name alone will be exalted.

Isaiah described the Day of the Lord this way. The Lord is angry with all the nations, and His wrath will be on their armies—they will be totally destroyed. Isaiah further says that all the stars in the Heaven will go dark and the sky will be rolled up like a scroll. The sword of the Lord will be covered in the blood of the slain from His fierce judgment. This is the day of the Lord's vengeance, which He planned to fulfill His purposes.

However, Scripture does not indicate how long the wrath lasts. The bowls may be poured out on the earth over a period of weeks, days, or hours.

Some Protected

Before we learn what each bowl brings, let's consider who will be subject to this wrath. The Bible states that the followers of Christ will not be subject to the wrath of God, so they are somehow protected from the bowls when they are poured out on the earth. Scripture also says that during this time of God's wrath, no one on earth will repent and turn to worship God. Therefore, the last warning calls of God to the world are during the time of the trumpets. Once the Bowls of Revelation begin, there is no changing paths; it's too late.

Now let's consider some of the specific details we are given about God's wrath. John tells us that he heard a loud voice from heaven telling the seven angels to pour out the Seven Bowls of God's Wrath on the earth. When the first bowl was poured out, ugly and painful sores broke out on the people who had the mark of the beast and who worshiped the beast's image. John saw the second bowl poured out on the sea, and every living thing in the sea died. The third bowl was poured out on the rivers and springs, and they turned to blood.

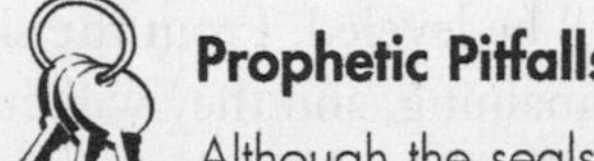

Prophetic Pitfalls

Although the seals and the trumpets of Revelation are associated with John's visions of devastation and death occurring on the earth, the Bowls of Revelation are specifically identified by Scripture as being God's wrath.

The fourth bowl was poured out on the sun, and the sun scorched people with fire and they were seared by the intense heat. John saw the people of the world curse God because of these plagues. They refused to repent of what they had done and glorify God. The fifth angel poured out his bowl on the throne of the Antichrist, and his kingdom was plunged into darkness.

—The Seven Bowls Timeline—

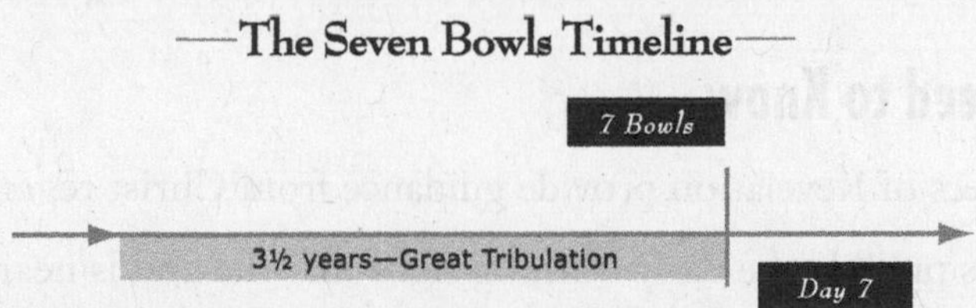

When the sixth angel poured out his bowl, it dried up the water from the Euphrates River to allow a way for the nations and kings of the Antichrist from the east. Then John saw evil spirits come from the Antichrist and the False Prophet. We are told that these are spirits of demons that perform miraculous signs and go out to the kings of the whole world to gather them for the great and final battle on the Day of the Lord.

The End Has Come

Finally, the seventh bowl of God's wrath will be poured into the air. When the seventh bowl is poured out, we are told that God's wrath will be complete. Then there will be flashes of lightening and peals of thunder and a great earthquake. The earthquake will be so tremendous that the great city of Jerusalem will split into three parts, and the cities of the nations will collapse. Every island will disappear, and the mountains of the earth will be leveled. From the sky, huge hailstones of about 100 pounds will fall on those remaining, and they will curse God because of the severe plagues. It should now be clear why many prophets refer to this as the great and dreadful Day of the Lord.

In the next few chapters, we discuss in more detail the events relating to final seals, trumpets, and bowls. We primarily examine the descriptions provided by the Old Testament prophets as they wrote about the coming Day of the Lord.

Now let's summarize. The seals of Revelation correspond to the birth pains that Jesus said would occur before the delivery of the Kingdom of God on earth at the end of Day 6. Scripture does not indicate how long the birth pains will last or when they start. On the other hand, the trumpets of Revelation will begin at the time of the abomination that causes desolation, which begins the Great Tribulation (see Chapter 11). The trumpets will continue to sound throughout the three and a half years of the Great Tribulation, culminating with the seventh and last trumpet when the Kingdom of God will arrive on earth.

The bowls of Revelation are the shortest in duration, and the plagues they bring are the Final Judgment and wrath of God on the earth as God's Kingdom is ushered in by the return of Jesus Christ, the Messiah.

The Least You Need to Know

- The letters of Revelation provide guidance from Christ regarding the Last Days.
- The seals provide the early warning signs that the end is near.
- The trumpets tell us there are just three and a half years left until the end of Day 6.
- Three angelic messages will be given during the Great Tribulation.
- The Bowls of Revelation contain the wrath of God that will be poured out on the unbelieving and disobedient world.

Part 4

The Great and Dreadful Day Is Dawning

When it comes to the Last Days, there is nothing the Bible talks about more than the Day of the Lord. This is huge. No student of the Bible can understand the biblical story without a firm grasp of the meaning of the Day of the Lord.

In Part 4, you will come to understand the awesome significance of the Day of the Lord to God's plan. You will also learn what "that day" means with respect to the promises God made to His people many years ago. You will also find out what "that day" means in terms of the Bible's Last Days.

When the Day of the Lord finally arrives, the world will go through some of the most cataclysmic changes since the days of Noah and the Great Flood. The Bible describes the changes that will occur on the Day of the Lord as literally earthshaking.

Chapter 16

The Day of the Lord

In This Chapter

- That great and dreadful day
- Scoffers and false prophets
- Judgment Day and God's wrath
- Deliverance and restoration

We have talked about the Day of the Lord (Day 7) in several previous chapters. Now we take a closer look at how the prophets describe the arrival of that day. Recall that the Day of the Lord is the seventh 1,000-year day of God's seven-day plan. We are currently in the last part of Day 6. Some of what we see in the prophets' descriptions will be things that will happen at the very end (days and hours) of Day 6. The remainder of the prophets' descriptions regarding the Day of the Lord describe events at the very beginning (hours and days) of Day 7.

In the next few chapters, we discuss in detail various aspects of that day's arrival as told by Christ and the prophets of God. We discuss the Messiah's Second Coming, the resurrection and rapture, the wedding banquet, and the Final Battle.

What a Difference a Day Makes

The prophets wrote about the coming of the great and dreadful "Day of the Lord." The Day of the Lord is one of the most significant events recorded in the Bible and is a key element of the *Gospel.* The Scripture regarding the Day of the Lord is so extensive that no other biblical event comes close to receiving such attention.

A Double Day

The Day of the Lord as presented in Scripture has a double meaning. First, the Day of the Lord is Day 7, the seventh and Last Day of God's seven-day plan. As we have discussed previously, Day 7 is the time of the 1,000-year reign of Christ on earth, also known as the Kingdom of God.

The Day of the Lord also refers to the start of Day 7, which I speak of as the transition from Day 6 to Day 7. Most of the biblical references to the Day of the Lord refer to this transition. Jesus also spoke of a change from the present age to the age to come. The present age ends with Day 6, and the coming age begins with Day 7, which is the Day of the Lord. We examine this transitional aspect of the Day of the Lord in this chapter.

def•i•ni•tion

The **Gospel** is the story and message of the Bible. The Gospel reveals who the God of the Bible is, who we (humans) are, and what God has done, is doing, and will do.

The Day of the Lord ushers in the 1,000-year Kingdom of God on earth, the Sabbath rest. It will be a great and glorious day for the people of God. However, because the kingdom's arrival also means the judgment and cleansing of all unrighteousness from the earth, it will also be a dreadful day, a day of God's wrath.

Don't forget that the Bible says that as we get closer to the Day of the Lord, persecution from the Antichrist and the False Prophet will become very severe for God's people as well, making the arrival of the Messiah even more glorious for them.

The Lord's Day

The expression the Day of the Lord is recorded 24 times in Scripture. In the Old Testament there are numerous synonyms for the Day of the Lord including the day, the day of God's wrath, the day of calamity, the day of battle, day of disaster, day of reckoning, the day of his burning anger, day of vengeance, the day of salvation, the day of clouds and darkness, the day of your watchmen, the day of calamity, the day of his coming, and that great and dreadful day of the Lord.

In the New Testament, there are also synonyms for the Day of the Lord, including the day of judgment, the day of our Lord Jesus Christ, the day of God's wrath, the day of the Lord Jesus, the day of redemption, the day of Christ Jesus, the day of slaughter, the day of God, the day of Christ, the great day of their wrath, and the great day of God Almighty.

So numerous are the references to the Day of the Lord in Scripture that most of the prophets and Gospel writers wrote "that day" or "the day" when referring to the Day of the Lord. When we read in Scripture about "that day" or "the day," it's important that we carefully examine the context because "that day" and "the day" have other meanings as well.

The Prophet Says

Peter says, "But the day of the Lord will come like a thief. The heavens will disappear with a roar; the elements will be destroyed by fire, and the earth and everything in it will be laid bare." (2 Peter 3:10)

Let's look at some passages that specifically use the expression "Day of the Lord." From these, we will be able to determine what will take place on that day. Then as we encounter "that day" or "the day" in Scripture, we will be able to determine whether or not the writer is talking about the Day of the Lord.

As we read biblical prophecies, we should always be alert to references to the Day of the Lord. Being familiar with the Day of the Lord will help determine the time frame of each part of a prophetic message. Old Testament prophets often received prophecies about several different events at one time. Some of the prophesied events would occur during the prophet's time, and others may not occur until the Day of the Lord. For example, the prophet Jeremiah received many prophecies that had application for his time as well as for the distant future, the End Times.

Last Days Timeline

— Jeremiah's Prophecies —

Day 1	*Day 2*	*Day 3*	*Day 4*	*Day 5*	*Day 6*	*Day 7*
1,000 years	2,000 years	3,000 years	4,000 years	5,000 years	6,000 years	7,000 years
Adam	Noah	Moses	David	Christ	Church	Kingdom
			↑ Jeremiah's Time			↑ End Times

In most of Jeremiah's prophecies, he warned his people about the destruction and exile that would come if they refused to repent and turn back to the Lord God. They did not, and Israel and Jerusalem were defeated by the Babylonians and exiled in about 586 B.C.

The prophet also received prophecies recorded in Jeremiah Chapters 50 and 51 that will be fulfilled in the End Times. Many of the prophecies in these two chapters will find their fulfillment when Mystery Babylon of Revelation Chapters 17 and 18 is destroyed just before the future Day of the Lord.

Good Old End Times Religion

Jeremiah also received prophecies depicting the state of affairs in religion as the world approaches the Day of the Lord. What he prophesied about the End Times was similar to what he was prophesying for his time. In his time he warned the people to repent because of the judgment that was approaching. But, the false prophets were assuring the people not to worry because God would deliver them from the trouble. The false prophets said, "No sword or famine will touch this land."

The prophet Ezekiel also received prophecies that were relevant to his time as well as to the future time of the end, leading to that day. In Ezekiel Chapter 13, he recorded a message from God for the false prophets of his time; this was also a message for the false prophets who would be prophesying in the End Times leading up to the Day of the Lord.

God told Ezekiel to prophesy against the so-called prophets of God who prophesy out of their own imagination. Here is God's message through His prophet Ezekiel.

False Prophets

The Lord warned the foolish prophets that they were in for a bad time because they were following their own ideas and had not heard or seen anything from God. Ezekiel referenced the judgment that the false prophets would face on the Day of the Lord because they did not speak according to God's word.

Ezekiel said that these false prophets will say that God has said things He has not. They will be so sincere in their lies that they will even expect them to come true. Ezekiel says that God will not be happy about the false prophets and their lies. God says He will be against them and that they will never enter the Kingdom of God or participate in the assembly of His followers. God will be very angry with their deceptive ways and will declare that their names will not be found in the Book of Life, nor will they participate in the age to come. When they are cast out, they will know that the Lord is Sovereign. Another thing these false prophets will do is tell God's people that there will be peace and security, when in reality God has prophesied tribulation and destruction.

Ezekiel said that not only will the false prophets not proclaim a message from God, but they also won't try to turn the people back to God from their own ways. These foolish prophets will fail to address the hypocrisy of the people; instead, they will just brush over their sins like someone who whitewashes over a weak levy. However, God says that when the rains and winds come, the whitewash will be washed away and the levy will not stand. God declares that they will be caught in His wrath and consumed by His destructive fury.

Ezekiel records this regarding the false prophets before the Day of the Lord:

- Foolish prophets will not have prepared God's people.
- False prophets will say, "The Lord says," although they will have seen nothing.
- The false prophets will not be listed in the Book of Life, nor will they enter the Kingdom of God.
- The false prophets will speak of peace when there is no peace.

So when we observe these types of behavior from people claiming to be from God, we should be alert that the Day of the Lord may be near.

Bad Shepherds

Ezekiel also prophesied about bad shepherds in the End Times. God told Ezekiel to warn the shepherds who only take care of themselves and do not take care of their flock. Ezekiel said that the shepherds allowed the sheep to be scattered and they did not go after them to bring them back. The bad shepherds ruled over their flock and did not feed them, strengthen them, care for them, or heal them.

Because the shepherds did not watch over their flock and care for them, Ezekiel prophesied that God was against these shepherds and that God would hold them accountable for His flock. Ezekiel said that God Himself would rescue His flock and He would care for them. God would bring them back from the nations where they had been scattered and He would shepherd them in the land of Israel. Ezekiel's prophecy indicated that this would take place when the kingdom had come and the Son of David would be the shepherd over Israel.

True Prophets

Not all prophets are false prophets. The prophets of God often carry a message that is very unpopular and are often persecuted for it. Scripture records that sometimes their message is so unpopular that the prophets have even been killed.

> **The Prophet Says**
>
> "Because of this, God in his wisdom said, 'I will send them prophets and apostles, some of whom they will kill and others they will persecute.' Therefore, this generation will be held responsible for the blood of all the prophets that has been shed since the beginning of the world." (Luke 11:49–50)

The prophet Malachi saw the coming Day of the Lord. He wrote that the Day of the Lord is coming and that when it does the earth will burn like a fiery furnace. The arrogant and the hypocrites will be consumed; nothing will remain. But those who revere the name of the Lord will be saved. God tells His servants to remember the laws and decrees that He gave Moses for Israel. Finally, God says through Ezekiel that God will send Elijah before the great and dreadful Day of the Lord comes, and Elijah will turn the children back to their fathers or God will strike the land with a curse.

Elijah is very likely one of the two witnesses we discussed in Chapter 11. Malachi indicates that Elijah will carry a message from the Lord, just as the two witnesses of Revelation will do during the three and a half years of the Great Tribulation. The two witnesses will also be able to afflict the earth with plagues as often as they like. Malachi says Elijah will strike the land with a curse if the people don't listen.

Unbelief

The Apostle Peter also warned of unbelief as the world moves closer to the Day of the Lord. He said that the people needed to understand that in the Last Days, scoffers (unbelieving teachers) will come and say, "Where is this 'coming' He promised?" This type of teacher will think that everything will continue on as it always has from the beginning of time. But they deliberately forget that God's word says that the present heaven and earth are destined for destruction and fire on the Judgment Day.

Peter says that the Lord is not slow in keeping His promise and reminds Christ's followers, "With the Lord a day is like a thousand years, and a thousand years are like a day." God is patient; He doesn't want anyone to be destroyed, but He wants everyone to repent.

Darkest Before the Dawn

Many of the prophets of God have described the time immediately before the Day of the Lord as a time of darkness; the sun, the moon, and the stars will not provide their light to the world.

The prophet Amos saw wailing in the streets and public places. Amos asks why anyone would wish for the Day of the Lord to come because that day will be a day of darkness. It will be like a man who goes from one disaster to another and can find no safe shelter anywhere. The darkness Amos describes seems to be both spiritual and physical. This fits with the prophecies of destruction and severe punishment that we have already discussed.

The prophet Zephaniah also describes an ominous, dark, and dreadful arrival of the Day of the Lord. I will list some of the descriptions so that you can picture what the prophet says is coming:

- The cry on the day will be bitter.
- It will be a day of wrath.
- It will be a day of distress and anguish.
- It will be a day of trouble and ruin.
- It will be a day of darkness and gloom.
- It will be a day of clouds and blackness.
- It will be a day of trumpet and battle cry.

This gloom and doom is not just written of in the Old Testament. In the New Testament, we have already looked at the wrath described in the Book of Revelation, but there are other examples. The Apostle Peter quoted from the prophet Joel when he spoke to the crowd visiting Jerusalem about the coming Day of the Lord. Here Peter is talking about the Last Days, Day 5 and Day 6. He goes on to tell them that God will show wonders in the sky and on the earth, including blood and fire and smoke; at the end of Day 6, the sun and moon will go dark before the great and dreadful Day of the Lord comes.

Judgment Day

"Judgment Day" and "the Day of the Lord" are synonymous. When this day arrives, the world will be judged. Scripture states that the people of God will be judged first, individually, and rewarded for their work. Then the world will be judged and punished. Judgment Day will be the time of individual rewards for the people of God, and the time of global punishment for the world. The Bible says that there is also an individual judgment for the disobedient that will not take place until the end of the 1,000 years of Day 7. Now let's see what the prophets and Christ have to say about Judgment Day.

Isaiah describes a day when God will judge Zion and Jerusalem. He says the Lord will wash away their filth and cleanse the blood from Jerusalem with fire. On that day, the "Branch of the Lord" (Christ) will be glorious, and the pride and glory of Israel will be her survivors, those who remain in Jerusalem. All in Jerusalem who are recorded in the Book of Life at that time will be saved.

Isaiah also saw the Lord coming with fire and chariots, like a whirlwind bringing down God's anger and fury from heaven. With fierce fire and His sword, the Lord will execute judgment on all men and will slay many on that Day of Judgment.

Jeremiah presents a similar view of the Day of Judgment. He was told that the Lord will roar from on high and thunder from His holy dwelling against His land. The Lord will shout against all those who live on the earth. Jeremiah's writing speaks of the tumult that will resound to the ends of the earth when the Lord brings charges against the nations, judges all mankind, and puts the wicked to the sword. He describes the disaster spreading from nation to nation like a mighty storm rising from the ends of the earth. Those slain by the Lord will be everywhere, from one end of the earth to the other.

The Prophet Says

James says, "Don't grumble against each other, brothers, or you will be judged. The Judge is standing at the door! Brothers, as an example of patience in the face of suffering, take the prophets who spoke in the name of the Lord." (James 5:9–10)

Jesus Spoke

Jesus taught on various occasions about the Day of Judgment. Let's examine what He said to His disciples about that day as He was preparing to send them out to preach about the Kingdom of God. He told them that if people do not welcome them or listen to their words, they should shake the dust off their feet as testimony against them as they leave that home or town. Jesus also told them that on Judgment Day, that town will experience something worse than the judgment that fell on Sodom and Gomorrah.

Jesus said everyone will have to give account on Judgment Day for every careless word they have spoken, saying, "By your own words you will be acquitted, and by your own words you will be condemned."

Jesus used a biblical analogy for this time of transition. He said it will be like "the days of Noah." In the days of Noah, the world had become corrupt in God's sight and full of violence. God decided He was going to put an end to the people because of their evil. God told Noah to build an ark to save his family from the flood. Then God sent the Great Flood, which took everyone on earth away except Noah and his family. Jesus said it will be like this when the Kingdom comes—the wicked will be judged and destroyed, and God's people will be saved.

The Prophet Says

"As it was in the days of Noah, so it will be at the coming of the Son of Man." (Matthew 24:37)

Day of Reckoning

Also in the New Testament, Jude reminds the followers of Christ about judgment on the great Day of the Lord. He says that God delivered His people out of Egypt, but then later destroyed them because of their unbelief. We are told that even the angels have been bound in chains until judgment on the great day. Like Jesus, Jude points to Sodom and Gomorrah, and the surrounding towns that gave themselves up to sexual immorality and perversion. The destruction of those towns serves as an example to those who will suffer the punishment of eternal fire.

The Old Testament prophet Isaiah wrote extensively about a coming day of reckoning when the nations will be measured on God's righteous scale and accounts will be settled. In Isaiah Chapter 13, he indicates that on that day God will command His mighty warriors to execute His wrath on the earth. Isaiah says the nations will be in uproar as they mass together for war. The Lord will lead His army for war; His warriors will come from the ends of the heavens with the weapons of God's wrath. Isaiah warns the people of the earth that the Day of the Lord is near; God's judgment and wrath are coming.

> "I have commanded my holy ones; I have summoned my warriors to carry out my wrath—those who rejoice in my triumph. Listen, a noise on the mountains, like that of a great multitude! Listen, an uproar among the kingdoms, like nations massing together! The Lord Almighty is mustering an army for war. They come from faraway lands, from the ends of the heavens—the Lord and the weapons of his wrath—to destroy the whole country. Wail, for the day of the LORD is near; it will come like destruction from the Almighty." (Isaiah 13:3-8)

Isaiah continues his warning, saying that the day will be an awful one. With God's wrath and fierce anger, He will destroy the land and the sinners within it. The stars in the heavens will go dark, and the sun and moon will not show their light. God will put an end to arrogance, and He will humble the proud. On the Day of the Lord, God will make man scarcer than pure gold and shake the earth from its foundation on the day of His burning anger.

The Prophet Says

"Terror will seize them, pain and anguish will grip them; they will writhe like a woman in labor. They will look aghast at each other, their faces aflame. See, the day of the Lord is coming—a cruel day, with wrath and fierce anger—to make the land desolate and destroy the sinners within it." (Isaiah 13:8–9)

Here's Isaiah's description of the Day of the Lord:

- The nations will mass together for battle.
- The sun, moon, and stars will be darkened.
- Heaven and earth will be shaken.
- The Lord will come with His army.
- God's wrath will be poured out.
- The Lord will put an end to sin.

Clearly, Isaiah presents a picture of an angry and punishing God, as does the prophet Joel, who wrote almost exclusively about the Day of the Lord. His prophecies capture the global scale of the coming great and dreadful day, and provide a few signs of that day's arrival.

Prophetic Pitfalls

The prophet Joel clears up any potential confusion regarding when the Day of the Lord will come. Joel says that the sun, moon, and stars will go dark *before* the great and dreadful Day of the Lord.

Joel said that the Day of the Lord will be a day of darkness and gloom. Like the dawn spreads across the mountains, a large and mighty army will come, before them a fire will devour and behind them flame will blaze. Nothing will escape their destruction. The nations will be in anguish; every face will turn pale.

Joel says that as God's mighty army approaches, the earth will shake, the sky will tremble, and the sun, moon, and stars will go dark. The Lord will thunder at the head of His army; His forces will be beyond number, and His mighty warriors will follow His command. The Day of the Lord will be dreadful, and who can endure it? Joel says that at that time, God will also restore the fortunes of Jerusalem and bring the nations into judgment concerning their treatment of God's people.

Joel describes the coming Day of the Lord thus:

- That day is close at hand.
- The sun, moon, and stars will go dark before that day.
- A large and mighty army will come for battle.
- The Lord will thunder at the head of His army.
- The earth and the sky will shake.
- That day will be great and dreadful.
- God will judge the nations.

As we examine each of the prophet's descriptions of the Day of the Lord, it should bring to mind our previous discussions about the feast of trumpets, the birth pains, the Great Tribulation, and the armies of the Antichrist. Many of these prophecies about the Last Days come into play as the Day of the Lord approaches, and a lot of the prophecies overlap or repeat. Let's consider what one more prophet had to say.

The Old Testament prophet Obadiah wrote that the Day of the Lord is near for all the nations and warned that as people have done, so it will be done to them—justice will be done. But on Mount Zion, there will be salvation and Israel will get its inheritance. The Messiah will be like a fire and the His enemies will be like stubble.

Based on these writings of Isaiah, Joel, and Obadiah, we can definitely see why the Day of the Lord is referred to as dreadful. Now let's look at descriptions of God's wrath.

Day of Wrath

The Day of the Lord will bring with it God's anger against sin and His judgmental wrath on the world. The Bible describes God's wrath as God's righteous judgment on an unbelieving and disobedient world.

David describes the Day of God's wrath as a time when God's hand will take hold of His enemies; David says that at the time of God's appearing, He will make His enemies like fuel for the furnace. God's wrath will swallow His enemies and His fire will consume them. God will also destroy their descendants from the earth and erase their posterity from mankind. The schemes of those who plot evil against Israel will not succeed because God will turn them around when He fights against them.

David's picture is one of destruction of God's enemies and redemption for Israel. Isaiah also had a vision of God's wrath. Let's examine it now.

The Prophet Says

Isaiah says, "According to what they have done, so will he repay wrath to his enemies and retribution to his foes; he will repay the islands their due. From the west, men will fear the name of the Lord, and from the rising of the sun, they will revere his glory. For he will come like a pent-up flood that the breath of the Lord drives along. 'The Redeemer will come to Zion, to those in Jacob who repent of their sins,' declares the Lord." (Isaiah 59:18–20)

The prophet Isaiah saw the Lord's garments stained red, like one who has been treading the winepress. Isaiah also wrote that God will tread the winepress alone; no one from the nations will help Him. When He tramples the nations in His anger, their blood will spatter His garments and stain His clothing. This day has been part of God's plan for a long time; He will work His salvation for His people, and His wrath will be on His enemies. Isaiah saw that God will trample on the nations in His wrath, their blood will be poured out on the ground.

As we can see, Isaiah describes God's wrath in terms of God treading a winepress, as does John in Revelation. John describes the armies of heaven, riding white horses and dressed in white linen, following Christ as He strikes down the nations and treads the winepress of the fury of God's wrath.

Jeremiah also saw the Day of the Lord as a day when God will pour out His wrath on the nations that do not acknowledge Him or call on His name. Jeremiah declares that the Lord is God, the living and eternal King who made the earth by His power and stretched out the heavens by His understanding. He also said that when God is angry, the earth trembles; it cannot endure His wrath. When God thunders from His dwelling, the heavens will roar, and He will send lightening, rain, and wind from His storehouses.

These insights into God's wrath provided by Isaiah and Jeremiah are quite terrifying. God's punishment of unbelievers and those who oppose Israel is unparalleled in its devastation. But the Bible also says that God is angry with Israel.

Starts with Israel

The Bible presents the work of man as worthless. Mankind's idols and images are considered to be frauds, and when judgment comes, they will all perish in the fire. The God of Jacob is presented as the one true God and the maker of all things, including Israel, the tribe of His inheritance. Let's see what Ezekiel tells us about God's anger at Israel in the Last Days.

Ezekiel declares, "The end has come"—an unheard-of disaster is coming against Israel. The time has come; that day is near—there is panic, not joy in Israel. The Lord is about to pour out His wrath and anger against her for her detestable practices. Ezekiel says that God will not have pity and will not spare Israel. He will repay her in accordance with her behavior and her detestable practices. Then Israel will know that it is the Lord who strikes the blow.

So at this point we can conclude that the Bible tells of God's wrath and anger being directed at His enemies and foes, including Israel, on the Day of the Lord. Another Old Testament prophet, Nahum, explains this by telling us that the Lord is a jealous and avenging God; he says God is slow to anger, and He will not leave the guilty unpunished. Nahum goes on to give us a picture, describing God's way as a whirlwind and a storm, rebuking the peoples of the world and burning up their ways of life. The nations will quake at His appearance and melt away. As we have learned from studying the prophets, the Bible describes the wrath of God as being "poured out" on the world. In the Book of Revelation, as you may recall, the wrath of God is depicted as being poured out from seven bowls. The bowls in Revelation hold God's wrath and judgment, which will be poured out on the earth on the Day of the Lord as the world moves into Day 7.

Now that we have studied the descriptions of God's punishment of the world, let's explore one detail that is mentioned in almost all prophecies about the return of Christ and the Day of the Lord: darkness.

Like a Thief in the Night

Paul wrote to the young church in Thessalonica to remind them of things he had taught about the coming Day of the Lord. In his first letter, Paul reminded them

> **The Prophet Says**
>
> Paul wrote, "While people are saying, 'Peace and safety,' destruction will come on them suddenly, as labor pains on a pregnant woman, and they will not escape. But you, brothers, are not in darkness so that this day should surprise you like a thief." (1 Thessalonians 5:3–4)

that the Day of the Lord will sneak up on the whole world like a thief in the night and will catch people by surprise. He said that while people are safe and secure, destruction will come on them suddenly, like labor pains on a pregnant woman, and they will not be able to escape.

Though most will be caught off guard and unprepared, Paul reminded them that believers in Christ will know what is coming and will not be in the dark about these things. He said the Day of the Lord will not surprise them like a thief because they are "of the light" and will be awake and alert.

Ready or Not

In Paul's second letter to the church in Thessalonica, he told them more about the Day of the Lord so that they would not become confused or deceived by anyone. Paul said that the Day of the Lord will not happen until after the Antichrist sets himself up in the Temple of God, proclaiming that he is God. We have already discussed this abomination that causes desolation and its timing in Chapter 9.

The Apostle Peter also taught that the Day of the Lord will come like a thief in the night to many. He said that the heavens will disappear with a roar and the elements will be destroyed by fire. He warned them to live holy and godly lives so that they can look forward to the Day of the Lord.

Deliverance and Restoration

I have already told you that the Day of the Lord is not destruction for everyone. Not only will the Day of the Lord be a day of wrath and judgment, but it will also be a day of deliverance and restoration. Let's explore further why the Bible says it is a great and glorious day for some.

The Apostle Paul wrote about this joyful aspect of the Day of the Lord in several of his letters. In his second letter to the Corinthian Church, Paul assures Christ's followers that the Word of God is written so they can read and understand it, and be prepared for the future tribulation. Paul also tells Christ's followers that he looks forward to the Day of the Lord (Day 7), when he will boast about their faith and perseverance in the Kingdom of God.

—Timeline to the End of the Age—

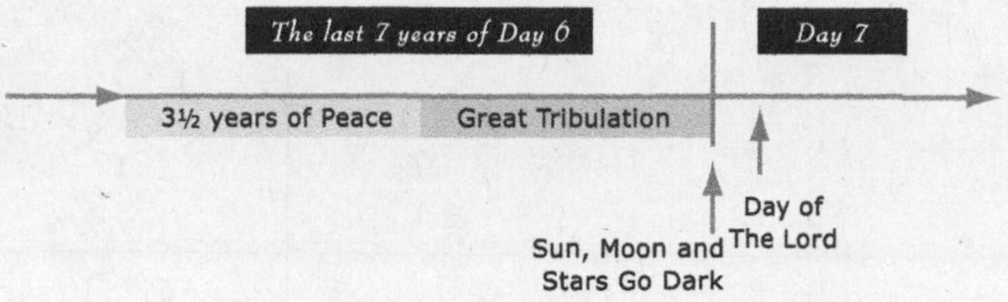

The last 7 years of Day 6

Day 7

3½ years of Peace

Great Tribulation

Day of The Lord

Sun, Moon and Stars Go Dark

We have already seen that day will come after the sun and the moon and the stars go dark, and after Elijah prophesies for three and a half years. Then the Lord will appear suddenly and return with all His mighty angels to punish the world. On Day 7, God will bring salvation and deliverance to His people as He establishes His kingdom in Jerusalem. This deliverance and restoration of God's people is the Gospel promise that was made to Abraham in the Old Testament and to Christ's followers in the New Testament. This is the day when the Bible says that God will restore everything as He said He would through His prophets. Throughout the Bible, God's plan for the future is repeated, and we are told that Christ will remain in heaven until it is time for the restoration: "He must remain in heaven until the time comes for God to restore everything, as he promised long ago through his holy prophets." (Acts 3:21)

God will remove the curse that He put on the earth because of man's disobedience in the Garden of Eden, and He will reestablish the kingdom in Jerusalem and reign over the whole world from David's throne on "the great day of God Almighty." (Revelation 16:14)

We talk more about the return of Christ and the restoration in the next chapters.

The Least You Need to Know

- The Day of the Lord is the Judgment Day as well as the Day of Salvation.
- The Bible says it will be too late to join Christ once God's wrath starts to be poured out.
- God's wrath will be severe and devastating.
- Judgment will start with Israel and the followers of Christ, and then encompass the whole earth.
- Followers of Christ who stand firm to the end will be saved and not subjected to His wrath.

Chapter 17

The Return of the King

In This Chapter

- After a long two days, He's back!
- Coming, complete with special effects
- The whole world will be changed
- Coming soon to a venue near you

It's hard to imagine that almost six days have gone by and that we are now very close to the end of the age, and the end of Day 6. How does the expression go? "How time flies when you're having fun"?

In the context of God's seven-day plan, we have been discussing the time just before the Day of the Lord and the Second Coming of Christ. Now we examine how the Bible describes Christ's return and the related happenings in heaven—and on earth.

Finally, the Second Coming

So far in this guide, we have studied many biblical prophecies relating to the Last Days, including those on the signs before the end of Day 6, the time of the Great Tribulation and God's judgment and wrath. We have discussed some of the prophetic events that the Bible indicates will occur in the last 24-hour days and hours of Day 6, and the first 24-hour days and hours of Day 7. The events packed into this period are some of the most supernatural and catastrophic recorded in Scripture. The Bible also provides numerous accounts of the Second Coming, which we need to understand if we are to get a full picture of the events of the Last Days.

— Last Days Timeline —

Day 1	*Day 2*	*Day 3*	*Day 4*	*Day 5*	*Day 6*	*Day 7*
1,000 years	2,000 years	3,000 years	4,000 years	5,000 years	6,000 years	7,000 years
Adam	Noah	Moses	David	Christ	Church	Kingdom

↑ Second Coming

The Second Coming of the Messiah (also called the Christ) is the appearing, from heaven, of the Messiah, the King of the Jews. This key biblical event—the coming of the King—is central to both the Jewish and Christian faiths. For the Jewish people, it is the appearing of the Son of David to deliver them from persecution and to establish His throne in Jerusalem. For Christians, it is the Second Coming of Jesus Christ to establish His Millennial Kingdom on earth. Though they are viewed differently by different faiths and religions, Scripture says that these two occurrences are one and the same.

First Things First

We previously discussed the Messiah's first visit to earth (First Coming), which occurred just as prophesied in Scripture. As you may recall, the prophet Daniel foretold the precise timing of the First Coming of the Messiah the King. Daniel also provides a roadmap of events that precede the end of Day 6 and the Second Coming.

The New Testament tells the story of the Messiah's visit to earth about 2,000 years ago in the person of Jesus Christ. When He finished everything He came to accomplish, He returned to heaven to wait for the time of His return. Jesus told His followers that one day He would come back to receive them into the Kingdom of God.

When Jesus left for heaven, He and His disciples were standing on the Mount of Olives, and Jesus was taken up into the sky before their very eyes. Then two men dressed in white appeared and told the disciples that Jesus will return from heaven in the same way they saw Him go.

The Prophet Says

"They were looking intently up into the sky as he was going, when suddenly two men dressed in white stood beside them. 'Men of Galilee,' they said, 'why do you stand here looking into the sky? This same Jesus, who has been taken from you into heaven, will come back in the same way you have seen him go into heaven.'" (Acts 1:11–12)

After a Long Time

The New Testament presents stories and parables from Jesus in which He tells his followers that He will be leaving and then, after a long time, He will return to claim His Kingdom. Once when Jesus was speaking near Jerusalem and the people were under the impression that the Kingdom of God was going to appear at once, Jesus told them a parable about a man of noble birth. In the parable, the man of noble birth represents Christ. Jesus said the man of noble birth left and went to a distant land to have himself appointed king and then return. He gave his servants work to do until he came back. But his subjects hated him and sent a delegation after him saying they didn't want him to be their king. However, according to this story, the man was made king and returned. This parable contains both prophecy and warning: God is telling His followers His plan and also warning them that some will rebel, to their detriment.

Second Coming Trailer

So what will the return be like? In addition to the many prophetic descriptions of the return, which we dig into soon, a passage in the Bible tells of a group that got to see a preview. Jesus was talking to a group about His return and told them that some who were standing there would see the Kingdom of God before they died.

About six days later, Jesus took some of them up onto a mountain to pray. As they were praying, Jesus' appearance changed and His clothes became as bright as a flash of lightening. Two men long deceased, Moses and Elijah, also appeared in glory. Moses and Elijah spoke to Jesus about His departure from Jerusalem, which was to happen shortly thereafter. Jesus told those present to keep this secret until after He had been raised from the dead.

The Prophet Says

"After six days Jesus took Peter, James, and John with him and led them up a high mountain, where they were all alone. There he was transfigured before them. His clothes became dazzling white, whiter than anyone in the world could bleach them. And there appeared before them Elijah and Moses, who were talking with Jesus." (Mark 9:2–4)

Those present had been given a prophetic vision of the Kingdom of God, with Jesus in His glory as King. Since this preview had limited viewing and is not in a theater near you, we will need to study what Jesus and some of the prophets said or wrote to complete our picture of the Second Coming.

Written by the Prophets

Scripture records several occasions when Jesus referred to himself as returning in glory and great power with His holy angels. On these occasions He would usually describe His return as a time when He would gather His faithful followers or judge mankind.

Jesus' descriptions of His Second Coming are often very similar to Old Testament descriptions of the coming of the Messiah. Let's now take a careful look at what the prophets wrote to learn what the Bible says will be happening at the Second Coming, when Christ returns.

Advent Similarities

One of the first Old Testament writers to prophesy about the Second Coming of the Messiah was Job. Job wrote about a time in the distant future when he would rise from the dead and see Israel's Redeemer with his own eyes. Job said that his Redeemer will stand on the earth at the end of the age. This is recorded in Job 19:25.

Another prophet, Zechariah, like Job, had a vision that the Messiah will stand on the earth at the time of the end. Zechariah saw that Christ, on the Day of the Lord, will stand on the Mount of Olives east of Jerusalem. So Scripture indicates that Jesus will return from heaven to the Mount of Olives at His Second Coming. This is interesting because when Jesus left after His First Coming, the Bible says He rose into the clouds and ascended into Heaven from the Mount of Olives.

Another similarity to the First Coming is that Jesus is described by the Old Testament prophet Malachi as coming into His temple at His Second Coming. Jesus also came to the temple of God at His First Coming. However, it is plain to see that the two advents are very different.

Now we know some of the similarities in the way the Bible describes His departure and return landing—heaven, clouds, the Mount of Olives, and the temple. Let's see what else the Bible says about His reappearance.

The Prophet Says

Zechariah says, "On that day his feet will stand on the Mount of Olives, east of Jerusalem, and the Mount of Olives will be split in two from east to west, forming a great valley, with half of the mountain moving north and half moving south." (Zechariah 14:4)

Jesus Is Coming, Look Busy

Isaiah is another Old Testament prophet with something to say about the Second Coming. Many of Isaiah's prophecies describe the reappearance of the Lord. He also touches on the "resurrection," which he describes as occurring at the Second Coming. Isaiah depicts the resurrection as the earth giving birth to the dead. Isaiah includes descriptions from the transition from Day 6 to Day 7 that we have already studied, such as the punishment of the people of the earth for their sins. Isaiah also tells us that the Lord will do battle on Mount Zion.

In Isaiah Chapter 64, Isaiah describes the Second Coming in the same way it is described in the Psalms. Isaiah writes that the Lord will open the heavens and come down. The mountains and the nations are described as trembling at His presence. Isaiah says the Lord will come to help those who do what is right and who remember His ways.

The Prophet Says

Daniel wrote, "In my vision at night I looked, and there before me was one like a son of man, coming with the clouds of heaven …. He was given authority, glory, and sovereign power; all peoples, nations, and men of every language worshiped him. His dominion is an everlasting dominion that will not pass away, and his kingdom is one that will never be destroyed." (Daniel 7:13–14)

Let's see what the Old Testament prophet Daniel can add. Among Daniel's many prophecies about the End Times, he, too, writes of visions of the Second Coming. In one vision, Daniel saw someone coming on the clouds of heaven. Daniel says this Son of Man was given authority, glory, and sovereign power over all the peoples, nations, and languages of the earth, and that his dominion will be everlasting and will never pass away or be destroyed.

By now you can't have helped noticing that the writers of the Bible are very consistent in how they describe the events of the Last Days. I think you have to be exposed to this repetition to get an idea of how the Bible presents the Last Days. We have now had several prophets mention power, domination, and battle in relation to the end of Day 6 and the Second Coming. Does the Bible tell us any more about what the Lord will do at His return?

Ready for Battle

The answer is, yes. But before we find out the details, let's review some of the events of the Great Tribulation, which starts three and a half years before the end of Day 6. Zechariah wrote that the armies of the nations will come against Jerusalem and capture it; her houses will be ransacked, and the women raped. Half of the city will go into exile, but the remainder of the people will stay in the city. Jerusalem will be devastated during the time of tribulation.

Zechariah says that after this tribulation, the Lord will fight against the nations on the day of battle. First, He will stand on the Mount of Olives, east of Jerusalem. From there, Scripture says, Jesus will enter Jerusalem, and from Mount Zion He will go out to do battle. When evening comes, there will be light, and the Lord will be king over the whole earth. The Bible says that on that day, the spirit of God will flow out from Jerusalem, half to the east and half to the west.

> **The Prophet Says**
>
> "Then the Lord will go out and fight against those nations, as he fights in the day of battle. On that day his feet will stand on the Mount of Olives, east of Jerusalem." (Zechariah 14:3–4)

When the Messiah returns, Jerusalem will be restored, never again to be destroyed. We are told that the Lord will strike all the nations that fight against Jerusalem with a plague, and their flesh will rot while they are still standing on their feet. On that day, men will panic; each one will seize the hand of another, and they will attack each other.

So when the Lord appears, there will be a final battle over Jerusalem and the world. We discuss the Final Battle in greater detail in Chapter 20. Now let's see what is written about the Second Coming in the Old Testament Book of Psalms.

As Written in Psalms

In Psalm 50, the Psalmist writes that God will appear in brilliant glory from Zion. At His coming, fire will go before Him and a tempest will rage around Him. The Lord will summon all His people from heaven above and the earth below to judge them. He will summon everyone who has made a covenant with Him by His sacrifice.

This account of the Second Coming touches on an aspect we discuss in more detail in the next chapter. For now, you should know that the Lord will have His angels gather His followers from heaven and earth. This gathering is mentioned several places in Scripture and was described by Jesus in the Olivet Discourse, recorded in Matthew 24:29–31. This gathering is referred to in Scripture as the harvest and the resurrection. A popular name for it is also the rapture.

> **The Prophet Says**
>
> Jesus said, "At that time … they will see the Son of Man coming on the clouds of the sky, with power and great glory. And he will send his angels with a loud trumpet call, and they will gather his elect from the four winds, from one end of the heavens to the other." (Matthew 24:30–31)

All Creation Affected

The Psalmist tells us that all creation will rejoice at the Lord's appearing. He says, Declare among the nations that the Lord will reign and judge His people fairly. The new heaven and the new earth we have discussed will be eternally established never again to be destroyed or changed. The Lord God will come to judge the earth and His people in truth and He will reign and the earth will be glad and rejoice.

Before this, the world will be in darkness, the sun and moon and stars will not give their light. Then suddenly He will appear like lightening in the sky and all the world will tremble at His appearing, Everyone will see the brilliance of His glory, blazing fire will go out before Him as He devours His enemies. When the battle is over, we are told that the heavens will proclaim His righteousness and justice will be the foundation of His throne.

King David's Account

The Psalms also repeat descriptions of the time of the Second Coming with which we are very familiar. In Psalm 18, David says the earth will tremble and quake, and the mountains will be shaken to their foundations because of the Lord's anger. David says smoke and fire will come from the Lord as He opens the heavens to come down. Dark clouds will be under His feet, and darkness will be all around Him. Out of the darkness His brightness will shine like lightning from heaven. He is described as soaring with the cherubim (powerful angels) on the wings of the wind. The voice of the Most High God will resound like thunder as He scatters His enemies.

The Prophet Says

David wrote, "He parted the heavens and came down; dark clouds were under his feet. He mounted the cherubim and flew; he soared on the wings of the wind. He made darkness his covering, his canopy around him—the dark rain clouds of the sky. Out of the brightness of his presence clouds advanced, with hailstones and bolts of lightning." (Psalm 18:9–12)

As we imagine the scene David is portraying, we should recall from the last chapter one of the signs that precedes the Day of the Lord. Before that day, the sky will be totally black because the sun, moon, and stars will have gone completely dark. It is out of this darkness that David describes the brilliance of the Lord's appearing.

In Psalm 144, King David repeats some of His descriptions from Psalm 18. Then David adds that the Lord will reach down His hand from heaven to rescue His people from the nations who are full of lies and deceit. This account captures a picture also found in several other prophecies of the Lord gathering His people to save them from the nations and armies of the Antichrist. Remember that the Bible says the Antichrist and his armies will come against Israel at the end of Day 6.

We have now discussed the accounts of several Old Testament prophets who described in considerable and vivid detail the return of the Messiah the King. Let's now see what the New Testament writers have to offer on the topic of the Second Coming.

Appearing Soon

When New Testament writers wrote about the Second Coming, they referred to it as His appearing, His revealing, and His coming. The word *coming* is one of the most popular New Testament terms used to describe the return of Christ, translated from the Greek word *parousia*, which also means "arrival" or "advent." Saying "the Second Coming of Christ" is the same as saying "the Second Advent" or "the Second Arrival." Let's see how the "coming" of Jesus Christ is expressed by the New Testament writers.

First, some confusion surrounds when the Bible says Christ's followers will be resurrected and changed.

—Timeline to the End of the Age—

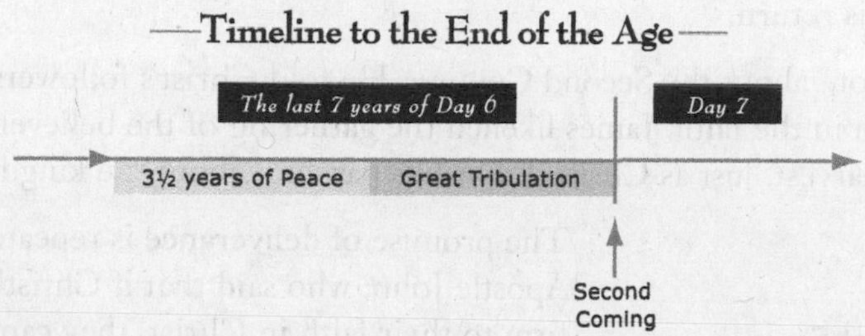

The term *coming* (*parousia*) was first used in the Olivet Discourse to refer to the Second Coming when the disciples asked Christ about His return at the end of Day 6. It was then used three times in Christ's description when He described the signs and events that will take place before His appearing.

The Apostle Paul penned one of the most popular passages about the "resurrection" and gathering that will take place at the Second Coming. Paul used the word *coming* (*parousia*) when describing the event popularly called the *rapture*. The rapture is the carrying of living followers into the clouds to meet Christ in the air when He appears.

Paul said that Jesus taught that those who are left alive will be changed in the resurrection at the Last Day. Later Paul wrote that the resurrection gathering of Christ's followers will not take place until after the Antichrist is revealed at the time of the Great Tribulation.

Prophetic Pitfalls

Paul clears up any confusion about when the Second Coming will take place when he tells the Thessalonians that the day cannot take place until the Antichrist is revealed.

Standing Firm

Often the New Testament writers encouraged Christ's followers to look forward to Christ's return. The Apostle Paul wrote that Christians should flee from the temptation of money and fight the good fight of the faith until the appearance of the Lord Jesus Christ. He said that God will bring about Jesus' appearing at the appointed time. Paul also wrote that the Gospel teaches Christ's followers to say no to worldly passions and to live a controlled and righteous life in this present evil age while they wait for the glorious reappearance of their God and Savior, Jesus Christ, the blessed hope.

Similarly, the author of Hebrews wrote that Christ will appear a second time to bring salvation and deliverance to all those who have put their faith in Him and who are waiting for His return.

James also wrote about the Second Coming. He told Christ's followers to be patient and stand firm in the faith. James likened the gathering of the believers at Christ's coming to a harvest, just as Christ did in His parables about the kingdom.

The promise of deliverance is repeated by the Apostle John, who said that if Christ's followers hold firm to their faith in Christ, they can be confident and not ashamed when they appear to be judged at His Second Coming. John also described the resurrection of their bodies. When Christ appears, the Bible indicates that His followers, both the living and the dead, will be resurrected and they will receive bodies like Jesus' resurrected body.

The Prophet Says

Paul says, "say no to ungodliness and worldly passions … while we wait for the blessed hope—the glorious appearing of our great God and Savior, Jesus Christ." (Titus 2:12–13)

The New Testament says that Christ sacrificed His life to pay for the sins of mankind, and that those who accept His gift are judged differently from those who don't, who are subject to God's wrath.

Seen from the Mount of Olives

Jesus provided His followers with a description of His Second Coming in His Olivet Discourse, recorded in Matthew Chapter 24, Mark Chapter 13, and Luke Chapter 21, some of which we have discussed previously. Jesus told the disciples that, immediately after the Great Tribulation, the sun will be darkened, the moon will not give its light, the stars will fall from the sky, and the heavens will be shaken. Jesus said that He will appear in the sky immediately after the Great Tribulation and that everyone will see Him returning from heaven to earth, coming on the clouds of the sky, with power and great glory. He also said that He will have His angels gather His followers from heaven and earth when He returns.

So we now have a pretty good picture of how the Bible presents Christ's return to the earth. Let's see what the Bible says about this from the perspective of heaven.

Seen from Heaven

As you may recall, in the Book of Revelation John writes that he was taken to heaven, where he saw a vision. John's vision includes both the supernatural and the natural. John says he saw a white cloud and that seated on the cloud was one "like a son of man," with a crown on his head and a sharp sickle in his hand. Christ swung the sickle over the earth, and the earth was harvested. This will be at the end of Day 6. After this harvest, an angel came out of the temple in heaven. This angel also had a sickle, which he used to gather the grapes, which he threw into the winepress of God's wrath. This picture of the harvest depicts Christ as gathering His followers and the angels separating out the rest of the earth for judgment and God's wrath.

In another vision of the Second Coming, John says he was in heaven and saw a white horse with a rider called "Faithful and True." John says this rider will make war on the world and judge it with justice. He describes the rider as having eyes like blazing fire and many crowns on his head. We are told that on this rider is a name that only the rider knows. The rider stands for Christ, and the armies of heaven follow Him riding on white horses and are dressed in fine white linen. John says that out of His mouth will come a sharp sword to strike the nations, and He will rule the nations with an iron scepter. John also says that Christ will tread the winepress of God's wrath, and that written on His robe and on His thigh are the names "King of Kings" and "Lord of Lords."

Prophetic Pitfalls

Many names and titles are used in Scripture to identify the Messiah, who is also called the Christ. In Revelation alone, John uses King of Kings, Lord of Lords, Faithful and True, God, the Lamb, Lord God Almighty, Word of God, Alpha and Omega, Beginning and End, the First and the Last, and Lord Jesus.

Once again, we see that the Bible describes Christ as appearing in glory when He comes back to earth. Now let's review some of the key things we know about the Second Coming and the Last Days.

The Coming Summary

In the days and possibly weeks before the Second Coming of Jesus Christ, the world will be in turmoil, and the bowls of God's wrath will have begun to be poured out on the world. The whole earth will have grown dark.

Out of this total darkness, Jesus Christ will appear. The Bible says He will come from heaven in glorious and brilliant light, accompanied by a supernatural army of angels numbering more than a hundred million and seen by all of creation. At the time of His appearing, Christ's holy angels will harvest the earth by separating the followers of Christ from the rest of the world. Christ's followers, both the dead and those left alive, will be gathered to Christ in the sky. Their bodies will be changed, in the resurrection, at the last trumpet.

In the next chapters, we discuss a royal wedding banquet in Jerusalem on Mount Zion, and the defeat of the Antichrist and the armies at the Final Battle.

The Least You Need to Know

- The Bible says that Christ came to earth once and that the same Christ will return again.
- At the Second Coming, Christ will appear out of the darkness with His angels in glorious light to the whole world.
- When Christ returns from heaven, His followers will be separated from the rest of the world.
- At the Second Coming, the followers of Christ will be gathered together with Christ.

Chapter 18

So This Is the Rapture

In This Chapter

- A critical spiritual change
- The dead will live again
- The living will not die
- Immediately after the tribulation

The resurrection is a foundational doctrine of the followers of Christ. Scripture describes the resurrection of the dead as foundational to the faith. *Resurrection* is the term used to describe the change that will take place in the bodies of the followers of Christ at the Second Coming.

The followers of Christ live in the Day 7 kingdom with their changed bodies. Scripture indicates that the change will occur in all believers, both dead and living. For the believers who died before the Second Coming, the change in their bodies is called the resurrection from the dead. For the believers who are still alive at the Second Coming, the change in their bodies is called the resurrection of the living, popularly referred to as the rapture. In this chapter, we explore Scripture on the resurrection of the living and the dead.

Children of the Resurrection

We have talked some about the Day 7 Kingdom of God, but we haven't talked about who will live in this kingdom. Jesus spoke and taught more on the Kingdom of God than on any other single topic. He said the secrets of the kingdom are hidden from many, but they are revealed to His followers. One of the mysteries about the Kingdom of God has to do with those who are included in the resurrection.

Individuals who will inherit the Kingdom of God are worthy to take part in the resurrection. Jesus calls these people "children of the resurrection." They will rule and reign with Christ in the Kingdom of God for the 1,000 years of Day 7. So who does the Bible say is worthy?

Inherit the Kingdom

On one occasion, Jesus was speaking about the work and mission of John the Baptist and said this about the Kingdom of God: "I tell you the truth: Among those born of women there has not risen anyone greater than John the Baptist; yet he who is least in the Kingdom of God is greater than he." Based on Jesus' statement, anyone who desires to enter the kingdom must be greater than John the Baptist, and John was the greatest human being.

On the surface this would make entrance into the kingdom impossible. However, when we take into consideration the rest of Scripture, we find that Jesus meant that no one will be able to enter the Kingdom of God unless and until they are born of the Spirit. Jesus explained that flesh gives birth to flesh, and the Spirit gives birth to spirit. John was born of woman (flesh), but those born of the Spirit will be greater than John.

The Prophet Says

Peter said, "For you have been born again, not of perishable seed, but of imperishable, through the living and enduring word of God." (1 Peter 1:23)

At some point, there will be "children of the resurrection" who will be greater in the Kingdom of God than John the Baptist was in the flesh. So who are those who are born of the Spirit, and when will they be greater than John? The Apostle Paul helps us understand this mystery when he tells us that flesh and blood cannot inherit the Kingdom of God. Paul says that a time is coming when those born of the Spirit will be changed from their present natural bodies into future spiritual bodies. The Bible says that the natural body is a mortal body, but the spiritual body will be immortal.

Paul tells us that the spiritual body does not come to life unless the natural body dies. He made an analogy to the planting of a seed. When you plant a seed, it eventually gives way to the plant. God gives each kind of seed its own body. There are heavenly bodies and there are earthly bodies. The Bible says that earthly bodies are one kind, and heavenly bodies another. Paul says that the resurrection of the dead will be as it is with a seed—the body is planted perishable but will be raised imperishable. We are told that this imperishable spiritual body will be raised in glory and in power. Scripture says that though the natural body is earthly, like the body of Adam, the spiritual body will be like that of Christ, who has already been resurrected.

We already know that the Bible says that when the Kingdom of God comes on earth, it will be imperishable because it is said to last forever. Now we know that the Bible says that those who inherit the Kingdom of God will also last forever—they will be immortal and imperishable. They will go from temporary natural bodies to eternal spiritual bodies. Paul calls this change in the natural body the "resurrection of the dead." We know that the resurrected body is like Christ's resurrected body, so let's see what Scripture says about Christ's resurrected body.

The Prophet Says

"Afterward Jesus appeared in a different form to two of them while they were walking in the country. These returned and reported it to the rest; but they did not believe them either. Later Jesus appeared to the Eleven as they were eating; he rebuked them for their lack of faith and their stubborn refusal to believe those who had seen him after he had risen." (Mark 16:12–14)

What do we know about Christ's resurrected body? Let's take a look at how the Bible describes Christ's body after He was raised from the dead. It seems that His resurrected body retained a likeness to His mortal body because we are told that His hands and feet still had the marks from His crucifixion. He also had the scar from where a soldier had pierced His side with a spear to determine whether He had died. However, we are also given the impression that Jesus' appearance was different because on several occasions close friends did not recognize Him at first. Of course, this could be due to the fact that they knew He had died.

Be Like Christ

Christ's resurrected body also possessed supernatural characteristics. For example, Jesus appeared to people without making an entrance. On two occasions He appeared and stood among the disciples even though the doors to the place where they were meeting had been locked.

In addition to descriptions of Christ's resurrected body, the Bible includes teachings by Jesus about the supernatural characteristics of the resurrected body. Jesus taught that the people who are worthy to take part in the resurrection from the dead will no longer die and will be like the angels in heaven. Jesus also taught that the resurrected will not marry or be given in marriage.

The Prophet Says

"Jesus replied, 'You are in error because you do not know the Scriptures or the power of God. At the resurrection people will neither marry nor be given in marriage; they will be like the angels in heaven.'" (Matthew 22:29–30)

This change in the mortal body is called the "resurrection of the dead" because the Bible says that Christ's followers who died before the coming of the Kingdom of God on earth will be raised to life and changed when the kingdom comes. According to Scripture, anyone who has put their faith in the Lord since the time of Adam will be raised to life when the kingdom comes.

I should point out that the Bible says that when followers of Christ die, they go to be with Christ, who is currently in Heaven. Therefore, before the resurrection, the dead in Christ have been in Heaven.

The Dead Will Rise

The resurrection is not just something from the New Testament. Several Old Testament writers and prophets wrote about it as well. Even though the Old Testament passages do not refer to it as the resurrection, they do describe the dead being raised to life in the end when everything is restored to Israel. Let's examine how the Old Testament writers described the resurrection of the dead.

In the Book of Job, Job writes that man dies and his body is laid to rest, and that after he takes his last breath, he is no more. Job then goes on to say that he himself will die and be buried, and will remain so while God punishes the world. Job also tells us that he looks forward to his future reward and to seeing God with his own eyes when God returns to earth.

Valley of Dry Bones

The Old Testament prophet Ezekiel provides a vivid description of the resurrection of the dead in a prophecy about a valley of dry bones. Ezekiel says he was put in the middle of a valley full of dry bones by the Spirit of God. There were many dry bones on the floor of the valley, and God asked Ezekiel if the bones could live. Ezekiel answered that only God knows. The Lord told Ezekiel to prophecy and to tell the bones to listen to the Lord. Ezekiel tells us that the Lord will make the bones come to life, that the Lord will attach tendons and add skin.

After Ezekiel told the bones that the Lord would bring them back to life, he says there was a noise, a rattling sound, and the bones came together, tendons formed, flesh appeared, and skin covered them. In the vision, the bones came to life and stood up on their feet, forming a vast army. The Lord told Ezekiel that this was the whole house of Israel, which God is going to bring up from the dead and back to the land of Israel.

The Prophet Says

Job said, "I know that my Redeemer lives, and that in the end he will stand upon the earth. And after my skin has been destroyed, yet in my flesh I will see God; I myself will see him with my own eyes—I, and not another. How my heart yearns within me!" (Job 19:25–27)

Daniel's Resurrection

Daniel also prophesied about God's people being raised from the dead. In Daniel Chapter 12, he describes the resurrection as coming after the tribulation. Let's review some of this prophecy. Daniel says that the Archangel Michael will arise for service. Daniel's prophecy describes the Great Tribulation as coming after Michael throws Satan to earth. After the Great Tribulation, Daniel says everyone whose name is written in the Book of Life will be delivered. Daniel describes all the dead as being woken up but says that some will receive everlasting life, and others shame and everlasting contempt. He describes God's people as shining brightly forever after they have been resurrected. You are probably getting the idea now that the resurrection is a popular topic among Old Testament prophets. Let's consider what a few more wrote—once again, the Bible uses repetition to reinforce the message.

The Prophet Says

"At that time Michael, the great prince who protects your people, will arise. There will be a time of distress such as has not happened from the beginning of nations until then. But at that time your people—everyone whose name is found written in the book—will be delivered. Multitudes who sleep in the dust of the earth will awake: some to everlasting life, others to shame and everlasting contempt. Those who are wise will shine like the brightness of the heavens, and those who lead many to righteousness, like the stars for ever and ever." (Daniel 12:1–3)

The Old Testament prophet Hosea tells how God will release His people from the power of the grave. The Old Testament Prophet Isaiah writes that the dead will live and their bodies will be raised to life. He says that the earth will give birth to her dead.

Several Old Testament prophecies describe the dead being raised in connection with the future redemption of Israel. We have already discussed that, at the end of Day 6 when the kingdom comes, God will gather all His followers into His kingdom. We now see that the Bible says God will raise the dead, gather His people, and resurrect them for Day 7. Does the Bible tell us anything else about what will happen to the living?

Rapture of the Living

When Jesus Christ returns to gather His followers on Day 7, all the Old Testament faithful and the New Testament saints will have died. As we have discussed, many New Testament saints will be killed during the last three and a half years of Day 6, during the Great Tribulation. However, Scripture indicates that some of Christ's followers will still be alive when Christ returns.

Jesus and the apostles taught about what would happen to the followers of Christ who are still alive at the time of the Second Coming. For example, the Bible tells of Jesus talking to Martha about her brother Lazarus, who had recently died. Jesus told Martha that Lazarus would rise again. Martha was quick to let Jesus know that she knew her brother would rise again in the resurrection at the last day. Apparently, Martha was familiar with Jesus' teaching on the topic of the resurrection.

Jesus then explained to Martha that He is the resurrection. Jesus told her that those who put their faith in Him will live, even though they die. Basically, the Bible's message is that anyone who dies believing in Jesus Christ will be raised to life in the resurrection at the last day, Day 7. We have already studied this, so it is nothing new. However, Jesus went on to tell her that those who believe in Him and are still alive at the last day will never die. Therefore, anyone who is left alive at the last day (Day 7) will be changed in the resurrection from a mortal body into an immortal body.

Catching Up with the Dead

The Apostle Paul also taught about living believers being changed in the resurrection on the last day. In his first letter to the Thessalonians, Paul described Christian doctrine regarding the resurrection. Paul said, according to Jesus' own words, that believers who are still alive and left at the Second Coming will be carried up into the clouds to meet the Lord in the air at the time of the resurrection of the living. He also explained that this will be the time when the dead will be raised (the resurrection of the dead).

def•i•ni•tion

The **rapture** is a nonbiblical term used to describe the catching up of living believers into the clouds to meet the Lord in the air at the return of Christ, as described in 1 Thessalonians 4:17.

It is from this description of the gathering and resurrection of the living that many people get the popular idea of the *rapture*. This passage from Paul's letter beautifully describes the sequence of events of the resurrection of the dead and the living at the Second Coming. Let's break it down. Here's the sequence of the resurrection and rapture:

1. The Lord will come down from heaven with a trumpet call.
2. The dead in Christ will rise (resurrection of the dead).
3. Those in Christ who are still alive will be carried up together with the dead in Christ into the clouds.
4. The dead and the living in Christ will meet Jesus Christ in the air.

This description of the resurrection and rapture by Paul confirms the timing of the resurrection and rapture. Because Paul says that Jesus comes down from heaven, the timing of this event must be at the beginning of Day 7. We know this because Scripture indicates in Acts 3:21 that Jesus must remain in heaven until it's time to restore everything. Because we know that Jesus will restore everything when He establishes the Kingdom of God on earth, the resurrection and rapture must be at end of Day 6 and the beginning of Day 7.

—Timeline to the End of the Age—

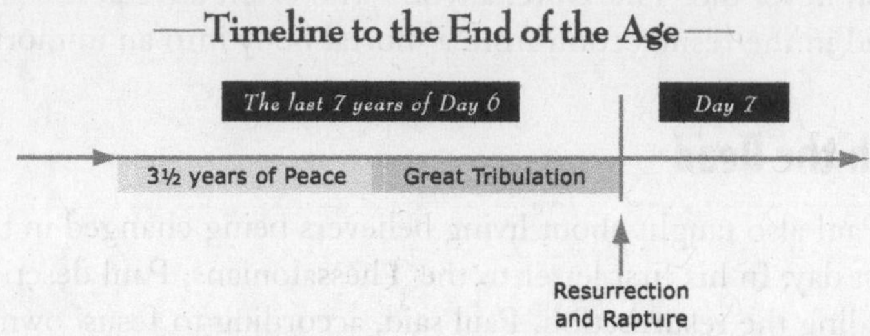

Paul also instructs Christ's followers about the resurrection and rapture in Chapter 15 of his first letter to the Corinthians. This teaching also places the timing of the resurrection and rapture at the beginning of the last day, Day 7. Let's examine this teaching and learn what else Paul has to say about the resurrection and its timing.

Rapture at the Last Trumpet

"Listen, I tell you a mystery," Paul begins, as he explains that when the resurrection takes place, all believers—the dead and the living—will be changed instantaneously, in a flash, in the twinkling of an eye. Paul also tells us that this will all happen at the last trumpet. We have already discussed the last trumpet in previous chapters. The last trumpet is the seventh trumpet of Revelation, which will sound at the time Christ establishes the Kingdom of God on earth.

—Timeline to the End of the Age—

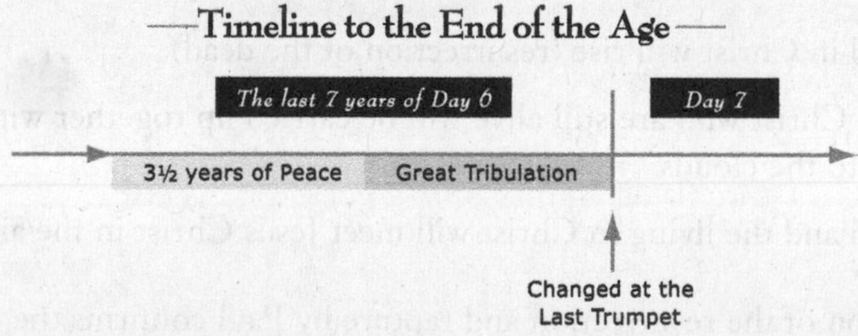

In this same teaching, Paul describes what happens to the human body when it is resurrected. He repeats a familiar refrain, that the body, which is currently perishable and mortal, must be changed into a body that will be imperishable and immortal, at which point the prophecy will be fulfilled that says, "Death has been swallowed up in victory."

This prophecy is recorded in Isaiah 25:8, and it will be fulfilled on the Day of the Lord when Jesus holds the wedding feast in Jerusalem. We discuss this event in more detail in the next chapter.

Harvest Gathering

Often the resurrection is mentioned in connection with the separation of believers and nonbelievers. Let's review a Last Days event that we have previously discussed. Jesus' depiction of the time of the resurrection and gathering of believers as a harvest at the end of the age (the end of Day 6) is recorded in Matthew Chapter 13.

Jesus told His followers a parable about the Kingdom of God and how things would be in the world until the end of Day 6. In the parable, a man sowed good seed in his field. However, while everyone was asleep, his enemy came and sowed weeds in the field. When the wheat sprouted, the weeds also appeared. The owner's servants asked the man if he wanted the weeds pulled up. The owner told his servants to let them both grow together until the harvest; then at that time, they could pull up the weeds and burn them, and then gather the wheat and bring it into the barn.

Kingdom Come

Later Jesus explained the parable of the wheat and the weeds to His disciples. Jesus said that He is the one who sowed the good seed. His field is the world, and the good seeds are the sons of the Kingdom of God. The Devil is the enemy, and the weeds are the sons of the Devil. The harvest is at the end of the age, and the harvesters are the angels of God. At the end of Day 6, Christ will send out His angels, and they will weed out of His kingdom everything that causes sin and all who do evil. The sons of the Devil will be thrown into the fire, where there is weeping and gnashing of teeth, and the resurrected righteous will shine like the sun in the Kingdom of God.

It is important to understand the connection of the harvest, the gathering, and the resurrection to have a correct timeline of the Last Days events.

From Heaven and Earth

As you know, Jesus also described the harvest of His followers at the end of the age in the Olivet Discourse. He said that immediately after the Great Tribulation, the sun, the moon, and the stars will go dark and the heavenly bodies will be shaken. Jesus said then He will appear, coming on the clouds of the sky with power and great glory. He will send His angels with a loud trumpet call, and they will gather His followers, the dead from heaven and those left alive from the earth.

Let's summarize the sequence of events as given in the Olivet Discourse.

1. The Lord will appear in the clouds of the sky.
2. The Lord will send His angels with a trumpet call.
3. The dead in Christ will be gathered from heaven to meet Christ in the clouds of the sky (resurrection of the dead).
4. The living in Christ will be gathered from earth to meet Christ in the clouds (resurrection of the living—rapture).

Able to Say When

Although Scripture repeats the sequence of events in several passages, there is still confusion about the timing, especially the timing of the rapture of the living. Deception regarding the timing of the resurrection of the dead and the rapture of the living has existed since at least the time of the New Testament.

Paul, like Christ, warned Christ's followers not to be deceived about the doctrine of the resurrection. In his second letter to Timothy, Paul warned Timothy that some who had left the faith were teaching a nonscriptural timing for the resurrection and were destroying the faith of some. These false teachers were saying that the resurrection had already taken place, causing some to think they had missed the resurrection. According to Scripture, a correct understanding of the resurrection of the dead is very important to faith in Christ. In the New Testament, Hebrews Chapter 6, the "resurrection of the dead" is listed as one of the six *elementary teachings about Christ*.

def•i•ni•tion

The **elementary teachings about Christ** include six topics that are foundational to the Christian faith: repentance from acts that lead to death, faith in God, instruction about baptisms, laying on of hands, resurrection of the dead, and eternal judgment. These six doctrinal teachings are also called the "elementary truths of God's word" and spiritual milk (as opposed to solid food, which is for the mature).

Paul Knows When

Paul again addressed deception about the timing of the resurrection and rapture in his second letter to the Thessalonians. He warned Christ's followers very strongly against believing anything that did not agree with what Jesus taught about the resurrection. Paul reminded them that the Second Coming and resurrection will take place after the Antichrist is revealed.

As you know from earlier chapters, the Antichrist is revealed when he sets himself up in God's temple and proclaims himself to be God in the middle of the last seven years of Day 6.

Prophetic Pitfalls

Do not be deceived in any way. The Second Coming will not take place until after the abomination that causes desolation. The Antichrist must set himself up in God's temple, declaring that he himself is God, before Christ will return.

Jesus Knows When

Jesus also warned about the deception regarding the timing of His Second Coming and the resurrection. Like Paul, Jesus was very clear when He told His followers that His return would come after the Great Tribulation. Recall that Jesus said that everyone in the world will see Him appear like lightening in the clouds of the sky.

Jesus also connected His coming to the Day of the Lord. Jesus said that He would not return until after the darkening of the sun, the moon, and the stars. He warned His followers repeatedly to hang on until the end of the age (Day 6) and assured them that this is when they will be saved.

John Knows When

The Book of Revelation also tells us when the resurrection of believers will take place. In one of John's visions of the future, he saw those martyred for their faith during the Great Tribulation come to life to reign with Christ for 1,000 years, Day 7. John explained that these people will be killed during the Great Tribulation because they will refuse to receive the mark of the beast (Antichrist) or will refuse to worship the Antichrist. Once again, Scripture is clear that the resurrection will take place after the Great Tribulation.

John also explained that this resurrection of believers at the beginning of Day 7 will be the first resurrection. He said that the rest of the dead will not come to life until the 1,000 years are over. When the 1,000 years are over, the rest of the dead (those who were not followers of Christ when they died) will come to life in the second resurrection, and they will be judged. Anyone whose name is not written in the Book of Life will be thrown into the lake of eternal fire.

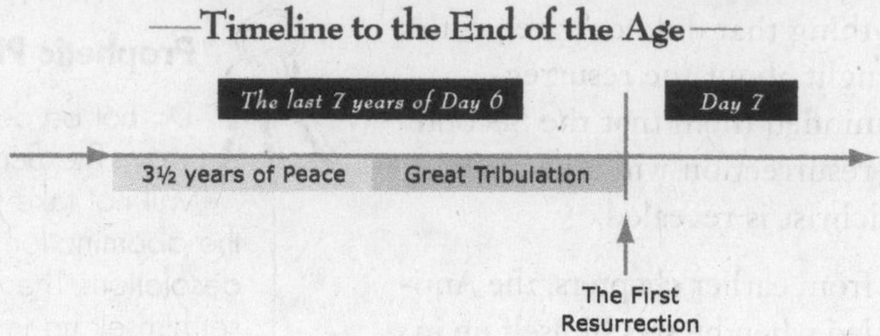

The Least You Need to Know

- Everyone who is to inherit the Kingdom of God must receive a spiritual body at the resurrection.
- Everyone in the Old Testament who put their faith in God will be resurrected from the dead at the time of the Second Coming.
- Those who put their faith in Jesus Christ and who die will be resurrected from the dead.
- Those who put their faith in Jesus Christ and remain alive until the Second Coming will be raptured and resurrected.
- The Bible places the resurrection of believers and the rapture as taking place immediately after the Great Tribulation, at the time of the Second Coming.

Chapter 19

The Royal Wedding Banquet

In This Chapter

- Planning a royal wedding
- Something about the bridegroom
- Something about the bride
- The wedding date

In this chapter, you learn more about how the Bible describes the coming together of Christ and His followers. One of the ways the Bible talks about the union between Christ and His followers is in terms of marriage. Jesus is the bridegroom, and the followers of Christ are the bride. Scripture portrays this union between Christ and His followers as taking place on the Day of the Lord, when Christ appears to gather His bride to Himself forever. One aspect of the marriage union is the wedding banquet or feast. In this chapter, we study this banquet and other details of the wedding.

The Wedding Plan

Not long after Christ appears and is united with His followers at the gathering and resurrection, He will hold a wedding banquet on Mount Zion in Jerusalem. Scripture describes Christ as the bridegroom and His followers as the bride. This wedding banquet will fulfill the prophecies about the Feast of Tabernacles. You learned about the Feast of Tabernacles in Chapter 3. The Feast of Tabernacles is described in the Old Testament and the New Testament; it is also called the Lord's Supper.

On Day 7, when the Kingdom of God has come, one of the first orders of business is the wedding banquet to celebrate the union between Christ and His bride. The "bride" is all human beings who have put their faith in the Lord God from the beginning of time.

To understand how the wedding banquet fits into the events of the Day of the Lord, let's see what the Bible says about it. As we consider each prophecy describing the wedding banquet, you will notice many other things that will be occurring during this time. Some of the things will sound very familiar because we have studied them in other aspects of the Day of the Lord. We are slowly bringing everything together so that we end with one big picture of how the Bible describes the Last Days. For example, you will again see references to the sun, moon, and stars going dark, which we know occurs before the Day of the Lord. You will also see references to the last trumpet call, which you know occurs on that day. The wedding banquet prophecies also touch on a battle and the pouring out of God's wrath. The Bible describes these two events as taking place after the banquet. We discuss the Final Battle in detail in the next chapter. Now let's go to the wedding banquet.

The Announcement

As usual, the Old Testament prophet Isaiah provides a comprehensive description of the wedding of the Lord to His bride. In the New Testament, we are told that part of Isaiah's prophecy was fulfilled by Christ during the time of His First Coming, at the beginning of Day 5. When Christ made the proclamation, He was essentially promising the future union with His followers.

— Last Days Timeline —

Day 1	Day 2	Day 3	Day 4	Day 5	Day 6	Day 7
1,000 years	2,000 years	3,000 years	4,000 years	5,000 years	6,000 years	7,000 years
Adam	Noah	Moses	David	Christ	Church	Kingdom

↑ Wedding Announcement (under Day 5)

The Bible tells us that the next part of Isaiah's prophecy will be fulfilled at Christ's Second Coming. Isaiah talks about the day of God's vengeance (the Day of the Lord) as a time when God will comfort those who mourn and grieve in Zion. We are told that God will bestow on Israel a crown of beauty, the oil of gladness, and a garment of praise. Apparently, this includes rebuilding Israel's ruins and her cities of old. There are also others to do the work. The prophecy says that foreigners will shepherd the flocks and work the fields and vineyards. God's people will be priests of the Lord and ministers of God. They will eat from the bounty of the nations.

The Wedding Gift

On the Day of the Lord, God's people will receive a double portion, and they will rejoice and be glad. When God's blessing is heaped on His bride, Isaiah says that Israel (the bride) will delight in the Lord (her bridegroom), clothed in garments of salvation and righteousness as a bride adorns herself with jewels and fine things. Clearly, his prophecy describes the restoration of Israel at the beginning of the age to come (Day 7) as starting with the union between the bride (spiritual Israel) and the bridegroom (Christ the Lord).

The Old Testament prophet Hosea also describes the Lord restoring everything to Israel at the time of the union between Israel and Himself. We also learn from Hosea's description that the whole earth will be restored at the same time Israel is restored. This is when there will be a new heaven and a new earth. Hosea also describes Israel's unfaithfulness to God. Let's examine how Hosea describes the breakup; then we talk about the beginning of the new relationship.

Hosea admonishes Israel for her unfaithfulness to God, describing her adultery as chasing after other lovers, those who give her what she thinks she needs. Because of her unfaithfulness, God is against her, and blocks her paths and causes her to lose her way. Hosea describes her as chasing after other lovers but not catching them; she looks for a way but does not find it. Basically, Hosea is saying that God's chosen people turned away from Him and to other gods and idols, and God is not happy about it.

Following this unfaithfulness we are told that Israel will attempt to turn back to God, thinking that she will be better off than she is now. However, she will not repent and acknowledge God. So God will punish her and expose her to the nations. God will stop her celebrations, her yearly festivals, her Sabbath days, and her appointed feasts. God will punish her for the days she chased after other gods.

In the end, though, the Lord will give Israel back her vineyards and make the Valley of Anchor a door of hope. The Valley of Anchor is thought to be a safe haven for Israel during the Great Tribulation. Some believe it to be the area of Petra inside Jordan. However, this is a theory without scriptural confirmation.

—Last Days Timeline—

Day 1	Day 2	Day 3	Day 4	Day 5	Day 6	Day 7
1,000 years	2,000 years	3,000 years	4,000 years	5,000 years	6,000 years	7,000 years
Adam	Noah	Moses	David	Christ	Church	Kingdom

Wedding

Following this, Hosea describes the marriage union. On the Day of the Lord, Israel will no longer call the Lord "My Master"; rather, Israel will call the Lord "My Husband." On that day, we are told that God will remove the name of the false Gods from her lips and make a new covenant with all of creation. On Day 7, bow, sword, and battle will be abolished from the land so that everyone will be able to lie down in safety. The Lord will marry Israel in righteousness and justice, in love and compassion. The Lord will marry her in faithfulness, and Israel will acknowledge the Lord.

The Menu

In Isaiah Chapter 25, we are told that the Lord Almighty will prepare a banquet of rich foods, the finest aged wines, and the best meats. Now, I feel certain that there will be comparably good stuff for the vegetarians and the teetotalers.

The Prophet Says

"Then he took the cup [of wine], gave thanks and offered it to them, and they all drank from it. 'This is my blood of the covenant, which is poured out for many,' he [Jesus] said to them. 'I tell you the truth, I will not drink again of the fruit of the vine until that day when I drink it anew in the kingdom of God.'" (Mark 14:23–25)

Earlier in this chapter, I told you that the wedding banquet fulfills New Testament prophecy regarding the Lord's Supper. When Jesus first celebrated the symbolic Lord's Supper with His disciples, He told them that He would not drink wine again until its fulfillment in the Kingdom of God. The wedding banquet on Mount Zion in Jerusalem will be that celebration. Jesus will have His first taste of wine, the finest of aged wines, at that banquet, after almost 2,000 years.

Now that we have a good idea of God's long-time planning for the wedding and banquet, let's look at some other passages that talk about the bridegroom.

The Bridegroom

Isaiah is the first prophet to refer to the Lord as the "bridegroom" of His people. Isaiah describes the union that will take place on Day 7 as the salvation of God's people and events of God's final plans for Israel. God says that He will not be silent until Israel's righteousness shines like the morning sun and her salvation is like a blazing fire. God declares that the nations will all see her righteousness and glory. The Lord says that Israel will be called by a new name, a name to be given by the Lord. Israel will be crowned with splendor and will be the pride of the nations.

Isaiah goes on to say that Israel will no longer be called deserted or desolate, but she will be a delight to the Lord and He will marry her.

Waiting on the Groom

The Bible portrays God as eagerly anticipating this wedding. God says that He has posted watchmen for Jerusalem and that they will be vigilant day and night. God says His followers should call on Him, give the bridegroom no rest, and take no rest until He marries His bride and makes Israel the praise of the nations. After the wedding, Israel will eat her own grain and drink her own wine; never again will she plant and see others eat the fruit of her labor.

When the Lord passes through the gate of His temple, he will be preparing a way for His people. The Bible describes the Lord as a banner for the nations and says He will save His people. He will bring His reward for His people with Him; salvation will

> **The Prophet Says**
>
> "Jesus answered, 'How can the guests of the bridegroom mourn while he is with them? The time will come when the bridegroom will be taken from them; then they will fast.'" (Matthew 9:15)

accompany Him. His people will be redeemed and thereafter be highly esteemed by the nations.

The Groom Calls

Joel, like Isaiah, envisioned God's people waiting for the groom. He also called for the sounding of the trumpet and a sacred assembly. Joel said to prepare by gathering the people, consecrating the assembly, and gathering the children because the bridegroom will leave His dwelling and the bride her chamber.

In addition to the Old Testament references to the coming wedding and the bridegroom, Jesus referred to Himself as the bridegroom when speaking to John's disciples. Jesus told them that the guests of the bridegroom should not mourn when He is with them. Then He said that the time will come when the bridegroom will be taken from them and then they will fast, to indicate that He would be leaving them and returning to heaven and then they would fast.

The Bride

In Paul's letter to the Ephesians, he explains that the relationship of Christ and His followers is like that of husband and wife. Paul says that as the husband is head of the wife, Christ is the head of the church. Just as when a man is united to his wife the two become one flesh, Paul says that the relationship of Christ and the Church is a profound mystery. He says that when Christ and His wife are united, they will become one in spirit.

Israel

This scriptural mystery of the union between Christ and His bride was first described in the Old Testament. Isaiah includes a couple of prophecies that describe the Lord God as the husband and Israel His wife. In one prophecy, Isaiah describes Israel like a wife who married young, only to be rejected and abandoned for a time. In anger God will turn away from her for a time, but then with eternal kindness He will have compassion on her.

The Prophet Says

John the Baptist said, "You yourselves can testify that I said, 'I am not the Christ but am sent ahead of him.' The bride belongs to the bridegroom. The friend who attends the bridegroom waits and listens for him, and is full of joy when he hears the bridegroom's voice." (John 3:28–29)

Once they are reunited, God declares His unfailing love for Israel. His bond will not be shaken, nor His covenant removed. Even though Jerusalem is an afflicted city, God will adorn her with precious jewels and make her gates and walls of precious stones.

This prophecy is echoed in the Book of Revelation Chapter 21. John sees a future vision of new Jerusalem, the bride of Christ, coming down from heaven beautifully dressed for her husband. Then John hears a voice from the throne saying, "Now the dwelling of God is with men, and he will live with them. They will be his people, and God himself will be with them and be their God." John also sees the bride and describes her in more detail.

Radiant Bride

Then an angel said to John, "Come, I will show you the bride, the wife of the Lamb." The angel showed John the Holy City of Jerusalem coming down from heaven. It is described as shining with the glory of God. Its brilliance is said to be like that of precious jewels and like jasper, clear as crystal. On its gates were written the 12 tribes of Israel, and on the foundation were written the 12 apostles of Christ. The city was made of pure gold, as pure as glass, and the foundations were decorated with all kinds of precious stones. The 12 gates to the city were made of 12 pearls.

Revelation Chapter 19 also depicts the wedding banquet, and here the bride is referred to as the "*Great Multitude.*" As John indicates, the Lord has begun to reign, and the Great Multitude roars from Mount Zion, the scene of the banquet. They declare that the Lord God Almighty reigns, as they rejoice in gladness. The time for the wedding banquet has come, and John says the bride will wear fine linen, white and clean. White linen stands for the righteous acts of the saints of God.

Now that we have studied how Scripture describes the bride and groom, let's see what else the wedding passages tell us about the Last Day, Day 7.

def•i•ni•tion

The **Great Multitude** is mentioned in Scripture only by the prophets Isaiah and John. It appears from Scripture that the Great Multitude is with Christ at the time He establishes the Kingdom of God on earth. This means that the Great Multitude is most likely the bride, who is with the bridegroom at the wedding banquet on Mount Zion.

Invitations

Jesus often taught about the Kingdom of God in terms of a wedding banquet. Let's examine some of Jesus' parables to understand more about this aspect of the coming Kingdom of God on earth.

In Matthew Chapter 22, one of Jesus' parables says that the Kingdom of God is like a king who prepared a wedding banquet for his son. The king in this parable is God the Father, and the son is Christ. God sent the prophets to issue the invitation, but the people refused to come. Then God tried again to get them to come, telling them that the banquet was prepared and everything was ready. But still they paid no attention and continued on their own way. Some even seized God's prophets and messengers, and mistreated and killed them.

The Bible tells us that God wants His banquet to be full, and He extends His invitations to everyone—but as we will see, not everyone accepts His invitation. Next, we will see that only those who accept receive proper wedding attire.

Proper Attire Required

God was enraged and sent His army, destroying those murderers and burning their city. Then God sent more prophets and messengers because those who had originally been invited did not accept the invitation. God sent His servants out to invite anyone they could find. They went out and invited all they could find, and the wedding banquet and the wedding hall were filled. Only those who accepted the invitation will be chosen. They will receive proper wedding clothes and be received into the banquet; all others will be thrown out into the darkness, where there will be weeping and gnashing of teeth. God said, "For many are invited, but few are chosen."

We find this theme of God extending invitations to everyone repeated throughout Scripture, but as we also see, there appear to be few RSVPs.

The Prophet Says

Jesus said, "But when the king came in to see the guests, he noticed a man there who was not wearing wedding clothes. 'Friend,' he asked, 'how did you get in here without wedding clothes?' The man was speechless. Then the king told the attendants, 'Tie him hand and foot, and throw him outside, into the darkness, where there will be weeping and gnashing of teeth.' For many are invited, but few are chosen." (Matthew 22:11–14)

RSVP

One of Jesus' recurring topics regarding the Kingdom of God was who would be worthy to be admitted to the banquet. The Bible tells us that someone once said to Jesus, "Blessed is the man who will eat at the feast in the Kingdom of God." Jesus responded with a story. He said that a man (God) was preparing a great banquet and had invited many guests. At the time of the banquet, He sent His servants to tell all those who had been invited to come. But they all excused themselves, saying that they had their own things to do. When the servant reported this to God, He became very angry and ordered His servants to go out into the streets and alleys, and bring in the poor, crippled, blind, and lame. When this had been done, there was still room, so God sent His servants out to invite more people. In His anger, God said that none of those who had turned down His invitation would taste of the banquet.

The Bible indicates that there will be some who are expected to be at the banquet but will not be granted entrance. The Bible sets a high standard for Christ's followers which involves belief in God and obedience through faith.

On one occasion, someone asked Jesus, "Lord, are only a few people going to be saved?" Jesus responded by saying that the road to the kingdom was a narrow way, but it was worth the effort. He went on to say that many will try to enter on that day, but only a few will be admitted. He said when the door to the banquet closes, there will still be many who will stand outside knocking and pleading to get in, but they will not be admitted. Then the bridegroom will say to them, "I don't know you or where you come from." They will insist that they know Him, saying that He had broken bread with them, drank wine with them, and taught in their towns. Again he will deny that he knows them, and they will not enter the banquet. Then they will weep and gnash their teeth outside the Kingdom of God.

Inside, Jesus said they will see Abraham, Isaac, and Jacob, and all the prophets. People will come from the east, west, north, and south, and take their places at the wedding feast in the Kingdom of God, but some who should have entered the kingdom will be thrown out.

Groom Comes Quickly

Another aspect of the wedding banquet is the bride's state of readiness for the bridegroom's return. Whenever Jesus taught about His return, He emphasized the need for His bride to stay awake and to keep watch. It appears from Scripture that one reason He did this is because His return will come very quickly. In several scriptural accounts regarding the wedding banquet, we find an indication that His return will be quick. Let's see how this is described.

The prophet Isaiah describes the Lord appearing quickly, breaking forth like the dawn, bringing salvation to Israel and protecting her at the time of His appearing. Isaiah said Israel will call on the Lord, and He will respond to her cry for help. Isaiah's prophecy about the Lord's appearing quickly mentions the wedding feast on the heights of Israel. Like Jesus' description of the wedding banquet, Isaiah mentions that the patriarch Jacob will be at the feast. Also like Christ, Isaiah tells the people that they must respond to God by keeping the Sabbath and not doing what they please on God's holy day. If they call the Sabbath a delight and honor it by not going their own way, they will receive their inheritance. The Bible tells us what God expects from those who will make it into the banquet. They will be ready and they will keep His day holy.

We can see that Scripture indicates that a lot of planning has gone into this wedding banquet. But what would a great wedding banquet be without a suitable location? So where will the wedding banquet be held? Let's see what Scripture has to say.

Location, Location, Location

Some confusion exists about the location of the wedding banquet. Some people think it is in heaven. I have told you it will be on Mount Zion. But what does the Bible say?

Whenever Jesus described the wedding feast to His audience, He invariably described it using earthly terms. This was true when He mentioned things related to the venue of the banquet as well as its menu. Let's take a look at how Jesus described the wedding banquet.

On Earth

Jesus often mentioned the banquet when teaching about the coming Kingdom of God. Here are some of His quotes.

Jesus described the wedding banquet by saying that the banquet was ready: "My oxen and fattened cattle have been butchered, and everything is ready. Come to the wedding banquet." (Matthew 22:4) When Jesus was sharing His Last Supper with His disciples and had taken His last sip of wine, He said, "I will not drink again of the fruit of the vine until the kingdom of God comes." (Luke 22:18) He included earth's livestock and vegetation as part of the menu.

Each of Jesus' accounts of the wedding feast creates the perception that the banquet will feature earthly delights and will be held on earth. An account of the feast from Isaiah also specifically tells us the location of the wedding feast. Let's see what Isaiah has to say about this.

Mount Zion, Jerusalem

In Isaiah Chapters 24 and 25, Isaiah describes events related to the Day of the Lord that will occur in Jerusalem and on Mount Zion. Isaiah says that the Lord Almighty will prepare a great feast of rich foods and the finest aged wines for a banquet on Mount Zion. At the time of the banquet, Isaiah says, God will swallow up death forever. The Sovereign Lord will wipe away the tears from His people and remove their disgrace, and the people will rejoice.

Based on the scriptural record, *Mount Zion* is God's holy hill and Jerusalem is His holy city. In biblical terms, there is no more holy place on earth. Therefore, the location of the wedding banquet is Mount Zion, Jerusalem, Israel.

The Wedding Date

Basically, we have now discussed the "who," the "what," and the "where" of the wedding banquet. To complete our examination, let's look more closely at the "when" of the wedding banquet.

We already know the sequence of events that indicate when the wedding date will be near. We also know that the union between Christ and His followers will take place when Christ appears from heaven, and that the wedding banquet will follow.

Even with what we already know, the Bible indicates that Christ's followers will need to know still more to be ready and able to enter the banquet. Once again, let's see what Scripture tells us about the wedding date.

Not Before It's Time

As we have already seen from the Bible, God has been planning this wedding and banquet for some time. He has set the appointed time in His weekly calendar and in His annual feasts. Scripture also indicates that the exact date of this event has been long established, even though God has chosen not to reveal it.

We already know, from Scripture, that the wedding and the wedding banquet will take place as the Kingdom of God arrives on earth. Therefore, when people were looking for the Kingdom of God to come at the First Coming, they were, in effect, looking for the wedding and the wedding banquet.

Jesus knew that His kingdom would not come into being during His First Coming. He consistently pointed His followers to the end of the age when He spoke and taught on the coming kingdom and the wedding banquet.

During Christ's First Advent, several times people tried to get Christ to usher in the kingdom. But each time He refused and resisted. However, Scripture indicates that Christ will not always resist. When the appointed time arrives, He will take concerted action to accomplish all that has been planned. Now let's take a close look at what the Bible says about that time and what Christ's followers must do to be ready.

Ready or Not

Jesus gave a very strong message to His followers in His Olivet Discourse about their need to stay awake and be watchful. In this parable, He once again described His relationship with His followers in terms of a marriage and a wedding banquet. In the parable, He described how the people will be at the time of the Second Coming. Jesus said the Kingdom of God will be like 10 virgins who went out to meet the bridegroom when He returned. Five were foolish and five were wise. The wise virgins were prepared when the bridegroom arrived. The foolish virgins were not prepared and were caught off guard with the rest of the world.

Prophetic Pitfalls

Jesus instructed His followers to always stay awake and keep watch for the signs of His return. He also indicated that all 10 virgins (His potential brides) would be asleep until the watchman sounded the warning of Christ's return. He told them to stay awake, yet they had fallen asleep. Jesus also said, "But if you do not wake up, I will come like a thief, and you will not know at what time I will come to you." (Revelation 3:3)

Jesus said that the bridegroom was a long time in coming, and all 10 virgins fell asleep, the foolish as well as the wise. When the watchman's call rang out that the bridegroom was coming, they all woke up and got ready for His arrival. The foolish virgins asked the wise virgins for help in getting ready, but there was not enough time for the foolish virgins. While the foolish virgins were still trying to get ready for the bridegroom, He arrived. The wise virgins, who were ready, went in with Him to the wedding banquet, and the door was shut. Later, when the foolish virgins came, they said, "Open the door for us." But the bridegroom said, "I tell you the truth, I don't know you," and they were left outside the banquet, where there was weeping and gnashing of teeth.

Jesus' message seems clear. Not everyone who thinks they are ready for His return and the wedding banquet will be. This brings us to our next topic. What does Jesus say is required of His followers for them to be ready for His return and the wedding banquet? Let's see what He says.

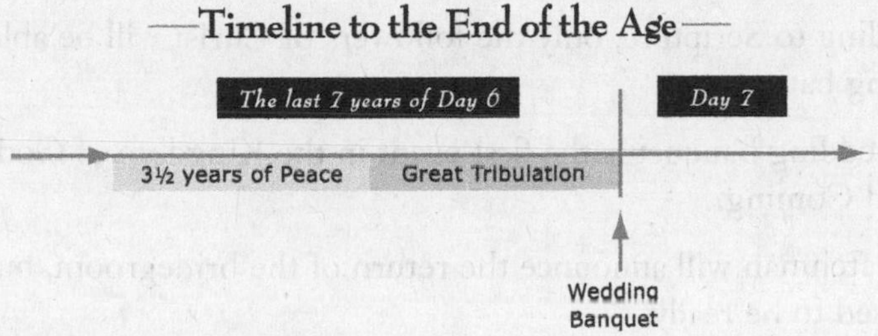

Watching and Waiting

Jesus repeatedly warns His followers to stay spiritually awake and keep watch for His Second Coming. He says that if they stay awake, the Day of the Lord will not surprise them, as it will the rest of the world. As a matter of fact, Jesus seemed very intent that His followers understand this warning because He ended many of His messages regarding His Second Coming with, "Keep watch."

Not only did Jesus tell His followers to keep watch, but He also described in detail just what they were to be watching for. The Bible tells His followers what to watch for, and we have discussed that already. Now let's see what Jesus said about watchfulness.

On one occasion, Jesus instructed His followers to remain spiritually alert so that they would not be caught off guard by His quick return. Jesus told them to be ready so that when He comes, they can immediately open the door for Him. He cautioned them that it will be good for them to be found watching when He returns. Jesus said He will have the followers who are ready recline at the banquet table, and He will come and wait on them. Jesus warned His followers that they must be ready, and He told them to keep watch!

This union of the bridegroom and bride leads quickly to the wedding banquet on Mount Zion in Jerusalem. Following the wedding banquet, the groom will leave the banquet to fight for His bride in what I call the Final Battle, discussed in the next chapter.

The Least You Need to Know

- Following the union between Christ and His bride, there will be a wedding banquet.
- According to Scripture, only the followers of Christ will be able to enter the wedding banquet.
- The wedding banquet is the first event in the Kingdom of God following the Second Coming.
- The watchman will announce the return of the bridegroom, but the bride is supposed to be ready.

Chapter 20

The Final Battle

In This Chapter

- Preparing for battle
- Where the Final Battle will be fought
- The prophets describe the Final Battle
- Israel is restored once and for all

In this chapter, we discuss the Final Battle, often called the Battle of Armageddon. Scripture tells us many things about the Final Battle, including that it is not at Armageddon, but at Jerusalem.

Before the Battle

In the last four chapters, we talked about several aspects of the transition from Day 6 into Day 7. We discussed the Day of the Lord, the Second Coming, the resurrection and rapture, and the wedding banquet. Now we discuss one of the final transitional events, the *Final Battle*.

The Final Battle will take place in the Kidron Valley, located in Israel between Jerusalem and the Mount of Olives. According to Scripture, the Antichrist and his armies will muster their forces at Armageddon, which is north of Jerusalem, and then will move to attack Jerusalem. Christ and His supernatural army from heaven will slaughter the armies of the Antichrist just outside of Jerusalem in the bloodiest battle of all time.

We have discussed many momentous events that the Bible says will take place on earth and in heaven during the transition from the end of Day 6 to the beginning of Day 7. Prophetic scriptural accounts allow us to determine the basic sequence of events during the transition and the Final Battle. However, even though there are many prophecies about the Final Battle, it is very challenging to sort out exactly when things happen. We have already seen how biblical prophecies move back and forth in time, like flashbacks in a movie. The prophecies relating to the Final Battle also follow this pattern. Complicating things further is the fact that many things are prophesied to occur in this short period of time.

However, we should be encouraged by two things. First, Scripture and history tell us that biblical prophecy is fulfilled in just the way it was predicted. Second, the Bible states that we are supposed to be able to read and understand what is written in the Bible. With these assurances, we will begin our examination of the Final Battle and try to figure out what will take place and when.

As I have already mentioned, the Final Battle will take place at the beginning of the Day of the Lord, Day 7. Previous chapters discussed how the Antichrist and his armies will come against Jerusalem three and a half years earlier, at the beginning of the Great Tribulation. During the three and a half years of the Great Tribulation, Jerusalem and Israel will be severely beaten down and ravaged by the Antichrist.

—Last Days Timeline—

Day 1	*Day 2*	*Day 3*	*Day 4*	*Day 5*	*Day 6*	*Day 7*
1,000 years	2,000 years	3,000 years	4,000 years	5,000 years	6,000 years	7,000 years
Adam	Noah	Moses	David	Christ	Church	Kingdom

↑ Final Battle

From the last few chapters, we know that the return of Christ (the Messiah), the gathering and resurrection of Christ's followers, and the wedding banquet will all take place at the very beginning of the Day of the Lord, Day 7. As I previously mentioned, these are transitional events as the world leaves Day 6 and enters Day 7, God's

Sabbath rest, also known as the Kingdom of God. The Final Battle is the last major transitional event.

Leading up to the Day of the Lord, we have seen that the Bible says that the superpower, Mystery Babylon the Great, is destroyed and that much of the world's population is killed by war, famine, and plague. Recall also that the wrath of God, which is contained in the seven bowls described in Revelation, is being poured out on the world. The nations that have survived to this time are in great turmoil from the wrath poured out on them by the God of Israel. It also appears, according to what is revealed by the prophets, that the God of Israel has returned to Jerusalem, and the whole world knows it. As we have already discussed, Scripture states that every eye will see the return of Jesus Christ. Christ is on Mount Zion with His bride celebrating the wedding banquet, which is also called the Feast of Tabernacles. It is time for the Final Battle.

Gathering for Battle

The world stage is set, and Jerusalem is center stage. For the past three and a half years, the Antichrist and the False Prophet have reigned supreme over the nations of the world. The God of the Bible has used the Antichrist to punish His people for their disobedience and unbelief, but that is all about to change. God has stopped punishing Israel, and He is about to turn His wrath on the Antichrist and all the nations that are aligned with him.

Let's review a little from previous discussions about this time and the Antichrist and the False Prophet. Just before their capture and destruction on the day of battle, demon spirits go out from them to the kings of the nations to gather the kings and their armies for the Final Battle. It appears that the Antichrist and the False Prophet, with their demon spirits, are behind a conspiracy among the nations to totally destroy, once and for all, the nation of Israel and take the world from the God of Israel. This plot and conspiracy are mentioned in some of the prophecies that we examine shortly.

The Prophet Says

The Psalmists say, "The One enthroned in heaven laughs; the Lord scoffs at them. Then he rebukes them in his anger and terrifies them in his wrath, saying, 'I have installed my King on Zion, my holy hill.'" (Psalms 2:4–6)

We learned from the Book of Revelation that the kings and their armies will be gathered in a place called Armageddon, a large plain northwest of Jerusalem. It seems like a perfect place to amass a great number of armies if your plan is to attack Jerusalem. Let's see what John says about this.

Across the Euphrates

John says that the great river Euphrates will dry up so that the kings east of Jerusalem can come quickly and gather at Armageddon. This is not a new idea. Isaiah described this occurrence thousands of years before. In Isaiah Chapter 11, Isaiah wrote about the Day of the Lord and said that God will dry up the Euphrates River with a scorching wind so that men can cross it on foot. Now let's learn more from the prophets about how the nations are gathered for the Final Battle against Jerusalem.

> **The Prophet Says**
>
> "The Lord Almighty has sworn, 'Surely, as I have planned, so it will be, and as I have purposed, so it will stand. I will crush the Assyrian in my land; on my mountains I will trample him down. His yoke will be taken from my people, and his burden removed from their shoulders.' This is the plan determined for the whole world; this is the hand stretched out over all nations." (Isaiah 14:24–26)

The Psalmists prophesied about the Final Battle between the Messiah and the kings of the earth. In Psalm 2, the nations are seen plotting and conspiring to take their stand against God's Anointed One. The nations want to free themselves from God, but the Lord laughs at them. He rebukes them in His anger and terrifies them with His wrath.

In Psalm 83, the prophet writes that God's enemies will conspire with cunning against God's people. His enemies say they will destroy Israel so they will be remembered no more. They plot together and form an alliance of Middle Eastern nations. But God will not be silent; He will not stand still. He will make them like a tumbleweed; fire will burn them like a forest ablaze. The nations will be consumed in His tempest and terrifying storm.

The prophet Joel describes the Lord as a jealous bridegroom coming from His room to take pity on Israel as His bride. Joel sees Israel leaving her chamber to be gathered by God for a sacred assembly. Joel says that never again will God's people be an object of scorn among the nations. God will ensure that His enemies know that the Lord is in Israel and that He is God.

Valley of Decision

The Messiah will lead the mighty army of supernatural warriors into the Final Battle against the nations. Joel says that the nations will be in anguish and that every face will turn pale at the sight of the Lord's army. At that time, the Lord will gather all the nations at Armageddon and bring them down to the Valley of Jehoshaphat, at Jerusalem. There the Lord will enter into judgment against them.

Prophetic Pitfalls

In Revelation, we are told that the kings of the whole world are gathered to a place called Armageddon for a battle. The passage does not say that the battle is in Armageddon. This is in keeping with traditional warfare—armies usually gather one place and then advance to the battlefield. Scripture indicates that the kings will attack Jerusalem and that the nations will be slaughtered in the Valley of Jehoshaphat at Jerusalem.

Similar to the other prophets, Joel describes the nations gathering their warriors and fighting men to attack. He says that all the nations will come quickly from every side and assemble at Armageddon. They will advance from there into the Valley of Jehoshaphat, where the Lord will engage them in battle. The Lord will swing His sickle and trample the grapes in the winepress of His wrath. Great is their wickedness, Joel writes: "Multitudes, multitudes in the valley of decision!" Joel describes the great wickedness of the enemy and concludes by referring to this final battle in the Valley of Jehoshaphat as the valley of decision.

We have now read of the same descriptions and sequence of events coming from several different prophets. Once again, the Bible repeats itself to emphasize key prophecies. From the prophets, we know that the armies of the nations will conspire to destroy Israel and free themselves from the God of Israel once and for all. The kings will gather their mighty armies at the plain of Armageddon and then advance to Jerusalem for the Final Battle. This battle will be in the Valley of Jehoshaphat, also known as the Kidron Valley, at Jerusalem.

The Prophet Says

"Multitudes, multitudes in the valley of decision! For the day of the Lord is near in the valley of decision. The sun and moon will be darkened, and the stars no longer shine. The Lord will roar from Zion and thunder from Jerusalem; the earth and the sky will tremble." (Joel 3:14–16)

When the armies of the nations arrive at Jerusalem, the final, winner-take-all battle will be fought.

The Army of the Lord

The Bible tells us that the Lord's army is composed of mighty warrior angels. Well, nobody said this was going to be a fair fight. Many prophecies about this battle give us a glimpse of the Lord's army, but the prophet Joel gives us the most comprehensive description.

The prophet Joel writes of a vision of the army of the Lord coming with Christ as He returns from heaven to earth. Joel describes the mightiest army of warriors the world has ever seen. They approach out of darkness, advancing in the brightness of their presence. He says they will come sweeping over the land, leaving devastation in their path. The nations tremble in fear, nothing stands in their way as they cut through the defenses in pursuit of victory. The earth shakes as the Lord thunders at the head of His mighty army.

> **The Prophet Says**
>
> "I have commanded my holy ones; I have summoned my warriors to carry out my wrath—those who rejoice in my triumph. Listen, a noise on the mountains, like that of a great multitude!" (Isaiah 13:3–4)

Joel describes a well-organized, highly disciplined, and powerful army. Now that we know something about both sides, let's learn a little more about the battle.

Battle for Earth

The Old Testament provides the greatest amount of prophetic information about the Final Battle. As usual, we examine Scripture to get the clearest picture that we can of this future conflict between the Messiah and His army, and the Antichrist and his armies.

So prolific are the prophets of the Old Testament about the Final Battle that cinematographers would have a relatively easy time choreographing the Final Battle scenes.

A Great Multitude

Isaiah, in Chapter 13, tells of the time after the Messiah has returned, gathered His people, and prepared a wedding feast on Mount Zion. They are gathered on Mount Zion to celebrate as the Lord prepares to carry out His wrath on the nations. The

Lord tells that He has commanded His holy angels and summoned His mighty warriors to carry out His wrath on the nations. As the Lord tells them His plan, His followers give a great cheer as they rejoice in His triumph.

Then Isaiah sees that the kings of the world will have met together in Armageddon and the Lord has summoned His army of mighty warriors for battle. Isaiah writes of the coming destruction and says that the whole world will be shaken, all hands will go limp, and every man's heart will melt with fear.

From Zion

The Lord will roar from Zion and thunder from Jerusalem; the earth and the sky will tremble, and He will bring down His warriors and protect Jerusalem.

In Psalm 110, David's prophecy, consistent with the other prophecies we have studied, seems to indicate that the Final Battle will take place after the Lord has returned to earth. David describes the Lord as extending His scepter from Zion and says the Lord will rule in the midst of His enemies. The Lord's troops will be ready for battle and arrayed in majesty. The Lord will crush the kings of the earth, judge the nations, and pile up the dead.

Like David, Isaiah gives us a good description of the battle. He says that the Lord will come as a devouring fire with thunder, a great earthquake, and great noise. This is what the nations that fight against Mount Zion will be facing. The sword of the Lord will shatter Assyria (Iraq and Iran) and He will strike them down. Isaiah sees the Lord Almighty come down and do battle on Mount Zion. The Lord will shield Jerusalem and rescue her from the nations. The nation of the Antichrist will fall by the sword; a sword not of mortals will devour them.

In Isaiah Chapter 34, the prophet warns the nations of the world to listen and pay attention. He says they should take notice of what is coming. Isaiah explains that the Lord Almighty is angry with them and there will be grave consequences for what they plan to do. God's wrath will be poured out on their armies and they will be totally destroyed. Isaiah describes the slaughter that will take place on that day. He says that the mountains will be covered with blood and the dead bodies will stink.

The returning Messiah is described by Isaiah as carrying a sword for battle. We find this same picture in Jeremiah and Revelation. Isaiah says the Lord's sword will drink its fill and the people will be totally destroyed. His sword is bathed in blood, for the slaughter is great east of Jerusalem. Isaiah says that this is the day of vengeance of the Lord, the year of retribution, to deliver Zion and establish God's kingdom on earth.

Now let's see how Jeremiah described the battle. Though these prophecies are often repetitive, it helps you get an idea of how often the Bible speaks of this bloody final battle.

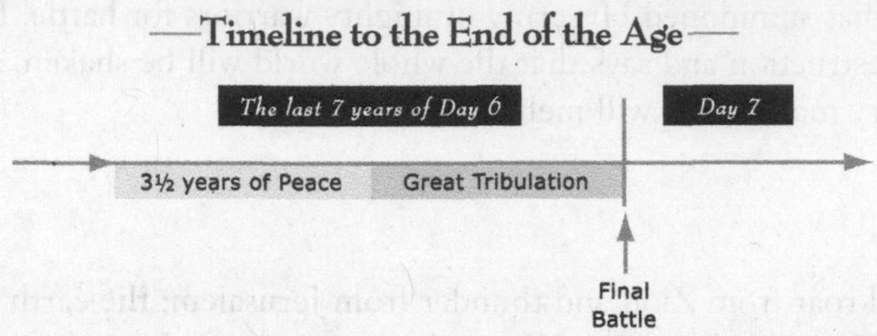

In Jeremiah's prophecy, he first refers to the Great Tribulation, the time of Jerusalem's punishment, and then he describes God turning His wrath on the nations. The Lord will call down a sword on everyone who lives on the earth. He will thunder from His holy dwelling against those who live on the earth like one treading grapes in the winepress. The tumult will resound to the ends of the earth. The Lord will bring judgment on all mankind and put the wicked to the sword. Those slain by the Lord will be everywhere—from one end of the earth to the other. The bodies of the slain will not be gathered or burned; rather, they will be like refuse on the ground.

Grapes of Wrath

John's visions in the Book of Revelation echo the prophecies of the Old Testament. John looked and saw the Lord seated on a white cloud with a crown of gold on His head and a sharp sickle in His hand. The Lord took His sickle and swung it over the earth, and the earth was harvested. Then an angel, who also had a sharp sickle, came out of heaven and swung his sickle over the earth and gathered the grapes and threw them into the great winepress of God's wrath. They were trampled in the winepress outside Jerusalem, and their blood rose as high as a horse's bridle.

Isaiah says the Lord's garments will be stained red. He says that the Lord has trodden the winepress alone, in His anger, and trod His enemies down so that their blood splattered His garments and stained His clothing.

Clean-Up Crew

In Revelation Chapter 19, John describes a white horse whose rider is called "Faithful and True" (Christ). Christ is dressed in a robe that appears to have been dipped in blood. Following Christ into battle are the mighty armies of heaven riding on white horses and dressed in white linen. In this vision, John also sees the Antichrist, the kings of the earth, and their armies ready to make war against Christ and His army. But the Antichrist and the False Prophet are captured and thrown into the lake of burning fire. The rest of the enemies are killed with the sword of the Lord. The Lord treads the winepress of the fury of the wrath of Almighty God. Then an angel cries out in a loud voice to all the birds to come and feast on the flesh of kings, generals, and mighty men—the flesh of all people, free and slave, great and small. Then all the birds gorge themselves on the flesh.

Isaiah also mentions the clean-up crew. He says that wild birds will feed on the bodies of the nation's fallen armies. On the mountains of Israel, the harvest will take place and the bodies will be left to the birds of prey and to the wild animals. Birds will feed on their bodies all summer and the wild animals all winter.

The Prophet Says

"This is what the Lord Almighty says: 'Look! Disaster is spreading from nation to nation; a mighty storm is rising from the ends of the earth.' At that time those slain by the Lord will be everywhere—from one end of the earth to the other. They will not be mourned or gathered up or buried, but will be like refuse lying on the ground." (Jeremiah 25:32–33)

The Prophet Says

"See, the Lord is going to lay waste the earth and devastate it; ... The earth will be completely laid waste and totally plundered. The Lord has spoken this word .... The earth is defiled by its people; they have disobeyed the laws, violated the statutes, and broken the everlasting covenant. Therefore, a curse consumes the earth; its people must bear their guilt. Therefore, earth's inhabitants are burned up, and very few are left." (Isaiah 24:1–6)

Ezekiel also describes the sword of the Lord coming against the Antichrist and his armies on the mountains of Israel. He says that God's judgment will cause every man's sword to turn against his brother and the bloodshed will be great. Ezekiel also sees

God pouring down torrents of rain, hailstones, and burning sulfur on the Antichrist and the nations with him. At that time God will show His greatness to the nations, and they will know that He is the Lord.

On more than one occasion, Ezekiel prophesied that the Lord will bring the Antichrist against Israel. But then after the punishment of Israel, the Lord will strike the weapons from the Antichrist on the mountains of Israel, and the nations with him will fall in the open field. At that time, their bodies will be given as food to the birds and wild animals as a feast. No longer will God's holy name be profaned; the nations will know the Lord, the Holy One of Israel.

Vultures Will Gather

Ezekiel repeats this same message over and over. I guess God believes His people need the repetition to get the picture. In the third prophecy on the topic, Ezekiel says the Lord will give the Antichrist and his armies a burial place in Israel. Ezekiel repeats that the Lord will slaughter the armies of the nations as a sacrifice, and the birds and wild animals will feed on them. The Lord will summon every kind of bird and wild animal to the mountains of Israel. There the Lord will give the birds a feast to eat, the flesh of mighty men and soldiers and the blood of princes to drink. The Lord will display His glory, and all the nations will see the punishment He inflicts on His enemies.

The description of the outcome of the battle is not unique to Revelation and the Old Testament prophets. In fact, when Jesus was teaching about His return, He also mentioned the clean-up crew. In the Olivet Discourse, Jesus said where there is a body, there the vultures will gather. Of course, those familiar with the Old Testament would have known that He was referring to the aftermath of the Final Battle over Jerusalem.

Let's list the key events we have seen so far, in chronological order.

1. The Lord will appear with His mighty angels.
2. The people of God will be gathered.
3. The heavens and the earth will be shaken.
4. The Lord will stand on the Mount of Olives.
6. The wedding banquet will be held on Mount Zion.
7. The Lord will go out to fight the nations.
8. The nation's armies will be slaughtered at Jerusalem.
9. Birds of the air will feast on the dead bodies.

Now that we have a good picture of what the Bible says will take place in Jerusalem, we need to consider what comes next. The prophets describe the Final Battle as being carried by the Lord from Jerusalem to the whole world. The wrath of God is not restricted to the territory of Israel. Let's see what the prophets say.

A Consuming Fire

It appears that after the battle in Jerusalem, the Lord goes first to the nations of the east that fought against Jerusalem. The Old Testament prophet Zechariah says the Lord will go out from Jerusalem and fight against those nations on the day of battle and will strike all the nations that fought against Jerusalem with a plague. Their flesh will rot while they are still standing, their eyes will rot in their sockets, and their tongues will rot in their mouths. We are also told again that men will be stricken by the Lord with great panic and they will attack each other.

Isaiah also describes the battle being carried to the nations of the Antichrist, those who fought against God's people. In Isaiah Chapter 10, the prophet describes what will happen to the armies of the Antichrist. The Lord will send a wasting disease on the Antichrist's sturdy warriors. As we know, the Lord will be like a blazing fire, and He will consume His enemies and the foes of Israel. The splendor of the Antichrist's forests and fields will be laid waste and completely destroyed. A few people will survive, but so few that a child will be able to count them.

The Prophet Says

"I will display my glory among the nations, and all the nations will see the punishment I inflict and the hand I lay upon them. From that day forward, the house of Israel will know that I am the Lord their God." (Ezekiel 39:21–22)

His Burning Anger

The Bible is very clear that God is angry and administering justice. The Bible says that on that day, the Lord will punish the world for its evil and the wicked for their sins. He will put an end to arrogance and humble the proud. Man will become scarcer than pure gold. At that time, the heavens will tremble and the earth will be shaken from its place at the wrath of the Lord Almighty in the day of His burning anger.

Again in Isaiah Chapter 14, the Lord declares that He will rise up against Babylon (present-day Iraq) and cut off her descendants. He will turn her into a place for owls and sweep her with the broom of His destruction.

The Prophet Says

Isaiah wrote, "For the day of vengeance was in my heart, and the year of my redemption has come. I looked, but there was no one to help, I was appalled that no one gave support; so my own arm worked salvation for me, and my own wrath sustained me. I trampled the nations in my anger; in my wrath I made them drunk and poured their blood on the ground." (Isaiah 63:4–6)

Everlasting Covenant

In Isaiah Chapter 24, the prophet continues his description of this time of God's wrath. He says the Lord will lay waste to the whole earth and devastate it. On that day, He will scatter its inhabitants with impartiality; it will be the same for everyone, regardless of their standing. The earth will be completely laid waste and dried up. Isaiah says the earth has been defiled by its people. They have disobeyed God's laws, violated His statutes, and broken the everlasting covenant; therefore, a curse will consume the earth and its people will be held accountable. The earth's inhabitants will be burned up, though a small number will survive. However, those who do survive will raise their voices, shout for joy, and give glory to the Lord.

So there will be a few survivors of God's fiery wrath. We will learn more about them later. Keep in mind that God's people have already been gathered for Day 7, so those survivors were not included among them. Now let's see what Scripture says about how things will be at the end of the battle.

To the Victor the Spoils

In the Psalms, God says Israel will inherit the world. After the Lord completely removes wickedness from the earth, He will rule over the nations with an iron scepter. God warns the rulers of the earth and kings of the nations ahead of time, to be wise and serve the Lord with fear and trembling or He may become angry. His wrath can flare up in a moment.

Deliverance

From that day forward, the house of Israel will know that the Lord is their God. Though Israel was the subject of God's anger for a time, now God will bring back His people from exile and He will have compassion on all the people of Israel. Then they will be allowed to forget their shame and their unfaithfulness toward God.

The Prophet Says

"I will show wonders in the heavens and on the earth, blood and fire and billows of smoke. The sun will be turned to darkness and the moon to blood before the coming of the great and dreadful day of the Lord. And everyone who calls on the name of the Lord will be saved; for on Mount Zion and in Jerusalem there will be deliverance, as the Lord has said, among the survivors whom the Lord calls." (Joel 2:30–32)

Then Jerusalem will be lifted up and be secure in its place; never again will it be destroyed. On that day, the Lord will be king over the whole earth. The few survivors from the nations that attacked Jerusalem will go to Israel year after year to worship the King, the Lord Almighty, and celebrate the Feast of Tabernacles. As you may recall from our previous discussions, the Feast of Tabernacles is the final fall feast that signifies that God tabernacles (lives) with His people.

All Things New

As we have seen, many of the prophecies about Day 7 describe great changes in the whole earth. In Isaiah Chapter 40, the prophet says every valley will be raised, every mountain and hill leveled, and the rough ground and the rugged places made smooth. On that day, the glory of the Lord will be revealed on Mount Zion, His holy mountain.

The Prophet Says

"Behold, I will create new heavens and a new earth. The former things will not be remembered, nor will they come to mind." (Isaiah 65:17)

The Least You Need to Know

- Although the Final Battle is often called the Battle of Armageddon, it will be fought at Jerusalem.
- When the Lord appears from heaven, He will hold a wedding feast before He fights the Final Battle.
- The Final Battle will spread from Jerusalem to the whole world.
- After God's wrath and judgment have been poured out, Day 7 begins and Jerusalem will be the center of God's kingdom on earth for all eternity.

Part 5

The Sabbath Rest

After the world has gone through the transition from this present age and has arrived in the age to come, things on earth will be very different. The Bible tells us what it will be like during the Last Day.

Many of the aspects of the Kingdom of God on earth will be very appealing even to the casual observer, but other aspects … well, let's just say they're different from what we're used to.

Finally, there are different points of view about when Jesus Christ will return to gather up His followers and establish His kingdom on earth. So that you are informed, I present the alternative positions. Then I point out what Scripture says regarding each.

Chapter 21

In the Kingdom of God

In This Chapter

- Who will make it into the Kingdom of God
- There will be subjects in the kingdom
- There will be owners of the kingdom
- About the change in the nature of things

When the Kingdom of God (Day 7) comes on earth, there will be some big changes. Not only will there be an admissions test for residents of the kingdom, but the very nature of things on earth will be different. Scripture describes the change as a total restoration.

Residents of the Kingdom

In the last few chapters, we have been discussing the transitional events that will take place as the world enters into Day 7. We discussed the Second Coming of the Messiah, the gathering and resurrection of the followers of Christ, the wedding banquet, and the Final Battle. Now we talk about who will live in the Kingdom of God and some of the other changes that will take place.

Separating Sheep and Goats

Let's review a little. Christ's angels will weed out of the kingdom everything that causes sin and all who do evil. This separating of God's subjects from Satan's subjects is described many times in Scripture. We have discussed most of the biblical passages in this book, including the parables about separating the wheat and the weeds, separating the good fish and the bad fish, and separating the sheep and the goats. Each of these teachings describes separating the wicked from the righteous for God's kingdom.

> **The Prophet Says**
>
> Peter wrote, "For if God … did not spare the ancient world when he brought the flood on its ungodly people, but protected Noah, a preacher of righteousness, and seven others; if he condemned the cities of Sodom and Gomorrah by burning them to ashes, and made them an example of what is going to happen to the ungodly." (2 Peter 2:4–6)

As I previously mentioned regarding the removal of the wicked, Jesus said that the coming of the Kingdom of God would be like it was in the days of Noah. In those days, God brought the Great Flood to weed out everyone who did evil. Besides the animals on the Ark, only Noah and his family were saved when God sent the Great Flood that took away all the ungodly people who lived on the earth. At the time of the Great Flood, God promised that He would never again wipe out the world with a flood.

In the New Testament, the Apostle Peter tells us that God will wipe out the wicked in the world again, but this time with fire. Peter points to the burning of the ancient cities of Sodom and Gomorrah as an example of what is going to happen to the world when the Day of the Lord arrives. In Chapter 19, we also studied several prophecies in which Christ is described as a fire that will consume His enemies on the Day of the Lord.

As He did with water in the days of Noah, God is planning to do with fire as the world passes from the present age of Day 6 to the coming age of Day 7.

— Last Days Timeline —

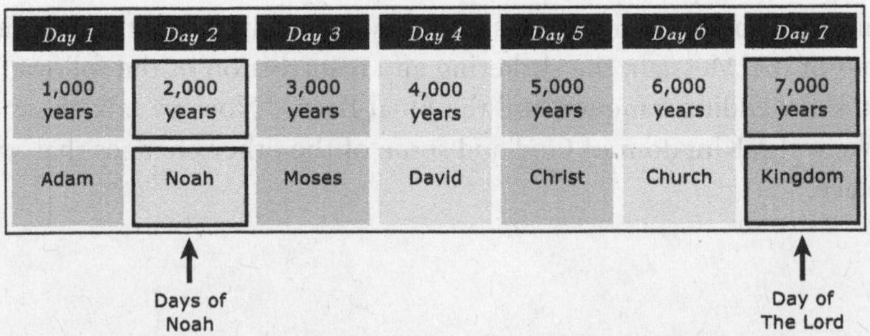

Day 1	Day 2	Day 3	Day 4	Day 5	Day 6	Day 7
1,000 years	2,000 years	3,000 years	4,000 years	5,000 years	6,000 years	7,000 years
Adam	Noah	Moses	David	Christ	Church	Kingdom
	↑ Days of Noah					↑ Day of The Lord

According to Jesus, not only will the ungodly be weeded out of His kingdom and burned, but the sons of God will be gathered into His kingdom. This brings us to the question, who are the Sons of God who will enter the Kingdom of God on earth when it comes, and will anyone else make it?

Sons of the Kingdom

Jesus described those who will be considered worthy to take part in the resurrection, inherit the kingdom, and become immortal like the angels in heaven.

The resurrection will include individuals who died before the Second Coming, as well as those alive at the time of the Second Coming. First, let's examine the resurrection of the dead. Who will be in the group resurrected from the dead? Scripture indicates that there will be individuals from the time covered by the Old Testament included in the resurrection of the dead. Old Testament prophet Job prophesied that he himself will be raised to life and see Israel's redeemer in the end. Similarly, the prophet Daniel recorded in the last words of his prophecies that God told him that at the end of the age, Daniel will rise to life and receive his portion of the inheritance.

A Multitude of Heirs

In addition to his prophecy about his own resurrection, Daniel prophesied about a great multitude of people who will rise from the dust of the earth at the end of the age. He said that these people will shine like the brightness of the heavens and that they will be glorious forever and ever.

In the New Testament, Jesus taught about the resurrection at the last day. Jesus said He will give eternal life to those who believe in Him, and He will raise them up at the last day. You may recall the conversation Jesus had with His friend Martha, which we also discussed in an earlier chapter. Jesus told Martha that whoever believes in Him will be raised to life at the last day, even if they had died.

We also know that some people who believe in Christ will survive the Great Tribulation

The Prophet Says

Jesus said, "And this is the will of Him who sent me, that I shall lose none of all that He has given me, but raise them up at the last day. For my Father's will is that everyone who looks to the Son and believes in Him shall have eternal life, and I will raise him up at the last day." (John 6:39–40) and will still be alive at the Second Coming at the end of Day 6. Jesus told Martha that those still alive at the last day who believed in Him would not die. They will be resurrected from life to eternal life.

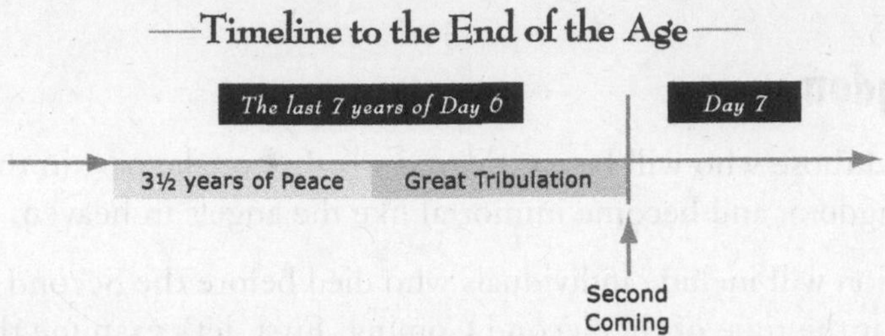

The Apostle Paul taught the Corinthians the same thing when he wrote to them in his first letter. Paul indicated that both the dead and the living will be instantly changed from their temporary, perishable, mortal bodies to their permanent, imperishable, immortal bodies when Christ returns.

Therefore, the Bible indicates that at the Second Coming, Jesus will resurrect and change all the dead who have believed in Him from the beginning of Day 1 to the end of Day 6. He will also change those who continue to believe in Him to the end of Day 6. These are the people who inherit the Kingdom of God.

Legitimate Heirs

So who will be the legitimate heirs of the Kingdom of God, and how does the Bible define belief in Christ?

def•i•ni•tion

The word **believe** in the New Testament is translated from a Greek word that means to be totally convinced of something and faithful to it. In the biblical context, to believe in Christ means to be totally convinced of who He is and obedient to Him.

First, you should know that the Bible states that Jesus Christ is God. Therefore, people of the Old Testament period who knew God also knew Christ because Christ is God. Similarly, people of the New Testament period who know Christ also know God.

So, what does *believe* mean? The Bible provides a great amount of information to answer this question. Not only is there a wealth of information regarding who qualifies as one of Christ's followers, but the Bible also is concise and to the point regarding what belief in Christ means.

To understand what is meant by "believe," it helps to consider the meaning of the Greek word that is translated to "believe." The Greek word *pisteuo* means to be totally convinced of something and faithful to that belief. In the case of belief in Christ, it means to be totally convinced of who He is and obedient to Him.

Now, we know who the Bible indicates will participate in the resurrection and inherit the Kingdom of God on Day 7. However, two other groups of people will reside in the kingdom.

Subjects of the Kingdom

The Kingdom of God will be occupied by more than just the "new" immortals. There will also be mortals in the kingdom. Actually, Scripture describes two groups of mortals as surviving the Wrath of God. These survivors will be subjects in the kingdom while the immortals rule and reign with Christ for the 1,000 years of Day 7. These two groups of mortals are a remnant from Israel and the survivors from the nations. Let's see how they are described in the Bible.

The Remnant

The prophets indicated that when Christ returns and God's wrath is poured out on the world, a remnant of Israel will survive God's wrath. This remnant is a group of people who did not put their faith in Christ. If they had, they would have been part of the resurrection. This remnant of Israel will survive to the return of Christ, recognize Him, and accept Him as God when He appears. This remnant will enter the Kingdom of God in their mortal bodies.

Isaiah said that a surviving remnant of Israel will return and trust in the Holy One of Israel when the Day of the Lord arrives. Isaiah said that even though the people of Israel will have a large population when the Day of the Lord begins, only a few will survive and turn to the Lord.

The prophet Jeremiah also mentioned the remnant of Israel that will turn to the King in Israel on the Day of the Lord. Jeremiah describes the remnant as being drawn to Israel when Christ appears as King in Israel.

The Prophet Says

Isaiah wrote, "A remnant will return, a remnant of Jacob will return to the Mighty God. Though your people, O Israel, be like the sand by the sea, only a remnant will return. Destruction has been decreed, overwhelming and righteous. The Lord, the Lord Almighty, will carry out the destruction decreed upon the whole land." (Isaiah 10:21–23)

Jeremiah also says that God will put shepherds over them, shepherds who will care for them.

Jeremiah describes the remnant of Israel as coming from the land of the north and from all over the world. He says that the lame, the blind, and expectant mothers will be among them. They will come weeping, singing, and praising God.

We know that this remnant is not part of the resurrection because Jeremiah says that they will procreate, be fruitful, and increase in the land. This means that the remnant is mortal because those of the resurrection will not marry. Therefore, since those of the resurrection will not be having babies and multiplying, this remnant is not of the resurrection group.

Micah also prophesied about this remnant. Micah said that the Lord will assemble the exiles and the lame, those who had been driven away from Israel, and will rule over them from that day on, forever.

def•i•ni•tion

Children of the resurrection is a title Jesus gave to those people who will take part in the resurrection and eternal life in the Kingdom of God. In this book, I also refer to them as the immortals because when they are resurrected, they will become immortal.

This is another reason we know these people are not part of the resurrection: the Lord says that He will rule over them. Scripture indicates that those of the resurrection will be rulers with Christ and coheirs of the Kingdom of God with Christ. They will be priests in the kingdom, not subjects of the kingdom.

Therefore, in the kingdom, in addition to the *children of the resurrection*, there will be a mortal remnant from Israel. Let's see if the prophets identify any others.

The Survivors

In the Old Testament, the Psalmist describes the Day of the Lord as a day when God will punish the world and judge the nations. The Psalmist says that God's wrath against men will bring God praise and that the survivors of His wrath will be restrained.

The prophet Zechariah also speaks of survivors of the Day of the Lord. He says that the survivors of the nations, even those that attacked Jerusalem, will go to Jerusalem year after year to worship the King, the Lord God Almighty, and celebrate the Feast of Tabernacles.

So three groups of people will reside in the Kingdom of God: the immortal children of the resurrection, the mortal remnant of Israel, and the survivors of the nations.

Scripture is very clear about how the children of the resurrection qualify for their residency; however, no direct statements in Scripture appear to indicate how some from Israel and the nations survive and qualify for residency in the Kingdom of God, Day 7.

The Prophet Says

Zechariah says, "Then the survivors from all the nations that have attacked Jerusalem will go up year after year to worship the King, the Lord Almighty, and to celebrate the Feast of Tabernacles." (Zechariah 14:16)

The Bible does say that God will totally destroy the wicked of the world in His wrath. Since we are told by the prophets that some will survive God's wrath and enter the kingdom, there must be a few unbelievers whom God will not consider wicked. Therefore, to summarize, those who have believed in Christ will enter the kingdom in resurrected bodies, a few nonwicked (the survivors and the remnant) will enter the kingdom in their mortal bodies, and the rest of the world's population will be destroyed.

Owners of the Kingdom

We know Christ's followers will live in the kingdom, but what is their role in the kingdom? Also, what is their relationship to the subjects of the kingdom, the mortal survivors? Once again, let's see what the Bible says.

In the New Testament, Jesus says that His followers will inherit the Kingdom of God. However, the idea of inheriting the kingdom was first written about in the Old Testament. For example, Psalm 37, written by King David, tells us that the meek and the righteous, those who put their hope in the Lord, will inherit the land, but the wicked will be cut off and will have no part in the kingdom. This picture should be very familiar to us at this point.

Prophetic Pitfalls

Scripture is consistent and clear that all followers of Christ will inherit eternal life, enter the Kingdom of God on earth, and reside with Christ in His kingdom forever. Heaven is not their eternal home; it will be the Kingdom of God on earth.

Inheritance

If you inherit property, you become the owner of the property and are given possession of it. Therefore, in the biblical context, Christ's followers, the children of the resurrection, will take possession of the Kingdom of God. With that in mind, let's see what else the prophets say about the ownership of the kingdom.

Like David, the Old Testament prophets wrote about the righteous inheriting the earth. In a very interesting prophecy, Isaiah contrasted the fate of Satan, the Antichrist, and Satan's followers to that of the righteous people of God. Isaiah describes the pride and ambition of Satan and his resulting destruction at God's hand. Isaiah says Satan and his followers will go down to the pit, but the righteous will inherit the land and cover the earth with their cities.

Prime Real Estate

In other prophecies about the coming Kingdom of God, Isaiah describes in some detail the fate of the people of God. In his descriptions, he mentions that they will inherit a double portion as their inheritance, that they will rejoice in their inheritance, and that their inheritance will be everlasting. In another prophecy, Isaiah tells us that God's people will receive their inheritance when God creates the new heaven and a new earth. We know that the new heaven and the new earth will be created on the Day of the Lord—which we discuss in more detail shortly.

Now let's look at what else Jesus says about God's people inheriting the Kingdom of God. As we have already discussed, a major theme of Jesus' ministry was the Kingdom of God. In one of His earliest teachings, called the Sermon on the Mount, Jesus describes those who will be found worthy to inherit the Kingdom of God.

When Jesus taught about inheriting the kingdom, He often spoke of it as inheriting eternal life as well. Only those who have been changed from mortal to immortal in the resurrection will inherit the Kingdom of God. Paul made this very clear when he wrote his first letter to the Corinthians. In Chapter 15 of Corinthians, Paul says that flesh and blood cannot inherit the Kingdom of God—only those who have been changed in the resurrection.

The Prophet Says

Jesus said, "But those who are considered worthy of taking part in that age and in the resurrection from the dead will neither marry nor be given in marriage, and they can no longer die; for they are like the angels. They are God's children, since they are children of the resurrection." (Luke 20:35–36)

Not All Heirs Are Equal

In Chapter 19 of the Gospel of Luke, Jesus is recorded as telling a parable about a man of royalty. The man was going away on a long trip to have himself made king. Before he left, he called his servants together and gave them assignments to carry out while he was gone. He gave each servant some money to put to work. He said when he returned, he would settle up with them based on what they had done with the money.

The man went away and was made king, and after a long time he returned to settle accounts. He called his servants together to find out what they had done with the money he had given them. The first servant came and said, "Sir, your money has earned 10 times what you left with me." The king said, "Well done, my good and faithful servant," and gave the servant 10 cities. The second servant came and told the king that his money had earned five times what he left. To this the king said, "Well done, good and faithful servant." Because the servant had been trustworthy with a small amount, he gave him five of his cities.

The Prophet Says

Jesus said, "'Well done, my good servant!' his master replied. 'Because you have been trustworthy in a very small matter, take charge of 10 cities.' The second came and said, 'Sir, your mina has earned five more.' His master answered, 'You take charge of five cities.'" (Luke 19:17–19)

This parable indicates what it will be like when the Messiah returns and His followers inherit their portion of the kingdom. This parable may even describe a specific aspect of how the followers of Christ will be rewarded when they inherit the kingdom and receive their reward.

The last mention of Christ's followers inheriting the kingdom is recorded in Chapter 21 of the Book of Revelation. In this vision, John sees a new heaven and a new earth. He said the first heaven and the first earth were no more. The new earth was different than the first earth, in that the new earth had no sea. John also describes Christ's bride coming down to earth from heaven in this vision. We are familiar with this event from our discussions of the gathering of the followers of Christ in the clouds of the sky and their coming with Christ to earth. In this vision, John calls the bride of Christ, "new Jerusalem" and he says that now God will live with His people.

John also connects the inheritance of Christ's followers to that day when the new heaven and the new earth comes, just as we have seen in the prophecies of Isaiah.

Now let's take a closer look at what Scripture says about the new heaven and the new earth.

New Heaven and New Earth

In Chapter 18, we discussed the details provided by the prophets regarding the Final Battle. The Final Battle and the subsequent consuming fire of God's wrath occur at the time when the old earth is destroyed and the new heaven and the new earth come into being.

> **The Prophet Says**
>
> Peter wrote, "That day will bring about the destruction of the heavens by fire, and the elements will melt in the heat. But in keeping with his promise, we are looking forward to a new heaven and a new earth, the home of righteousness." (2 Peter 3:12–13)

The idea of a new heaven and a new earth does not necessarily mean that God will totally destroy everything and start over. Like it was in the days of Noah, the earth was not totally destroyed by the flood. When the water receded, the earth was still there. Then Noah, his family, and the surviving animals began to repopulate the earth. Based on what is revealed in Scripture about the Day of the Lord, something like the days of Noah will happen, except that instead of water, it will be done with fire. Then a new earth will emerge and those mortals who survive will repopulate the earth.

Long Live the Mortals

I should also point out that when the earth was destroyed in the flood, it was also changed. Before the flood, Scripture records that people were living a long time, hundreds of years. Genesis Chapter 5 records that Methuselah lived to be 969 years of age. After the flood, lifespans on earth changed to be like they are today.

> **The Prophet Says**
>
> Isaiah says, "Never again will there be in it an infant who lives but a few days, or an old man who does not live out his years; he who dies at a hundred will be thought a mere youth; he who fails to reach a hundred will be considered accursed." (Isaiah 65:20)

Isaiah was the first to refer to the new heaven and new earth. Some of the changes he mentioned sound like things will be restored to the way they were before the flood. As we have just discussed, before the flood people were living hundreds of years. Isaiah says when the kingdom comes, there will be no infant deaths, nor will there be a man who does not live out his years. Isaiah goes on to say that if a man dies at a hundred years of age, he will be considered to have died in his youth. Also, at that time, if a man fails to reach the age of a hundred, he will be considered cursed.

In the New Testament, the Apostle Peter also spoke of a new heaven and a new earth that would be coming with the Day of the Lord. Like Jesus and the Apostle Paul, Peter said that the Day of the Lord will come like a thief in the night and catch the people by surprise. At that time, the earth will disappear with a great noise and be destroyed by fire. Peter said that day would bring about the destruction of the heavens and the earth by fire, and that the elements will be melted in the heat.

The last mention of the new heaven and the new earth is recorded in the Book of Revelation with another vision by the Apostle John. John received this vision at the same time He saw the bride of Christ coming down from heaven as the new Jerusalem, which we discussed earlier. During John's vision, he is told by Christ that His followers will inherit all that he sees and that they will reign with Him forever and ever.

Back to the Future for Mother Nature

When the new heaven and new earth come into being, there will be a number of changes to good old "Mother Nature." We have already discussed that the life expectancy of mortals will be in the hundreds of years, as in the days before Noah and the Great Flood. However, that change in life expectancy is not the only part of the natural environment that will be altered.

At this point, I should also remind you that Scripture indicates that when Christ returns on Day 7, He will restore everything. In part, that means that the curse God placed on the world as a result of man's disobedience will be removed. When the curse is removed, the very nature of things will revert back to the way it was originally, as it was in the Garden of Eden. The Bible indicates that nature will remain like this forever. With this in mind, let's see what Isaiah says about "Mother Nature" going "back to the future."

The Prophet Says

"He must remain in heaven until the time comes for God to restore everything, as he promised long ago through his holy prophets." (Acts 3:21)

Once again Isaiah provides a good description of the way things will be in Day 7, God's Sabbath rest. Isaiah describes changes that indicate that the very nature of creation will be altered on that day. He describes several predators and their prey, in this age, as living in harmony together; the wolf and the lamb, the leopard and the goat, and the calf and the lion and the yearling will all lie down together. Children will be able to play without fear of animals that in our age are considered dangerous. Vipers and cobras will not threaten or harm infants. Meat-eating animals of our age will no longer kill for food in the age to come. They will eat straw like the ox and the cow.

In the prophecies of Ezekiel and Revelation about the Day of the Lord, the city of Jerusalem is described as having trees on the banks of the river that never drop their leaves and bear their fruit every month. It appears that when God restores everything, the land will be extremely productive, and the creatures of the earth will live in harmony with one another and with mortal man.

As we can see, there will be some very big changes in the order of things when the new heaven and the new earth are created for God's kingdom on earth. In addition to the changes in the nature of things, the order of things will change as well. In the next chapter, we examine these changes as described in the Bible.

The Least You Need to Know

- By God's definition, all the wicked and those who do evil will be weeded out of the kingdom.
- Only people who believe in and are obedient to God will be admitted into His kingdom.
- Those who pass the final will be the new owners of the new earth.
- The new earth will not be like the old earth.

Chapter 22

Lord of the Sabbath

In This Chapter

- The immortals are in charge
- The kingdom infrastructure
- The King's way
- Day 7, start to finish

So far, we have talked about some things that will be part of the Day 7 Kingdom of God. In this chapter, we will see what else the Bible says will happen during the 1,000-year reign of Christ, the Lord of the Sabbath, and His immortals.

Getting Started

In the last chapter, we discussed that during Day 7, immortal humans (resurrected followers of Christ) will rule over mortal humans (those who survived God's wrath). We also discussed some of the changes that are prophesied to occur, including mortal humans living hundreds of years and wild animals living in harmony.

Day 7 is popularly called the *Millennium*—a thousand years. This can be a little confusing because, as you know, the Bible also says that the Kingdom of God will last forever. Therefore, not only does the Kingdom last for 1,000 years, but the Kingdom of God will also continue on long after the completion of God's Sabbath rest, Day 7.

def•i•ni•tion

The **Millennium** is a nonbiblical term popularly used to refer to the thousand-year reign of Christ on earth in Revelation 20:2–7.

In Chapter 18, we discussed the Final Battle, God's wrath, and the clean-up crew during the transition from Day 6 to Day 7. However, it appears from the words of the prophet Ezekiel that the clean-up crew leaves a few things to be dealt with.

Division of Labor

In Ezekiel Chapter 39, Ezekiel tells us that after the Final Battle, the people who live in Israel will regularly go out and clean up weapons and bodies of the enemy nation's warriors. It will take seven months for the bodies to be buried and seven years for the clean-up to be finished, and people will be regularly employed to perform this clean-up.

Right from the beginning, there will be physical labor going on in the Kingdom of God during Day 7. Another job described as occurring in the kingdom is rebuilding. The prophet Isaiah tells us that after the Lord's return, the people will rebuild the ancient ruins, raise up old foundations, repair broken walls, and restore cities, streets, and dwellings.

Not only does the Bible tell of the labor that will be done, but it says who will be doing it. Isaiah says that the survivors of the nations that attacked Israel will serve the remnant of Israel. The mortal survivors will rebuild Israel's walls, shepherd her flocks, and work her fields and vineyards.

Immortals Rule

The Bible says that the resurrected people will inherit the earth and will be owner-operators of the kingdom in Day 7. However, there is much more to their responsibilities than that. Isaiah says that these people will be called priests of the Lord and ministers of God's kingdom. Isaiah says the immortals will inherit a double portion and will feed on the wealth of the nations.

In his last prophecy, Isaiah tells us that the Lord will appoint priests to serve in the new heaven and the new earth. The Lord says that as the new heaven and new earth endure, so will His priests. Isaiah goes on to describe how all mankind will come and bow down before the Lord from one new moon celebration to another, and one Sabbath to another. So the immortals will serve as priests to the nations as they reign with Christ.

The Prophet Says

John heard, "You [Christ] have made them to be a kingdom and priests to serve our God, and they will reign on the earth." (Revelation 5:10)

This idea is not limited to Isaiah's writings. Several times we are told in the Book of Revelation that Christ's followers will be priests in the Kingdom of God and that they will rule with Christ for 1,000 years.

Looks Like an Angel

In addition to the physical labor of the mortals and priestly responsibilities of the immortals, the Bible tells of visible angels in the kingdom. Angels will ascend from earth to heaven and descend from heaven to earth. This was described by Jesus when He was talking to a man named Nathanael. During the conversation, Nathanael was amazed by Jesus and declared that Jesus was the Son of God and the King of Israel. Jesus responded to him by saying that Nathanael would see greater things than that. Jesus said, "You will see heaven open, and the angels of God ascending and descending on the Son of Man."

There is no indication in the Bible that Nathanael saw what Jesus described. So it is likely that Jesus was describing something that would take place in the distant future, in the Kingdom of God. Since Nathanael was a follower of Christ, Nathanael will likely be an immortal in the kingdom and will see angels ascending and descending in the presence of Christ as He rules over His kingdom.

The Prophet Says

Paul says, "Do you not know that the saints will judge the world? And if you are to judge the world, are you not competent to judge trivial cases? Do you not know that we will judge angels?" (1 Corinthians 6:2–3)

As an immortal in the kingdom, Nathanael will have a spiritual body and will be able to see the angels. Mortals generally cannot see angels, even though the Bible tells us they are present in this age. Here is an interesting statement about immortals and angels by the Apostle Paul. In his second letter to the Corinthians, Paul explains to Christ's followers how to judge disputes and tells them that one day they will judge the world and will also judge angels. Therefore, when the followers of Christ enter the kingdom and become immortals, they will even have authority over the angels in heaven.

Every kingdom needs its infrastructure, and the Kingdom of God is no exception. Now that we know a little about the hierarchy in the kingdom, let's see where the worship will take place.

Kingdom Structure

The Bible provides various descriptions of the Temple of God and the temple complex. The temple itself consists of two sections, called the Holy Place and the Most Holy Place. In the Old Testament descriptions, the Holy Place is where the articles of worship were; the Most Holy Place is where the Ark of the Covenant was. The temple complex consists of all the buildings and structures that surround the temple.

The Architect

The Old Testament prophet Ezekiel provides the most comprehensive architectural description of the Temple of God in the Bible. Ezekiel wrote his description of the future temple (found in Chapters 40–47) shortly after the destruction of Solomon's temple around 586 B.C. Recall that Solomon's temple was the first permanently constructed Temple of God. Therefore, Ezekiel's detailed description was written before the second temple was built, before Herod's reconstructed second temple, before the future third temple, and before the future Millennial Temple. Let's list the various temples mentioned in the Bible so we see where Ezekiel's prophecy fits in.

> **The Prophet Says**
>
> The angel Gabriel said, "He will be great and will be called the Son of the Most High. The Lord God will give him the throne of his father David, and he will reign over the house of Jacob forever; his kingdom will never end." (Luke 1:32–33)

Temples described in Scripture:

- Solomon's temple, about 960 to 586 B.C.
- Ezekiel's temple prophecy
- The second temple, about 520 to 14 B.C.
- Reconstructed second temple, about 14 B.C. to A.D. 70

- The third temple, about A.D.____? to the end of Day 6
- Millennial Temple, from beginning of Day 7 to eternity

Since Ezekiel's prophecy was written before several of God's temples were built, it is most likely that his prophecy speaks of future temples because no temple has ever been built to the design described in this prophecy. Other prophecies predict things that will happen at different periods of time in the future. This seems to be the case with Ezekiel's prophecy about God's temple. Therefore, for our purposes, in Ezekiel Chapters 40–47, we need to focus on the parts of the prophecy about the Day 7 temple, or Millennial Temple.

Since we are discussing the Millennial Temple in this chapter, I will show you the parts of the prophecy that relate to it. However, keep in mind that two temples prophesied about in the Bible remain to be built. The third temple is to be built before the end of Day 6 (see Chapter 7), and the Millennial Temple is to be built in Day 7.

The outside dimensions of the Millennial Temple are said to be 750 feet, the length of two and a half football fields, on each side. By comparison, Solomon's temple was only 180 feet by 90 feet. So the Millennial Temple would be very large and would almost totally cover the Temple Mount as it exists in Jerusalem today.

Ezekiel's prophecy describes all the details of the temple, including rooms for the priests (immortals), gateways, gates, steps, porticos, parapets, courts, and alcoves. Ezekiel's description is so thorough that it could be the basis for an architectural plan for a future temple complex.

When we started our discussion of the temple, I made a distinction between the temple itself and what I called the temple complex because the Bible states that there will be no temple in Jerusalem during Day 7. In the Book of Revelation, there are many references to God's temple in heaven. However, when it comes to the temple in the Kingdom of God on earth, John, in telling of his vision of the future, wrote, "I did not see a temple in the city, because the Lord God Almighty and the Lamb are its temple." (Revelation 21:22) Okay, so there will be no temple, per se.

However, it is possible that the throne of God will be in the place of the Holy of Holies and Holy Place in the Millennial Temple. Previous temples had a room set aside as the Holy of Holies, which housed the Ark of the Covenant. The Ark of the Covenant signified the presence of God. But in the Millennial Kingdom, God Himself will be present, and, therefore, His throne will likely be in the Holy of Holies, in place of the Ark.

As we discussed in Chapter 3, God promised King David that one day His son would rule on David's throne in Jerusalem. God also said that once the "Son of David" begins to reign, His Kingdom will be an everlasting kingdom. So putting this together, it seems that there is to be a large temple complex with a throne.

> **The Prophet Says**
>
> John says, "Then the angel showed me the river of the water of life, as clear as crystal, flowing from the throne of God and of the Lamb." (Revelation 22:1)

It seems that a river will flow out from the Millennial Temple. This unique river is mentioned in several prophecies about this temple. In one prophecy, this river is called the river of life. This river is likely a symbol for the spirit of God flowing from His presence. Now that we know something about the temple, let's see what else Ezekiel tells us about Day 7.

The Surveyor

Ezekiel describes how Israel will be divided up among the tribes of Israel, the priests (immortals), and the Lord. Ezekiel tells us the dimensions and identifies the location of the allotments. There are also allotments for the sacred district of Jerusalem and for common use. The Lord's portion of the land is described as being at the center of Israel between the portions of Judah and Benjamin and surrounding Jerusalem.

The total territory identified by Ezekiel's prophecy is larger than current-day Israel. It encompasses all the land from Syria in the north, to Egypt in the south, to the Mediterranean on the west, and to the Arabian Desert on the east.

King of the Jews

We have already discussed that, in the Kingdom of God, Christ's followers will rule with Him. But what does the Bible say about the Lord's reign on earth during this period?

The Old Testament prophet Zechariah says that the Lord will be King over the whole world and that He alone will be King. Isaiah also says that the Lord alone will be exalted on the Day of the Lord. Ezekiel says Israel will totally rely on the Lord on that day and will recognize that the Lord is God. The prophet Micah tells us that from that day on and forever, the Lord will rule from Mount Zion.

Iron Scepter

One thing that is very obviously missing from the Kingdom during Day 7 is democracy. For that matter, all worldly forms of governance seem to have disappeared with the old earth. God is King, and He sets and disseminates the law from Jerusalem. Scripture indicates that this is universally accepted, and there appears to be no difference of opinion—at least, for a while.

The Prophet Says

Zechariah says, "On that day living water will flow out from Jerusalem, half to the eastern sea and half to the western sea, in summer and in winter. The Lord will be king over the whole earth. On that day there will be one Lord, and his name the only name." (Zechariah 14:8–9)

The Bible tells us that on the Lord's Day, Christ will rule with an iron scepter. Right off the bat, that sounds like a firm management style. We first read this in Psalm 2. The author goes on to warn the nations and their rulers to be wise and to serve the Lord with fear and trembling, or He may dash them to pieces.

In the Book of Revelation, we are told three times by John that the Lord will rule with an iron scepter and will strictly manage the nations. Isaiah tells us that the nations of the world will serve the Lord during Day 7 and that they will rebuild Israel's walls. The rulers will bring their wealth to the Lord, and those who will not serve the Lord will perish.

In Ezekiel's prophecy about the future kingdom, he tells us that the Lord will have requirements that must be met. Ezekiel says that the Lord will require offerings, choice gifts, and holy sacrifices.

The prophet Zechariah tells us that if any of the peoples of the earth do not go to Jerusalem to worship the Lord, they will get no rain. Zechariah also says that the Lord will bring a plague on those who do not take part and celebrate in the annual Feast of Tabernacles.

The Prophet Says

Zechariah says, "If any of the peoples of the earth do not go up to Jerusalem to worship the King, the Lord Almighty, they will have no rain. If the Egyptian people do not go up and take part, they will have no rain. The Lord will bring on them the plague he inflicts on the nations that do not go up to celebrate the Feast of Tabernacles." (Zechariah 14:17–18)

So it appears that even though the Kingdom of God has arrived on earth, it still is not a perfect world. There are other indications in Scripture that everything in the kingdom is not yet perfect. In the Book of Revelation, we are told some things about the holy city of Jerusalem during Day 7.

John says that nothing impure, shameful, or deceitful will enter the city, but only those whose names are written in the Book of Life. This indicates two things about how the world will be during the kingdom. First, some people will be considered impure and capable of doing shameful, deceitful things. These people will not have access to the holy city of Jerusalem. Second, only those whose names are written in the Book of Life will be permitted entrance to the city. This probably means that only immortals will be able to enter Jerusalem during the Millennium because they are the only people the Bible describes as having their names written in the Book of Life.

Just Scepter

The Bible always describes God as one who is fair and just, and who makes judgment without partiality. The Bible also indicates that God is unchanging. Based on this, we should expect to find indications that His justice, fairness, and impartiality will continue. From the Old Testament Psalms and prophets to the Book of Revelation, the Bible records a theme of righteousness and justice as the hallmark of the Kingdom of God when it comes.

The Psalmist tells us that the Lord will reign from His throne of righteousness, that He will govern and judge with justice. In one Psalm, the scepter of the Lord's eternal kingdom is described as a scepter of justice. We are told that the Lord loves righteousness and hates wickedness, and that is why He has put His followers in charge.

The Prophet Says

"But about the Son he says, 'Your throne, O God, will last for ever and ever, and righteousness will be the scepter of your kingdom.'" (Hebrews 1:8)

The Old Testament prophet Isaiah tells us that when the Lord's kingdom comes, He will be called, "Wonderful Counselor, Mighty God, Everlasting Father, Prince of Peace." When His kingdom comes, peace will reign and justice will be upheld. Righteousness will prevail from that time on and forever.

From this small sample from the Old Testament, we can see that the Lord's management style is described as one characterized by firmness and fairness. We also have seen that everything in the kingdom is not yet perfect, so the need for righteous judgment remains.

Kingdom Style

I have already mentioned that the Lord, the Messiah, will be King over the whole world. Not only will He be King, but the Bible says that everyone will know who He is. We are told that there will be a global awareness of the Lord and His ways. Isaiah says that all mankind will know who the Lord is. Isaiah says the eyes of the people will no longer be closed, and their ears will listen and understand. This knowledge and understanding of the Lord's ways applies to the mortal humans in the kingdom.

Remember that those who were resurrected, the immortals, have been united with the Lord spiritually. Not only are they intimately acquainted with the Lord's ways, but they also know Him. What else is there?

> **The Prophet Says**
>
> Isaiah says, "They will neither harm nor destroy on all my holy mountain, for the earth will be full of the knowledge of the Lord as the waters cover the sea." (Isaiah 12:9)

No More War

While we can see that the world is not yet perfect during Day 7, we also find additional encouraging prophecies about the Kingdom. For example, we are told that there will be no violence. Isaiah says that people in the kingdom will not harm each other, nor will they destroy.

In another of Isaiah's prophecies about God's kingdom, he tells us that the nations will stream to Israel to learn the Lord's ways so they can live by them. Isaiah also tells us that the Lord will settle disputes and judge between the nations, and that the nations will convert their weapons of war into tools for harvesting crops. He also says that the nations will no longer prepare for war, for there will be no more war.

So the world will seek after the ways of the Lord and there will be no more violence or war, but what about the economy?

> **The Prophet Says**
>
> Isaiah says, "He will judge between the nations and will settle disputes for many peoples. They will beat their swords into plowshares and their spears into pruning hooks. Nation will not take up sword against nation, nor will they train for war anymore." (Isaiah 2:4)

Deindustrialized

Another of the many things that seem to have been destroyed is the stuff brought by the Industrial Revolution. What we seem to find is a more agrarian type of economy where people have their own land, build their own houses, and tend their own crops. People may be involved in various trades, but there are no indications of an industrialized society.

Now this absence of modern technology may be explained by the fact that the writers of Scripture were themselves from an agrarian and nonindustrialized society. Or it may indicate that there will be no need for all the stuff we have today. Let's consider a couple of passages to see how things are described.

Isaiah says people will build their houses, plant their vineyards, and eat their fruit. He says no longer will they build houses and others live in them, or plant and others eat the fruit of their labor. They will enjoy the work of their hands and they will be blessed, they and their descendants with them.

As we read about the kingdom, it is hard to imagine industrialized factories, shopping malls, and mass transportation. It seems out of place to think of the world today with its economic, political, and military struggles. What is portrayed by the Bible seems to be a productive natural environment in which people live a basic agrarian lifestyle with their families in a society of peace and security.

For 1,000 Years

Now that you have a pretty good idea of how the Bible describes Day 7, let's turn our focus to the end of Day 7. First, let's step back and review a little. From the Book of Revelation Chapter 20, we know that Satan has been thrown into the Abyss, where he is said to be bound for 1,000 years. We are also told that while Satan is locked and sealed in the Abyss, he can no longer deceive the nations of the world. This may explain why everyone will know who the Lord is during Day 7.

In Revelation, John also tells us about the thrones of the immortals being set up at the beginning of the 1,000 years. As we have already studied extensively, the dead and the living followers of Christ are resurrected and reign with Christ for the 1,000 years. John tells us that this resurrection is the First Resurrection. So what about the other dead? John tells us that the rest of the dead, those who had not been followers of Christ, will not come to life until the 1,000 years of Day 7 (the Last Day) are over.

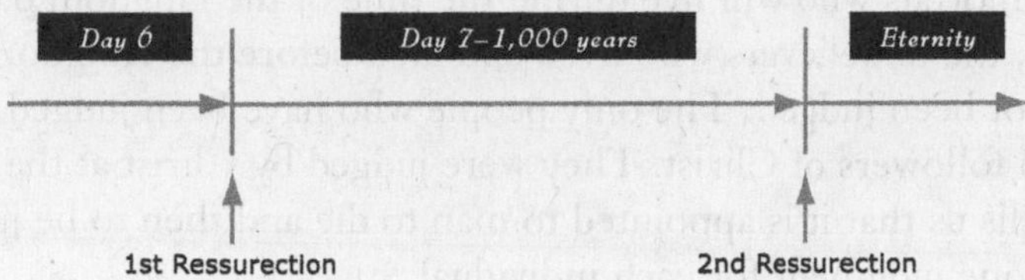

The dead who will come to life after the 1,000 years will rise in the Second Resurrection. Sometimes Scripture speaks of the resurrection as a resurrection of the righteous and a resurrection of the wicked. The First Resurrection is the resurrection of the righteous, and the Second Resurrection is the resurrection of the wicked. The First Resurrection will take place at the beginning of the 1,000 years, and the Second Resurrection will take place at the end of the 1,000 years. We will talk more about those of the Second Resurrection later. For now, let's consider the ultimate fate of the Day 7 mortals.

Decisions, Decisions

The remnant of Israel and the survivors from the nations who were not followers of Christ before the Second Coming are people who had not yet decided for or against Christ. Scripture indicates that they must decide during their lifetime, like everyone else. The major difference is they are living in the kingdom, and everyone else lived before the kingdom came.

In other words, by Day 7, every human being who lived on earth from Adam and Eve until the Second Coming of Christ fits into one of three categories:

- Everyone who was considered to be a follower of Christ at the Second Coming is an immortal in the kingdom.
- The unbelievers and the disobedient of the world died or were killed at the Second Coming.
- A few others somehow survived and entered the Kingdom of God in their mortal bodies.

Prophetic Pitfalls

Scripture clearly connects the destiny of Christ's followers to Christ, who is currently in heaven. However, Scripture also indicates that Christ will return to earth one day and then Christ's followers will be with Him on the new earth, for all eternity. Earth, not heaven, is the final destination of Christ's followers.

None of the mortals or their children will have yet made a decision for or against Christ. The mortals who will live during the time of the kingdom have not yet been judged. Also, the unbelievers who lived and died before the Kingdom of God came on earth have not been judged. The only people who have been judged are the immortal (resurrected) followers of Christ. They were judged by Christ at the Second Coming. The Bible tells us that it is appointed to man to die and then to be judged. So, there will be only one judgment for each individual.

Now, let's go back again to John's vision about Satan and the Abyss. John says that Satan will be released for a short time after he has been locked in the Abyss for 1,000 years. John says Satan will then go out and deceive the nations of the whole earth and stir up a rebellion against God's people and His holy city. John tells us that Satan will be able to gather a great number of people to march against Jerusalem. John also tells the outcome of Satan's rebellion. God sends fire down from heaven, and the fire devours all those who joined Satan. Then Satan is thrown into the lake of burning fire, where the Antichrist and the False Prophet were thrown at the beginning of the 1,000 years, Day 7.

The Prophet Says

John says, "If anyone's name was not found written in the book of life, he was thrown into the lake of fire." (Revelation 20:15)

Final Decision

Next, in John's vision of the end of Day 7, he describes the dead being raised in the Second Resurrection. Recall that the Second Resurrection will include everyone from the beginning of time who died without becoming a follower of Christ. After the Second Resurrection, Christ will sit on a great white throne and judge the people of the Second Resurrection.

Everyone whose name is not found written in the Book of Life is thrown into the burning lake of fire, which is where Satan was thrown.

Eternity

It appears from what is written that after the great white throne judgment, only people who are followers of Christ are left in the Kingdom of God. The Apostle Paul prophesied about the end of Day 7 this way: "When he has done this, then the Son himself will be made subject to him who put everything under him, so that God may be all in all." This is where Scripture leaves off: the rest is eternity. You have now completed your journey through Day 7, last of the Last Days.

In the next and final chapter, I discuss alternative interpretations of what is written about the Last Days and Christ's return.

The Least You Need to Know

- The immortals will be the owner-operators of the Kingdom of God.
- Detailed descriptions of the Day 7 kingdom were written long ago.
- God is described as a firm and just King who will rule from Jerusalem.
- There is still more to come at the end of the 1,000 years of Day 7.

Chapter 23

Last Days Points of View

In This Chapter

- The Last Days lingo
- The Great Tribulation short view
- The Millennium long view
- Improving your view

This last chapter on the Last Days discusses some of the terminology and different views regarding the return of Christ. You will see that people have come up with some very different ways of interpreting Last Days prophecy.

Familiarity with the terminology and views presented here will enable you to stand your ground in any eschatological discussion—and you'll also be able to impress your friends with words like eschatological.

Eschatology

The Bible has been around for a long time. The Old Testament was written between about 3,450 and 2,450 years ago. The New Testament was written between about 1,995 and 1,950 years ago. For centuries, people have been trying to figure out when the Last Days prophecies will be fulfilled and when the Kingdom of God will come on earth. Numerous *eschatological* theories have developed over the years, most seeking to answer the question of when the Messiah will come in relation to two time periods mentioned in the Bible. The first period is called the Great Tribulation. The second period we call the Millennium.

def•i•ni•tion

Eschatology is the branch of theological study of last things. It deals with death, the end of the world, and the ultimate destiny of mankind. In Christian doctrine, eschatology deals with the Second Coming, the resurrection of the dead, and the final judgment.

As we discuss the various Last Days viewpoints regarding the return of Christ, I point out what the Bible says. My approach is that all fulfilled biblical prophecies have been fulfilled in a normal, literal manner, so all prophecies relating to the future will also be fulfilled completely and, literally, the way one would expect if they believed what was being said.

Let's review a couple of biblical timelines so we can see where the Great Tribulation and the Millennium fit in.

Great Tribulation

The next chronological period described in the Bible that history will come to is the Great Tribulation. The Great Tribulation is a relatively short Last Days' period that the Bible says will occur in the last three and a half years of the thousand years that make up Day 6. The Last Days, Day 7, begin immediately after the Great Tribulation. Let's place the Great Tribulation in a timeline.

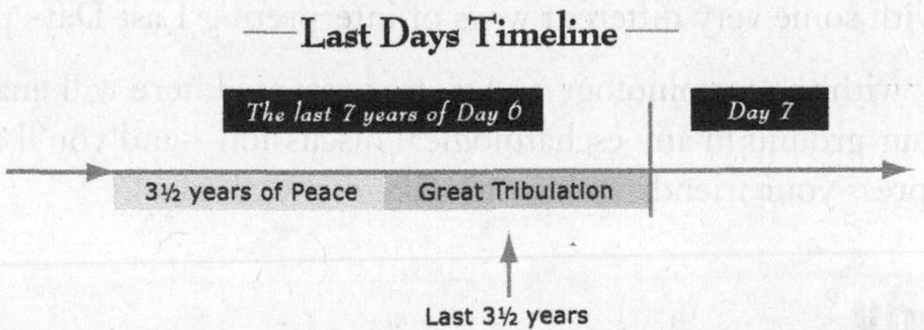

The Great Tribulation is described by Jesus in the Olivet Discourse as the worst period of tribulation since the beginning of time. The Great Tribulation is the only period of tribulation mentioned in relation to the Last Days. Therefore, whenever I refer to "the tribulation" or "the Great Tribulation," I am always referring to the last three and a half years of Day 6.

Now let's review the Millennium time period.

The Millennium

Immediately after the Great Tribulation, Day 7 begins. The 1,000 years of Day 7 is popularly called the Millennium. During these 1,000 years, the Bible tells us that Jesus Christ will reign and rule on earth with His followers. Following the 1,000 years of the Millennium comes eternity. Now let's place the Millennium in a timeline.

— Biblical Timeline —

Day 1	Day 2	Day 3	Day 4	Day 5	Day 6	Day 7
1,000 years	2,000 years	3,000 years	4,000 years	5,000 years	6,000 years	7,000 years
Adam	Noah	Moses	David	Christ	Church	Millennium

↑ The Great Tribulation

Tribulation Views

It is generally believed that the Great Tribulation is the next period to come on the biblical timeline. The Preterists, however, hold that the Great Tribulation has already occurred.

Unlike other theories that emphasize the Second Coming, the resurrection, and the gathering of living believers (the rapture), the Preterist view emphasizes the belief that other events are related to the Great Tribulation.

The Past in Review

The Preterist view is that all End Times prophecies, including the Book of Revelation, were fulfilled by A.D. 70. They hold that the Roman General Titus was the Antichrist and fulfilled the abomination that causes desolation when his army destroyed the Jewish Temple in A.D. 70.

According to the Jewish historian Josephus, the Roman army totally burned the temple during the battle over Jerusalem. The troops celebrated their victory by setting up their ensigns at the eastern gate of the temple and declared that Titus was imperator (commander in chief). The Preterist view is that this event fulfilled the prophecy regarding the abomination that causes desolation.

The Preterists generally view the Book of Revelation as symbolic of early church conflicts with the Roman government. They deny that Revelation and the New Testament predict future events, and they generally interpret unfulfilled prophecy allegorically. Preterists believe that Jesus Christ is currently reigning over earth from His throne, even though that is not visible nor is it evident by world conditions.

The Prophet Says

Daniel said this about the Antichrist: "He will confirm a covenant with many for one 'seven.' In the middle of the 'seven' he will put an end to sacrifice and offering. And on a wing of the temple he will set up an abomination that causes desolation, until the end that is decreed is poured out on him." (Daniel 9:27)

Let's talk a little about the abomination that causes desolation. Recall from Chapter 9 that before the abomination that causes desolation, the Antichrist confirms a covenant with Israel, then declares that he is God in God's temple.

Titus did not confirm this covenant with Israel. Furthermore, General Titus did not proclaim himself to be God, and Titus it seems was not the Antichrist. While others, like Titus, have defeated Israel and done abominable things in the temple, no one has yet to enter the temple and proclaim himself to be Almighty God.

—The Preterist View —

Day 1	*Day 2*	*Day 3*	*Day 4*	*Day 5*	*Day 6*	*Day 7*
1,000 years	2,000 years	3,000 years	4,000 years	5,000 years	6,000 years	7,000 years
Adam	Noah	Moses	David	Christ	Church	Kingdom

↑ The Preterist Great Tribulation A.D. 70

The Preterists also hold that Jesus said that everything that He described in the Olivet Discourse would be fulfilled within a generation of A.D. 32. However, this is not exactly what He said. In speaking of the End Times, Jesus said that the generation that sees all these things happen will be the generation that will see the kingdom come. Jesus said, "Even so, when you see all these things, you know that it is near, right at the door. I tell you the truth, this generation will certainly not pass away until all these things have happened." (Matthew 24:33–34)

The Prophet Says

John says, "They came to life and reigned with Christ a thousand years …. Blessed and holy are those who have part in the first resurrection. The second death has no power over them, but they will be priests of God and of Christ and will reign with him for a thousand years." (Revelation 20:4–6)

The Preterist view also holds that the Millennial Reign of Christ is being carried out today during this present age. Their interpretation is that descriptions of the Kingdom of God and Christ's reign are purely allegorical.

The Pre-Tribulation View

The Pre-Tribulation view places the Great Tribulation at the end of Day 6. However, the Pre-Tribulation view adds something new to the discussion of the Second Coming of Christ. It adds an additional coming of Christ between the First Coming and the final return.

The Pre-Tribulation view holds that Jesus Christ will come down from heaven before the Great Tribulation and gather His followers to meet Him in the air. Under this theory, the followers who have died will be resurrected from the dead, and those who are left alive will be caught up in the clouds with them to meet the Lord in the air. Then Christ and His resurrected followers return to heaven for the wedding banquet, which they say will take place in heaven.

Prophetic Pitfalls

Many opinions exist about when Jesus will return and gather His followers into His kingdom, but Jesus said, "Immediately after the tribulation …. they will see the Son of Man coming on the clouds of heaven with power and great glory, and He will send his angels with a loud trumpet call, and they will gather His elect …." (Matthew 24:29–31)

They will stay in heaven until after the Great Tribulation is over. Then Christ will leave heaven again for another resurrection and gathering. This resurrection will be for those who turn to Christ during the Great Tribulation. Some Pre-Tribbers call these new followers Tribulation Saints. The Pre-Tribbers say these two comings of Christ are two parts of the same Second Coming, even though they say the two parts are separated by several years. The first part they call the rapture, and the second part the glorious arrival and Second Coming.

This relatively new Pre-Tribulation view has become very popular with many people since it was introduced about 200 years ago. It rose to popularity from a new theology called Dispensationalism that was developed by John Nelson Darby (1800–1882).

The Prophet Says

The Apostle Paul says, "This mystery is that through the gospel the Gentiles are heirs together with Israel, members together of *one body*, and sharers together in the promise in Christ Jesus." (Ephesians 3:6)

In addition to the view of Christ's Pre-Tribulation return, this new theology holds that there are two distinct peoples of God: Israel and the Christian Church. Dispensationalists hold that the Church is separate from Israel, and Old Testament promises to Israel are not transferable to the Church. This division of God's people creates the need for the two-part Second Coming of Christ. The first coming (rapture) is for the Church and the second part (Second Coming) is for new believers.

This new theology is very popular because it holds that the followers of Christ will not go through the Great Tribulation. Rather, they are removed from the world before it starts. However, the Pre-Tribulation view has major problems when it comes to Scripture.

First, the Bible contradicts the idea of a division of God's followers into two groups. For example, the writers of the New Testament say that Christ's followers, both Jew and Gentile, form one body and all share in the promises to Israel.

The Apostle Paul wrote in his letter to the Ephesians that those who are Gentiles by birth and formerly separate from God's people have been brought into citizenship in Israel. Paul explained that they are all one in Christ. No longer is there a separation between Jew and Gentile; rather, by faith they are united in citizenship, joint heirs and members of God's household. Paul explained that this union between Jew and Gentile in the faith was previously a mystery of God, but now the Gentiles with Israel form one body and share in the promises of God as people of God.

The dispensational theology, which holds to a separation between the Jewish and Gentile followers of God, is attempting to divide what the Bible says God has united into one body. Therefore, the Pre-Tribulation view seems to lack scriptural support.

However, not only does it lack support because of this division, but there appears to be no biblical support for a two-part Second Coming of Christ. Even the Scripture that Pre-Tribbers use to support their view actually points to a different conclusion. Let me show you what I mean.

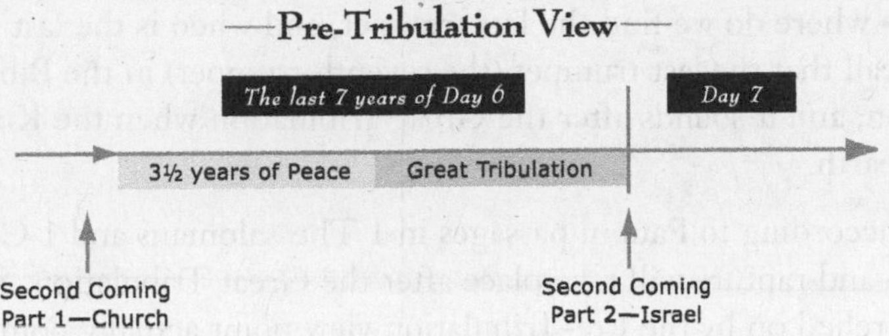

The #1 Pre-Tribulation passage:

"For *the Lord himself will come down from heaven*, with a loud command, with the voice of the archangel and with the trumpet call of God, and the dead in Christ will rise first. After that, we who are still alive and are left will be caught up together with them in the clouds to meet the Lord in the air. And so we will be with the Lord forever." (1 Thessalonians 4:16–17)

The Pre-Tribulation view holds that this passage describes the gathering (resurrection and rapture) of Christ's followers as occurring before the Great Tribulation. Now, notice that in this passage it says that the Lord will come down from heaven. Therefore, the Lord leaves heaven at the time of this resurrection and rapture.

Now let's read this passage in Acts 3:21: "He [the Lord] *must remain in heaven until the time comes for God to restore everything*, as he promised long ago through his holy prophets." Notice that the first passage says Christ will come down from heaven before the resurrection and rapture of His followers, and the second passage says that Christ must remain in heaven until it is time to restore everything. Since we already know that God restores everything when His kingdom comes after the Great Tribulation, this means that the resurrection and rapture will also take place after the Tribulation. So the passage in Thessalonians used by Pre-Tribbers actually points to a Post-Tribulation resurrection and rapture.

So what about their #2 Pre-Tribulation passage? Let's see what it says:

"Listen, I tell you a mystery: We will not all sleep, but we will all be changed—in a flash, in the twinkling of an eye, *at the last trumpet*. For the trumpet will sound, the dead will be raised imperishable, and we will be changed." (1 Corinthians 15:51–52)

This passage from First Corinthians is part of Paul's discourse to the church about the resurrection and rapture. Notice that Paul says that not everyone will die before the resurrection. Then he says that the resurrection and rapture will take place "*at the last trumpet.*" So where do we find the last trumpet, and when is the last trumpet sounded? You may recall that the last trumpet (the seventh trumpet) in the Bible is in the Book of Revelation, and it sounds after the Great Tribulation when the Kingdom of God is coming on earth.

Therefore, according to Paul in passages in 1 Thessalonians and 1 Corinthians, the resurrection and rapture will take place after the Great Tribulation. So, the #1 and #2 passages relied on by the Pre-Tribulation view point actually point to a Post-Tribulation resurrection and rapture.

The Mid Way

The next Tribulation view has historically been called the Mid-Tribulation view. However, today it is also called the Pre-Wrath view. This interpretation shares some of the tenets of the Pre-Tribulation view. For example, it involves a two-part resurrection and rapture.

The main difference between the Mid-Tribulation view and the Pre-Tribulation view is the timing of the first part of the Second Coming. It places the first part of the resurrection and rapture as occurring just before the bowls of God's wrath are poured out on the world. We covered the bowls of God's wrath in Chapter 13. This places part one of the Second Coming just before the end of the Great Tribulation. Here is how it looks on the timeline.

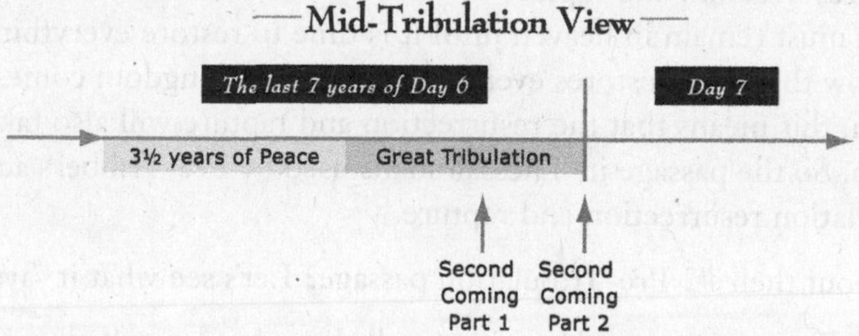

Because of the similarities with the Pre-Tribulation view, this view shares several of the same problems with the Pre-Tribulation view. However, this view has one scriptural problem all by itself. The Mid-Tribulation view holds that God will cut short the Great Tribulation to something less than three and a half years. They hold this view because Jesus said that those days will be shortened. Here is how He said it.

"For then there will be great tribulation, unequaled from the beginning of the world until now—and never to be equaled again. If those days had not been cut short, no one would survive, but for the sake of the elect those days will be shortened." (Matthew 24:21–22)

Jesus does say that the days of the Great Tribulation will be shortened. However, He does not say they will be shortened from three and a half years to something less. He just says they will be shortened for the sake of the elect. When the Great Tribulation is cut short, it will be cut short to three and a half years. How do I know this? Daniel 7:25 says that the saints will be persecuted by the Antichrist for three and a half years. So, according to Scripture, the followers of Christ will be persecuted for three and a half years, and the Tribulation will also be cut short.

The After View

The Post-Tribulation view is the view we have been studying and discussing all the way through this guide to the Last Days. This view places the resurrection of all God's people after the Great Tribulation, or Post-Tribulation. Let's see this in our timeline.

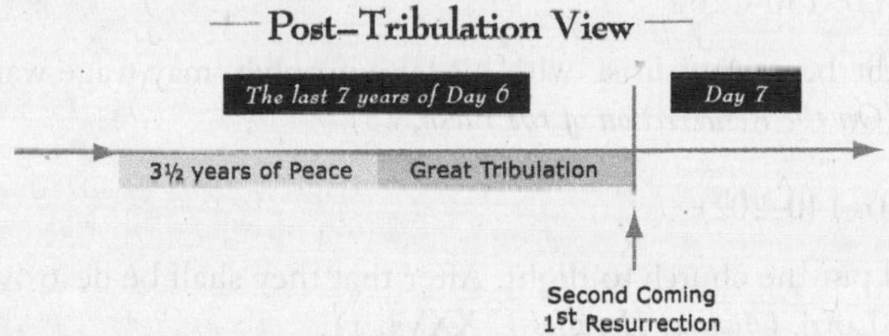

Not only is the Post-Tribulation view in harmony with Scripture, but it was also the most prevalent view among the early church writers. Let's read some excerpts from their writings.

Historical View

The following list of early church writers held that the followers of Christ will face the Antichrist in the Great Tribulation and then be delivered at the return of Christ—Post-Tribulation.

From Ages Digital Library—The Master Christian Library—Version 8:

Didache (A.D. 100):

> Then shall appear the world-deceiver as Son of God, and shall do signs and wonders, and the earth shall be delivered into his hands, … but they that endure in their faith shall be saved from under the curse itself. And then shall appear the signs of the truth; first, the sign of an out-spreading in heaven; then the sign of the sound of the trumpet; and the third, the resurrection of the dead; yet not of all, but as it is said: The Lord shall come and all His saints with Him. Then shall the world see the Lord coming upon the clouds of heaven. (Didache—Chapter 16)

Justin Martyr (A.D. 100–168):

> Two Advents of Christ have been announced: the one, in which He is set forth as suffering, inglorious, dishonored, and crucified; but the other, in which He shall come from heaven with glory, when the man of apostasy, who speaks strange things against the Most High, shall venture to do unlawful deeds on the earth against us the Christians. (*Dialogue of Justine*, Chapter 110)

Tertullian (A.D. 150–220):

> That the beast Antichrist, with his false prophet, may wage war on the Church of God. (*On the Resurrection of the Flesh*, 25)

Irenaeus (A.D. 140–202):

> … and put the church to flight. After that they shall be destroyed by the Coming of our Lord. (*Against Heresies V*, XXVI, 1)

Cyprian (A.D. 200–258):

> [T]he Lord hath foretold that these things would come. With the exhortation of His foreseeing word, instructing, and teaching, and preparing, and strengthening the people of His Church for all endurance of things to come. He previously warned us that the adversary would increase more and more in the last times. (Treatise 7)
>
> For you ought to know and to believe, and hold it for certain, that the day of affliction has begun to hang over our heads, and the end of the world and the time of Antichrist to draw near, so that we must all stand prepared for the battle …. The time cometh, that whosoever killeth you will think that he doeth God

> service .... Nor let any one wonder that we are harassed with increasing afflictions, when the Lord before predicted that these things would happen in the last times. (*Epistles of Cyprian, LV,* 1, 2)
>
> Nor let any one of you, beloved brethren, be so terrified by the fear of future persecution, or the coming of the threatening Antichrist, as not to be found armed for all things by the evangelical exhortations and precepts, and by the heavenly warnings. Antichrist is coming ... but immediately the Lord follows to avenge our sufferings and our wounds. (*Epistles of Cyprian, LIII,* p. 722)

Victorinus (A.D. 269–271):

> He shall cause also that a golden image of Antichrist shall be placed in the temple at Jerusalem, and that the apostate angel should enter, and thence utter voices and oracles .... The Lord, admonishing *His churches concerning the last times and their dangers, ... three years and six months, in which with all his power the devil will avenge himself under Antichrist against the Church.* (*Commentary on the Apocalypse,* 20:1–3)

Hippolytus (A.D. 160–240):

> ... the one thousand two hundred and three score days (the half of the week) during which the tyrant is to reign and persecute the Church .... (*Treatise on Christ and Antichrist,* 61)

Augustine (A.D. 354–430):

> ... the kingdom of Antichrist shall fiercely, though for a short time, assail the Church .... (*The City of God, XX,* 23)

Roger Bacon (A.D. 1214–1274):

> ... future perils [for the Church] in the times of Antichrist .... (*Opus Majus II,* p. 634)

Martin Luther (A.D. 1483–1546)

> [The book of Revelation] is intended as a revelation of things that are to happen in the future, and especially of tribulations and disasters for the Church .... (*Works of Martin Luther, VI,* p. 481)

John Knox (A.D. 1515–1572):

> [T]he great love of God towards his Church, whom he pleased to forewarne of dangers to come … to wit, The man of sin, The Antichrist …. (*The Historie of the Reformation etc.*, 1, p. 76)

Roger Williams (A.D. 1603–1683):

> Antichrist … hath his prisons, to keep Christ Jesus and his members fast. (*The Bloody Tenent etc.*, p. 153)

Charles Hodge (A.D. 1797–1878):

> … the fate of his Church here on earth … is the burden of the Apocalypse. (*Systematic Theology, III*, p. 827)

Carl F. Keil (A.D. 1807–1888):

> … the persecution of the last enemy Antichrist against the Church of the Lord …. (*Biblical Commentary*, YXMV, p. 503)

It's plain to see that the early church writers believed that the followers of Christ will face the Antichrist during the Great Tribulation and then Christ will return.

Now you are familiar with the major views on the timing of the Tribulation and the resurrection and rapture. Now let's discuss the various Millennial views.

Millennial Views

Following the Great Tribulation, at the conclusion of Day 6, the 1,000-year reign of Christ begins. Once again, one's Millennial viewpoint is determined by when one believes the Second Coming will take place in relation to the coming of the Kingdom of God, also known as the Millennium. There are three basic viewpoints: Premilliennial, Amillennial, and Postmillennial.

Premillennial View

The Premillennial view holds that Christ will return before the Millennium. It follows from the Tribulation views because each of the Tribulation views hold that Christ will return at the beginning of the Millennium. The Premillennial view is the view that I have been presenting in this guide. Let's see how this looks in a timeline.

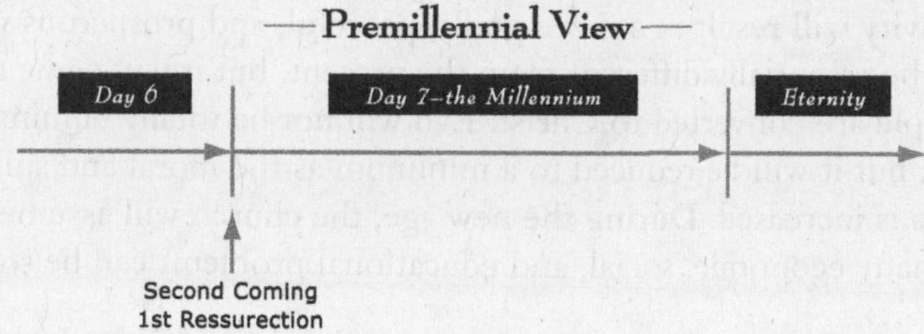

The Premillennial view holds that the Second Coming will be preceded by signs that include wars, famines, earthquakes, the appearance of the Antichrist, and the Great Tribulation. These events will culminate in the Second Coming, at which time Christ will establish His Kingdom on earth. His Kingdom will be established suddenly and supernaturally.

The Jews will figure prominently in the future age because the Premillennial view holds that they will be converted at the appearance of Christ at the time of the Second Coming. God will remove the curse from nature and Christ will restrain evil during the coming age by His authoritarian power. The Premillennial view also holds that during the thousand years of Day 7, the resurrected followers of Christ, the immortals, will intermingle with the surviving mortal inhabitants of the earth.

Amillennial View

Amillennial is the name given to the belief that there will be no literal 1,000-year reign of Christ. The prefix *a* in amillennial means "no" or "not." Hence, *amillennial* means "no millennium."

The Amillennial view holds that the Bible does not tell of a literal period of Christ's reign on earth before the final judgment. According to this view, good and evil will continue in the world until the Second Coming of Christ, when the dead are raised for the final judgment. The Amillennial view holds that the kingdom of God is now present in the world and that Christ currently rules His church from heaven through the Spirit. They hold that the scriptural passages about a future, glorious, and perfect kingdom refer to the new heaven and a new earth with life in heaven.

Postmillennial View

The Postmillennial view holds that the Millennium is not a literal period, but a long period that will come as a result of Christian preaching and teaching. It is believed that this activity will result in a more godly, peaceful, and prosperous world. The new age will not be essentially different from the present, but it will come about gradually as more people are converted to Christ. Evil will not be totally eliminated during the Millennium, but it will be reduced to a minimum as the moral and spiritual influence of Christians is increased. During the new age, the church will assume greater importance, and many economic, social, and educational problems can be solved.

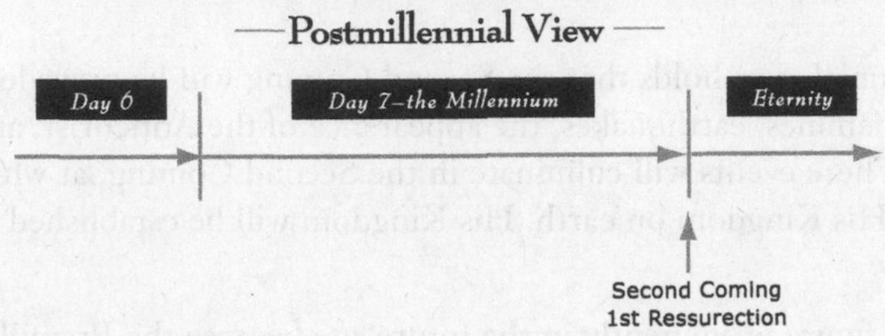

Under this theory, the period is not necessarily limited to a thousand years because the number may be symbolic. The Millennium closes with the unexpected and sudden Second Coming of Christ, the resurrection of the dead, and final judgment. Some who hold the Postmillennial view believe that the Second Coming will occur after Christians, not Christ, have established the Kingdom of God on earth.

Now that you have been exposed to the varying Millennial views, let's talk about some other eschatological terminology.

The Eschatologicalisms

There seems to be no end to the scholarly terminology related to the study of the Last Days and the return of Christ. It appears that every new idea that man has had about this topic requires its own "ism." But so you know what the scholars are talking about, I mention some of them here. First, let's talk about Futurism.

Futurism

Futurism is pretty simple. It basically says that the prophecies that haven't happened yet are still in the future. Therefore, unfulfilled prophecies in the Old and New Testament, including Revelation, are still to occur. This interpretive approach generally holds a literal and physical view of what will take place in the Last Days. Futurism includes divergent theologies including covenantal theology (which holds to the covenants of God) as well as dispensational theology, which we discussed.

Futurism places the Second Coming and the Kingdom of God in the future. In contrast, there is Historicism.

Historicism

Historicism is a form of eschatology that interprets the events of the Book of Revelation and other New Testament prophecies as having to do with the church's beginnings in the New Testament period. Historicism finds literal and symbolic earthly fulfillments of prophecy in the early Protestant and Roman Catholic conflicts. One very controversial aspect of this eschatology is that it holds that the Antichrist will come from the Roman Catholic papal succession. It also holds that the Roman Catholic Church is Mystery Babylon of Revelation Chapter 17. While these positions are very old, even today there are still related theories lingering about the Roman Catholic Church.

The Prophet Says

"Fallen! Fallen is Babylon the Great! She has become a home for demons and a haunt for every evil spirit, a haunt for every unclean and detestable bird. For all the nations have drunk the maddening wine of her adulteries. The kings of the earth committed adultery with her, and the merchants of the earth grew rich from her excessive luxuries." (Revelation 18:2–3).

Many of the tenets of this historic belief system have been discredited by Scripture. One that is most interesting to me is that Historicism seems to hold that the Antichrist comes out of Mystery Babylon. Yet according to Revelation Chapter 17, the Antichrist and his kingdom will destroy Mystery Babylon the Great. This would mean that the Antichrist would destroy his own kingdom. Not likely, nor is this consistent with biblical prophecy.

Idealism

Idealism, also called the "Spiritual View," is how some approach the Book of Revelation and biblical prophecy. Idealism holds that the Book of Revelation is full of symbols and imagery that are perpetually and cyclically being fulfilled in a spiritual sense. They hold that the imagery is symbolic of the on-going struggle between the Kingdom of God and the forces of Satan since the First Coming of Christ.

This belief system does not believe that any biblical prophecies will be fulfilled in a literal way. This approach seems to disregard the preponderance of biblical prophecies that have already been fulfilled in a very literal sense. For example, it does not address the Old Testament prophecies about the First Coming that we discussed previously. Recall that Christ rode into Jerusalem on the colt of a donkey, exactly as the Old Testament prophet Zechariah foretold.

Let's talk about one more "ism" and call it Realism because that is how I view eschatology—realistically.

Realism

Since the Bible has a perfect record in predicting future events, this view holds to the idea that one can, realistically, expect that to continue. To date, some Bible students and historians estimate that half of biblical prophecy has already been fulfilled, which leaves the other half to be fulfilled.

Of the people who believe that the Bible's prophecies were written before the event prophesied occurred, most see a perfect batting record. So accurate are the predictions that many doubters feel that the prophecies must have been written after the events they predict. Some people have said that the prophecies of Daniel are so accurate that the only logical explanation is that they were written after the fact.

As we know, Daniel predicted the events and timing of the First Coming of the Messiah. Just recently, around 1948, over a thousand ancient scrolls were discovered in the desert of Israel in an area called Qumran. These historic discoveries are called the "Dead Sea Scrolls." The scrolls found include most of the Old Testament writings as we have them today. The discoveries dated many of the scrolls at about 200 B.C. Included in the scrolls were the prophecies of Daniel, which predicted the events and timing of the First Coming in A.D. 32. In other words, the Book of Daniel was written at least hundreds of years before the events he predicted. Once again, the biblical record appears to be realistic.

> **The Prophet Says**
>
> "Go your way, Daniel, because the words are closed up and sealed until the time of the end." (Daniel 12:9)

We are now at the end of this guide to what the Bible says about the Last Days. I hope you have enjoyed it and found the discussions helpful. The Bible hasn't changed what it's saying about the future, but the future is getting closer and closer. For me, during the past several years the Bible has shown things about today's world that have never been visible before. It's as though the Bible and today's news are converging. Even though the Bible doesn't change what it says, the events shaping the world's future are changing. At some point, what is described in biblical prophecy will be happening before our eyes.

When Jesus was teaching His disciples about the Last Days, He directed their attention to the Old Testament prophet Daniel as a key to His return and the coming Kingdom.

Daniel was told that his prophecies would be closed (not understood) until the time of the end. As we move closer to the end of the age, Daniel's prophecies will become more and more open, until that day when the Messiah returns and the Kingdom of God arrives on earth. Then every eye will see.

The Least You Need to Know

- Eschatology is all about the Last Days.
- The Great Tribulation comes before Christ returns, and when it arrives, it will last three and a half years.
- The Millennium period comes after the Great Tribulation, and it will last for 1,000 years.
- The Realistic view of eschatology is your best bet for interpreting the Bible's prophecies.

Appendix A

Glossary

This glossary is provided to help our understanding of terms used in this guide. With each term is a list of synonyms followed by a definition.

abomination that causes desolation Describes the event when the Antichrist shows up in the Temple of God and proclaims himself to be God. This abominable act of blasphemy starts a time of death and destruction that will cause the desolation of many.

Abyss The place located either on or in the earth where God secures demons and fallen angels. Satan will be locked and sealed in the Abyss at Christ's return and will remain there for a thousand years.

Antichrist The Beast, the man of lawlessness; the world leader who will rise to power out of the Fourth Beast Kingdom, as prophesied in Daniel 7:23–24. He will confirm a covenant with Israel and then, after three and a half years, will put a stop to the sacrifice and offering in the temple when he proclaims himself to be God. During the Great Tribulation, he will receive power from Satan as he deceives the world and attempts to destroy the people of God.

Armageddon The place in northern Israel where the Antichrist and the nation's armies will gather in preparation for the final battle at Jerusalem, as in Revelation 16:16.

Babylon the Great, Mystery Mystery Babylon; a Last Days superpower that will hold a position of great influence over the world until she is destroyed by the Antichrist and the Fourth Beast Kingdom, as in Revelation Chapters 17 and 18.

Bible Scripture, the Word of God. The Bible is made up of two parts. The Old Testament, usually containing 39 books, was written before the First Coming of Jesus Christ. The New Testament, usually containing 27 books, was written following the First Coming of Jesus Christ.

birth pains Seven seals of Revelation; a prophetic term used by Jesus and the Old Testament prophets to describe certain signs and events that will take place on earth before the coming of the Kingdom of God. The birth pains, like the seals of Revelation, are the earliest warnings of the end of Day 6 and the coming Day of the Lord (Day 7). Some people believe that the first of the birth pains has already occurred and that the first seal has already been opened.

Beast, the Antichrist, man of lawlessness; the final leader of the Fourth Beast Kingdom, as in Daniel 7:24. This incredibly successful world leader will receive power from Satan (Revelation 13:3) and attempt to destroy the people of God (Revelation 13:7).

Beast Kingdom, Fourth The fourth world kingdom will rise to power during the last days and rule over the whole world. This kingdom will initially have 10 kings; then the Antichrist will arise among the 10 and overthrow 3 of the kings. Then the kingdom will have 7 heads and 10 horns, as in Daniel 7:24.

believers Saints, chosen, elect, servants of God, followers of Christ, Christians, Church, Body of Christ, Bride of Christ; those who have placed their faith in Jesus Christ have their names written in the Book of Life.

Book of Life God's record of all those who put their faith in Jesus Christ.

children of the resurrection A title Jesus gave to those people who will take part in the resurrection and eternal life in the Kingdom of God. In this book, I also refer to them as the immortals because when they are resurrected, they will become immortal.

Christ Messiah, Anointed One, Son of God; a title for the anointed one of God, the Messiah who has come into the world and will return to establish the Kingdom of God on earth.

Day of the Lord Day of Wrath, Day of Salvation, Day of Redemption; the day when Jesus Christ returns to gather His elect, punish the unbelieving world, and establishes the Kingdom of God on earth. The Day of the Lord is a very significant event in God's prophetic plan. It is referred to by name 24 times in Scripture and is written about so often that the prophets abbreviated its name by referring to it as "the day" or "that day." Several times in Scripture it is called "the great and dreadful day" because it will be both the day of deliverance and a day of judgment.

Dead Sea Scrolls A collection of almost 1,000 ancient (circa 200 B.C.) parchment scrolls and the Copper Scroll that were discovered in the caves of Qumran from 1947 to 1956. Qumran is a mountainous desert area about 13 miles east of Jerusalem near the Dead Sea.

elementary teachings about Christ Elementary truths of God's Word, spiritual milk, and the foundation. The elementary teachings about Christ include six doctrinal teachings that are foundational to the Christian faith. They are listed as repentance from acts that lead to death, faith in God, instruction about baptisms, laying on of hands, resurrection of the dead, and eternal judgment.

end of the age One of the terms Jesus used to refer to the time of the harvest and His return, when He will gather His elect and judge the world.

eschatology The branch of theological study relating to last things, concerning death, the end of the world, and the ultimate destiny of mankind. For example, in Christian doctrine, eschatology concerns the Second Coming, the resurrection of the dead, and the final judgment.

False Prophet The second beast of Revelation Chapter 13 who comes out of the earth and deceives the whole world by performing miraculous signs, causing the inhabitants of the earth to worship the first beast. He and the first beast are thrown into the lake of fire at the end of the Great Tribulation.

Final Battle Battle on the Great Day; the battle that will take place in the Kidron Valley between Jerusalem and the Mount of Olives. According to Scripture, the Antichrist and his armies will muster their forces at Armageddon, north of Jerusalem, and then come and attack Jerusalem. Christ and His supernatural army from heaven will slaughter the armies of the Antichrist just outside of Jerusalem in the bloodiest battle of all time.

Gospel The story and message of the Bible. The Gospel reveals who the God of the Bible is, who man is, what God has done, and what He will soon do.

harvest, the The separating out of the kingdom everything that causes sin and all who do evil, and the gathering of Christ's followers into the Kingdom of God at the end of the age.

Jews Jews, Jewish people, Israelites, and Hebrews are terms used interchangeably in this guide to the Last Days to refer to the people of God. For our purposes, this terminology does not refer just to people who live in a certain country.

judgment seat of Christ The judgment of believers that will occur at the return of Jesus Christ. This is when the saints will receive their reward for what they have done in Christ, as in 2 Corinthians 5:10.

Kingdom of God Christ's kingdom; the final earthly kingdom that will be ruled by Christ and His followers. There are other aspects to the Kingdom of God, such as the Kingdom of God in heaven and the kingdom that exists in each believer. But for the purposes of this study, whenever we refer to the kingdom, it is in reference to the coming earthly Kingdom of God.

Last Days End Times; the period of time leading up to the return of Jesus Christ and the end of the age.

Lord's Day Seventh Day, Sabbath, Sabbath rest. The Lord's Day is recorded only once in Scripture, in Revelation 1:10. However, the day that is the Lord's is well established in the Bible. In Isaiah 58:13, the Sabbath is defined as the Lord's Day. In the New Testament, we are told that Christ is the Lord of the Sabbath. Therefore, the Lord's Day according to the scriptural record is Saturday, the Sabbath.

man of lawlessness Antichrist, the beast; the leader of the Fourth Beast Kingdom. This incredibly successful world leader will receive power from Satan and attempt to destroy the people of God.

Michael the Archangel The archangel who protects the people of God (Daniel 12:1) and who, in the Last Days, will battle Satan and throw him to earth (Revelation 12:7).

Millennium The nonbiblical term for the thousand-year reign of Christ on earth, as in Revelation 20:2–7.

prophecy A prediction of the future, under divine guidance or influence. Biblical prophecy is like history written in advance.

prophet A person who proclaims a message from God by divine guidance, often about things that will take place in the future.

rapture The resurrection of the living; a nonbiblical term used to describe the resurrection, bodily change, and catching up from the earth of living believers into the clouds to meet the Lord in the air, at the Second Coming. Recorded in 1 Thessalonians 4:17.

rebellion, the The Falling Away, the Apostasy; the event Paul referred to in 2 Thessalonians 2:3 as marking the turning away from faith in Jesus Christ that will likely take place during the Great Tribulation.

restrainer, the Michael the Archangel. Michael, the Great Prince of the spiritual world, protects the people of God by restraining Satan. Satan will attempt to kill all God's people during the Great Tribulation, when he is no longer held back.

Resurrection, First Resurrection of believers; the bodily change that will take place in all the followers of Christ, both dead and living, at His return, as in Revelation 20:5. Scripture explains this as the raising of the dead and the changing of those left alive at that time.

Resurrection, Second A nonbiblical term for the raising of the rest of the dead at the end of the thousand-year reign of Christ on earth, as in Revelation 20:5.

Revelation, the Book of The last book in the Bible. It is the revelation of Jesus Christ for His followers to show them what will quickly take place. Jesus made the revelation known to His servant John through an angel.

Satan The devil, the great dragon; a powerful angel who rebelled against God and strives to rise to the throne of God by destroying the people and plans of God. He will be thrown to earth by Michael at the time of the abomination that causes desolation. Satan will give his power to the Antichrist during the Great Tribulation until he is captured and bound in the Abyss for a thousand years.

Scripture Bible, Word of God, Word of Truth; the holy written and infallible Word of God.

Second Coming Second Advent, return of Christ; a nonbiblical term for the return of Jesus Christ from heaven to earth.

Temple of God House of God; the structure called the House of God and the place of Jewish worship in Jerusalem. Solomon built the first temple. The second temple was rebuilt during the time of Nehemiah, and Herod restored it to a state of grandeur during the time of Christ's First Advent. The second temple was completely destroyed in A.D. 70, just as Jesus had prophesied. A third temple will be built sometime in the future.

trumpet, last The seventh trumpet of Revelation 11:15, which will signal the resurrection of the living and the dead in Christ, as in 1 Corinthians 15:51,52.

Tribulation, Great Time of Jacob's trouble; the three and a half year period of unparalleled persecution and suffering brought on by Satan through the Antichrist and False Prophet. This is the most documented period of time recorded in Scripture, being referred to as: 42 months; 1,260 days; and a time, time, and half a time. This period begins with the abomination that causes desolation and ends with the return of Christ at the end of the age, in Matthew 24:21.

white throne judgment, great The final judgment that will take place after the thousand-year earthly reign of Christ. The white throne judgment appears to be the judgment of everyone who did not take part in the First Resurrection, as in Revelation 20:11.

wedding banquet The wedding feast, the wedding supper; the celebration of the union between Jesus Christ and the Bride of Christ (all true believers). It will take place on Mount Zion in Jerusalem, as described in Isaiah 25:6–8.

Word of Truth Bible, Scripture, Word, Word of God; the holy written and infallible Word of God.

wrath of God God's judgment and punishment of the unbelieving and disobedient world that will be poured out on the Day of the Lord.

Appendix B

Last Days Timelines

Biblical Week to the Last Days

With the Lord a day is like a thousand years, and a thousand years are like a day (2 Peter 3:8).

First Days			*Mid Week*	*Last Days*		
Day 1	*Day2*	*Day 3*	*Day 4*	*Day 5*	*Day 6*	*Day 7*
1–1,000 years	1,000–2,000 years	2,000–3,000 years	3,000–4,000 years	4,000–5,000 years	5,000–6,000 years	6,000–7,000 years
Creation Adam and Eve	Adam to Flood 1,656 years Noah and the Great Flood	Adam to Egypt about 2,200 years Abraham, Isaac, Jacob, Joseph Egypt Persecution 1,550 B.C. Exodus 1,445–1,405 B.C. Joshua enters Promised Land King Saul	Israel in Promised Land King David 1,000 B.C. King Solomon 1st Temple 1st Temple destroyed 586 B.C. Daniel in Babylon 539 B.C.	Coming of Christ The King Christ Crucified and Risen A.D. 32 2nd Temple destroyed A.D. 70	Israel a Nation Mystery Babylon Tabernacle 3rd Temple Fourth Kingdom Antichrist Covenant Signed Abomination Great Tribulation	Christ Return 1st Resurrection Wedding Feast Final Battle 1,000 years Millennium 2nd Resurrection

Prophesies to be fulfilled

Timeline of Major Last Days Events

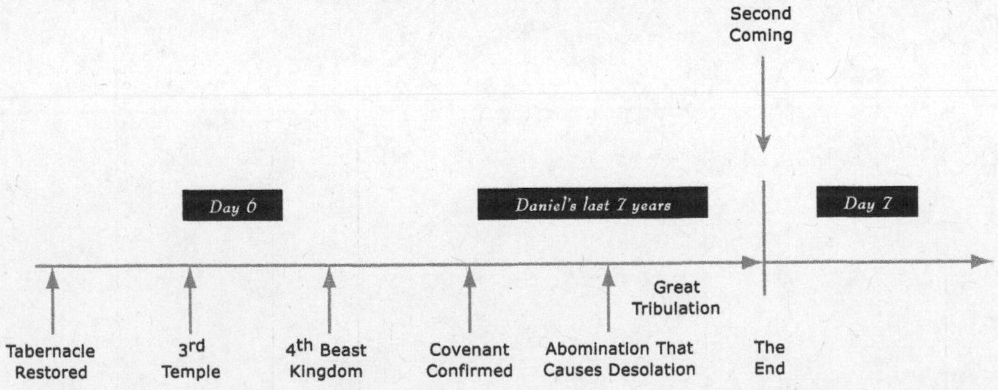

Second Coming

Day 6 — *Daniel's last 7 years* — *Day 7*

Tabernacle Restored → 3rd Temple → 4th Beast Kingdom → Covenant Confirmed → Abomination That Causes Desolation → Great Tribulation → The End

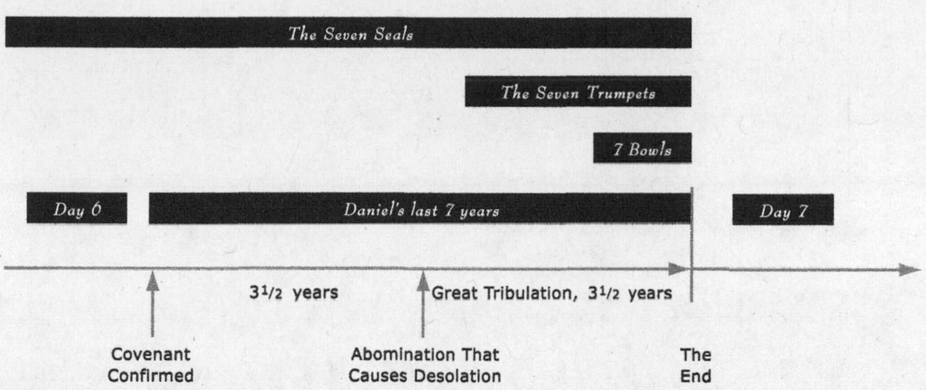
The Revelation Timeline
The Seven Seals
The Seven Trumpets
7 Bowls
Day 6
Daniel's last 7 years
Day 7
3 1/2 years
Great Tribulation, 3 1/2 years
Covenant Confirmed
Abomination That Causes Desolation
The End

Appendix C

Additional Reading

Anderson, Sir Robert. *The Coming Prince.* Grand Rapids, MI: Kregel Classics, reprinted 1957.

———. *Daniel in the Critics Den,* Fourth Edition. Edinburgh, England: Pickering & Inglis, n.d.

Bahnsen, L. Greg, and L. Kenneth Gengry. *House Divided, The Break-up of Dispensational Theology.* Institute for Christian Economics, 1977.

Barnhouse, Donald Gray. *Revelation: An Expository Commentary.* Grand Rapids, MI: Zondervan, 1971.

Beckwith, T. Isbon. *The Apocalypse of John.* Eugene, OR: Wipf and Stock Publishers, 2001.

Blaising, Craig A., and Darrell Bock. *Progressive Dispensationalism.* Wheaton, IL: Victor, 1993.

Bultman, Rudolf. *Jesus Christ and Mythology.* New York: Charles Scribner Sons, 1958.

Caird, G. B. *The Revelation of St. John the Divine.* New York: Harper & Row, 1966.

Cook, Terry L. *The Mark of the New World Order.* Springdale, PA: Whitaker House, 1996.

Erickson, Millard J. *A Basic Guide to Eschatology: Making Sense of the Millennium.* Grand Rapids, MI: Baker Books, 1998.

Fruchtenbaum, G. Arnold. *The Footsteps of the Messiah.* Tustin, CA: Ariel Ministries, 1982.

Gentile, B. Ernest. *The Final Triumph.* Grand Rapids, MI: Chosen Books, 2001.

Gentry, Kenneth. *The Beast of Revelation.* Institute of Christian Economics, 1989.

Gregg, Steve, ed. *Revelation: Four Views: A Parallel Commentary.* Nashville, TN: Nelson, 1997.

Grenz, Stanley J. *The Millennial Maze: Sorting Out Evangelical Options.* Downers Grove, IL: InterVarsity Press, 1992.

Gundry, Robert H. *The Church and the Tribulation.* Grand Rapids, MI: Zondervan, 1973.

———. *First the Antichrist.* Grand Rapids, MI: Baker Books, 1997.

Guthrie, Donald. *The Relevance of John's Apocalypse.* Grand Rapids, MI: Eerdmans, 1987.

Hanson, Paul. *The Dawn of the Apocalyptic.* Philadelphia: Fortress Press, 1979.

Hendrickson, William. *More Than Conquerors: An Interpretation of the Book of Revelation.* Grand Rapids, MI: Baker, 1944.

Hitchcock, Mark. *101 Answers to the Most Asked Questions About the End Times.* Sisters, OR: Multnomah Publishers, 2001.

Hobbs, Herschel. *The Cosmic Drama.* Waco, TX: Word Books, 1971.

Howard, Kevin, and Marvin Rosenthal. *The Feasts of the Lord.* Orlando, FL: Zion's Hope, 1997.

Ice, Thomas, and Timothy Demy. *The Truth About the Signs of the Times.* Eugene, OR: Harvest House, 1997.

Kuenzi, L. Vernon. *Restoring the Vision of the End-Times Church.* Salem, OR: Preparing the Way Publishers, 2001.

Ironside, H. A. *Lectures on the Revelation.* Neptune, NJ: Loizeaux Brothers, 1920.

Ladd, George. *The Blessed Hope.* Grand Rapids, MI: Eerdmans, 1956.

———. *A Commentary on the Revelation of John.* Grand Rapids, MI: WM. B. Eerdmans, 1972.

———. *The Presence of the Future.* Grand Rapids, MI: WM. B. Eerdmans, 1974.

———. *The Last Things.* Grand Rapids, MI: WM. B. Eerdmans, 1978.

LaHaye, Tim, and Jerry Jenkins. *Are We Living in the End Times?* Wheaton, IL: Tyndale, 1999.

Lenski, R. C. H. *The Interpretation of St. John's Revelation.* Minneapolis, MN: Augsburg, 1943.

Lightner, Robert. *The Last Days Handbook.* Nashville, TN: Thomas Nelson Publishers, 1997.

Lindsey, Hal. *The Late Great Planet Earth.* New York: Bantam Books, 1973.

MacPherson, David. *The Rapture Plot.* Simpsonville, SC: Millennium III Publishers, 2000.

McGinn, Bernard. *Antichrist: Two Thousand Years of the Human Fascination with Evil.* San Francisco: Harper, 1994.

Meeks, M. Douglas. *Origins of the Theology of Hope.* Philadelphia: Fortress, 1974.

Montgomery, Don. *Rapture, Post-Tribulation and Pre-Wrath.* Wnumclaw, WA: Winepress Publishing, 1995.

Morris, L. *The Revelation of St. John: Tyndale New Testament Commentaries.* Bedford Square, London: Tyndale, 1969.

Mounce, R. H. *The Book of Revelation.* Grand Rapids, MI: Eerdmans, 1977.

Nee, Watchman. *Come Lord Jesus.* New York: Christian Fellowship Publishers, 1976.

Newton, Sir Isaac. *Observations upon the Prophecies of Daniel and the Apocalypse of St. John.* Oregon Institute of Science and Medicine, reprinted 1991.

Palmer, Frederic. *The Drama of the Apocalypse.* Indianapolis, IN: Macmillan, 1903.

Pate, C. Marvin, ed. *Four Views of the Book of Revelation.* Grand Rapids, MI: Zondervan, 1998.

Perry, Richard. *Of The Last Days: Listen, I Tell You a Mystery.* Belleville, Ontario: Guardian Books, 2003.

Pieters, Albertus. *The Lamb, the Woman, and the Dragon.* Grand Rapids, MI: Zondervan, 1937.

Plantinga, Cornelius. *Not the Way It's Supposed to Be: A Breviary of Sin.* Grand Rapids, MI: Eerdmans, 1995.

Ramsey, William. *The Letters to the Seven Churches.* Grand Rapids, MI: Baker Book House, 1963.

Reese, Alexander. *The Approaching Advent of Christ.* Grand Rapids, MI: International Publications, 1975.

Rosenthal, Marvin. *The Pre-Wrath Rapture of the Church.* Nashville, TN: Thomas Nelson Publishers, 1990.

Ryrie, Charles. *Revelation.* Chicago: Moody Press, 1968.

Showers, Renald. *Maranatha Out Lord, Come.* Bellmawr, NJ: Friends of Israel Gospel Ministries, 1995.

Stedman, Ray. *God's Final Word: Understanding Revelation.* Grand Rapids, MI: Discovery House, 1991.

Swete, Henry Barclay. *The Apocalypse of St. John.* Grand Rapids, MI: Eerdmans, n.d.

Tenney, Merrill C. *Interpreting Revelation.* Grand Rapids, MI: Eerdmans, 1957.

Travis, Stephen. *The Jesus Hope.* Downers Grove, IL: InterVarsity Press, 1974.

Wainewright, Arthur W. *Mysterious Apocalypse: Interpreting the Book of Revelation.* Nashville, TN: Abingdon Press, 1993.

Walvoord, John. *The Rapture Question.* Findlay, OH: Dunham Publishing, 1957.

———. *Armageddon and the Middle East Oil Crisis.* Grand Rapids, MI: Zondervan, 1990.

———. *End Times.* Nashville, TN: Word Publishing, 1998.

———. *The Revelation of Jesus Christ.* Chicago: Moody Press, 1966.

Woodrow, Ralph. *Great Prophecies of the Bible.* Riverside, CA: Ralph Woodrow Evangelistic Assoc., 1984.

Appendix D

Websites to Explore

Anderson, Sir Robert
www.fbinstitute.com/Anderson/toc.html
His book: *The Coming Prince*

Bible Prophecy News
www.bibleprophecynews.com
World news as it pertains to the Bible prophecies

Blessed Hope Ministries International
www.bhm.dircon.co.uk
A basic study of Bible prophecy, with a particular emphasis on the Second Coming of Jesus Christ

Countdown to Armageddon
www.countdown.org
Information on Armageddon, the Mark of the Beast, 666, and the Antichrist

Daniel's 70 Weeks
www.sentex.netl-tcc/dan70.html
Daniel's Bible prophecies, explained in detail

End of the World and the Second Coming of Christ
www.secondcoming.freeservers.com
Aims to show how recent Middle East fulfillment of Bible prophecy shows that the present generation will see the Second Coming of Christ

End Times Prophecy: A Catholic Perspective
www.conventhill.com/endtimes
Collection of Catholic resources

Endtime
www.endtime.com
Examining world events from a biblical perspective; details of the radio show "Politics and Religion" and online magazine

Endtimes Now
www.endtimesnow.com/index.html
Analysis of world events with End Times significance, along with articles and chat

Eschatology
www.pbministries.org/Eschatology/eschatology.htm
Contains articles, books, and links on the study of Last Things

Focus on Jerusalem
www.focusonjerusalem.com
Bible prophecy newsletter and links

The Harpazo Network
www.harpazo.net
News and articles on biblical prophecy

HisTomorrow
www.historicism.com
Takes a pre-millennial historicism approach to Bible prophecy, with online books, articles, news, and essays

The Historical Alternative
www.historicist.com
Seeks to refute the futurist interpretation of the signs leading up to the Second Coming

Lambert Dolphin's Resource Library
www.ldolphin.org
Large collection of books, articles, and links to topics of interest in the fields of Christianity, science, and prophecy

Last Days in the News
http://lastdays.fattony.net
Videos, news, and audio clips aiming to show how Bible prophecy is being fulfilled today

LastDays.info
www.lastday.info
News and prophecy about the Last Days

Last Days Mystery
www.lastdaysmystery.info
Biblical studies on the Last Days and the Second Coming, with PowerPoint presentations and timelines

Messiah's Kingdom
www.messiahskingdom.com/default.html
A good resource on biblical prophecy

Posttribulationism
www.aboundingjoy.com/posttrib-fs.html
Biblical studies and answers for the post-Tribulation position

Prophecy Truths
ad2004.com/prophecytruths/indexB.html
Articles on the post-Tribulation and pre-Wrath raptures

The End Time Pilgrim
www.endtimepilgrim.org/index.htm
Articles and studies on the Second Coming and the post-Tribulation rapture

The Last Trumpet—Post-Trib Research Center
www.geocities.com/lasttrumpet_2000
Provides a comprehensive biblical explanation for post-Tribulation theology

The Moorings
www.themoorings.org/apologetics/69weeks/weeks2.html
Study on Daniel's 70 sevens prophecy

The Post Tribulation Rapture
www.apostolic.net/biblicalstudies/post/index.htm
Biblical studies and guest articles by Dave MacPherson

The Preterist Homepage
www.preteristhomepage.com
Bible prophecy from a Preterist (past fulfillment) perspective

The Prophecy Site
www.prophecy2.co.uk
A Bible-based prophecy site offering commentary and news, with a message board and links

The Rapture Theory
www.therapturetheaching.bravepages.com/The_Rapture_Th/Page_1x.html
A small post-Tribulation site with good articles

ProphecyUSA.com
www.prophecyusa.com
A look at the USA in Bible prophecy, with Bible studies and commentaries

Rapture Research Website
www.pretribulationrapture.com
An examination of the various rapture views

Restoring the Vision of the End Times Church
www.restoringthevision.com
Articles, links, and relations to the post-Tribulation rapture

Revelation Ministry
www.pioneer-net.com/-revrnin
An explanation of Daniel and Revelation

Scottish Preachers Hall of Fame
www.newble.co.uk/hall/links.html
Many articles and resources

Truth Research
www.geocities.com/athens/parthenon/3021/ascension1.html
A study on Daniel's 70 Sevens prophecy

Index

Numbers

A

B

C

E

F

J

K

L

M

N

O

P

Q-R

S

T

U-V

W-X-Y-Z